Lecture Notes in Computer Scie

Commenced Publication in 1973
Founding and Former Series Editors:
Gerhard Goos, Juris Hartmanis, and Jan van Leeuwen

Editorial Board

Thomas Stützle   Mauro Birattari
Holger H. Hoos (Eds.)

Engineering Stochastic Local Search Algorithms

Designing, Implementing and Analyzing
Effective Heuristics

Second International Workshop, SLS 2009
Brussels, Belgium, September 3-4, 2009
Proceedings

 Springer

Volume Editors

Thomas Stützle
Mauro Birattari
Université Libre de Bruxelles
IRIDIA, CoDE
Avenue F. Roosevelt 50, CP 194/6, 1050 Brussels, Belgium
E-mail: {stuetzle,mbiro}@ulb.ac.be

Holger H. Hoos
University of British Columbia
Computer Science Department
2366 Main Mall, Vancouver, BC, V6T 1Z4, Canada
E-mail: hoos@cs.ubc.ca

Library of Congress Control Number: 2009932137

CR Subject Classification (1998): E.5, E.2, F.2, I.1.2, I.2.8, F.2.2, H.3.3

LNCS Sublibrary: SL 1 – Theoretical Computer Science and General Issues

ISSN	0302-9743
ISBN-10	3-642-03750-X Springer Berlin Heidelberg New York
ISBN-13	978-3-642-03750-4 Springer Berlin Heidelberg New York

springer.com

© Springer-Verlag Berlin Heidelberg 2009
Printed in Germany

Typesetting: Camera-ready by author, data conversion by Scientific Publishing Services, Chennai, India
Printed on acid-free paper   SPIN: 12741809   06/3180   5 4 3 2 1 0

Preface

Stochastic local search (SLS) algorithms are established tools for the solution of computationally hard problems arising in computer science, business administration, engineering, biology, and various other disciplines. To a large extent, their success is due to their conceptual simplicity, broad applicability and high performance for many important problems studied in academia and encountered in real-world applications. SLS methods include a wide spectrum of techniques, ranging from constructive search procedures and iterative improvement algorithms to more complex SLS methods, such as ant colony optimization, evolutionary computation, iterated local search, memetic algorithms, simulated annealing, tabu search, and variable neighborhood search.

Historically, the development of effective SLS algorithms has been guided to a large extent by experience and intuition. In recent years, it has become increasingly evident that success with SLS algorithms depends not merely on the adoption and efficient implementation of the most appropriate SLS technique for a given problem, but also on the mastery of a more complex algorithm engineering process. Challenges in SLS algorithm development arise partly from the complexity of the problems being tackled and in part from the many degrees of freedom researchers and practitioners encounter when developing SLS algorithms. Crucial aspects in the SLS algorithm development comprise algorithm design, empirical analysis techniques, problem-specific background, and background knowledge in several key disciplines and areas, including computer science, operations research, artificial intelligence, and statistics. Ideally, the SLS algorithm development process is assisted by a sound methodology that addresses the issues arising in the various phases of algorithm design, implementation, tuning, and experimental evaluation.

In 2007, we organized a first workshop intended to provide a forum for researchers interested in the integration of relevant aspects of SLS research into a more coherent methodology for engineering SLS algorithms. This event attracted more than 50 participants and was widely considered a resounding success. It was therefore an easy decision to organize a second event, *SLS 2009, Engineering Stochastic Local Search Algorithms — Designing, Implementing and Analyzing Effective Heuristics*. Like the inaugural SLS 2007, SLS 2009 brought together researchers working on various aspects of SLS algorithms, ranging from more theoretical contributions on aspects relevant for SLS algorithms to the development of specific SLS algorithms for specific application problems. We believe that this second event further promoted the awareness and use of principled approaches and advanced methodology for the development of SLS algorithms and other complex heuristic procedures.

Of the 27 manuscripts submitted, seven were accepted as full papers for these workshop proceedings, which corresponds to an acceptance rate of about 25%.

During the workshop, each of these papers was presented in a 30-minute plenary talk. In addition, ten articles with promising, ongoing research efforts were selected for publication as short papers. The selected papers were chosen based on the results of a rigorous peer-reviewing process, in which each manuscript was evaluated by at least three experts. SLS 2009 also included the *Doctoral Symposium on Engineering Stochastic Local Search Algorithms (SLS-DS)*, which was organized by Frank Hutter and Marco Montes de Oca. All short papers and the contributions of SLS-DS were presented in poster sessions. This format was chosen in order to provide opportunities for extended discussion and interaction among the participants. The workshop program was completed by three tutorials on important topics in SLS engineering given by well-known researchers in the field.

We gratefully acknowledge the contributions of everyone who helped to make SLS 2009 a successful and lively workshop. We thank Frank Hutter and Marco Montes de Oca for the organization of the doctoral symposium, SLS-DS; everyone at IRIDIA who helped in organizing the event; the researchers who submitted their work; the Program Committee members and additional referees who provided valuable feedback during the paper selection process; the Université Libre de Bruxelles (ULB) for providing the rooms for the event. Finally, we would like to thank the Belgian National Funds for Scientific Research, and the French community of Belgium for supporting this workshop.

June 2009   Thomas Stützle
Mauro Birattari
Holger H. Hoos

Organization

SLS 2009 was organized by IRIDIA, CoDE, Université Libre de Bruxelles, Belgium.

Workshop Chairs

Thomas Stützle   Université Libre de Bruxelles, Belgium
Mauro Birattari   Université Libre de Bruxelles, Belgium
Holger H. Hoos   University of British Columbia, Canada

Program Committee

Thomas Bartz-Beielstein Cologne University of Applied Sciences,
                         Germany
Roberto Battiti   Università di Trento, Italy
Christian Blum   Universitat Politècnica de Catalunya, Spain
Marco Chiarandini   University of Southern Denmark, Denmark
Carlos Cotta   University of Málaga, Spain
Patrick de Causmaecker   Katholieke Universiteit Leuven, Kortrijk,
                         Belgium
Camil Demetrescu   Università La Sapienza, Italy
Yves Deville   Université Catholique de Louvain, Belgium
Luca Di Gaspero   Università degli Studi di Udine, Italy
Karl Doerner   Universität Wien, Austria
Marco Dorigo   Université Libre de Bruxelles, Belgium
Carlos M. Fonseca   University of Algarve, Portugal
Michel Gendreau   Université de Montréal, Canada
Bruce Golden   University of Maryland, USA
Walter J. Gutjahr   Universität Wien, Austria
Jin-Kao Hao   University of Angers, France
Richard F. Hartl   Universität Wien, Austria
Geir Hasle   SINTEF Applied Mathematics, Norway
Adele Howe   Colorado State University, USA
David Johnson   AT&T Labs Research, USA
Joshua Knowles   University of Manchester, UK
Chu Min Li   Université de Picardie Jules Verne, France
Arne Løkketangen   Molde University College, Norway
Vittorio Maniezzo   Università di Bologna, Italy
Catherine C. McGeoch   Amherst College, USA
Daniel Merkle   University of Southern Denmark, Denmark

Frank Neumann	Max-Planck-Institut für Informatik, Germany
Luis Paquete	University of Coimbra, Portugal
Paola Pellegrini	Università degli Studi di Trieste, Italy
Steven Prestwich	University College Cork, Ireland
Günther Raidl	Vienna University of Technology, Austria
Celso Ribeiro	Universidade Federal Fluminense, Brazil
Andrea Roli	Università di Bologna, Italy
Ruben Ruiz	Valencia University of Technology, Spain
Michael Sampels	Université Libre de Bruxelles, Belgium
Andrea Schaerf	Università degli Studi di Udine, Italy
Marc Schoenauer	Université Paris Sud, France
El-Ghazali Talbi	University of Lille, France
Dirk Thierens	Universiteit Utrecht, The Netherlands
Jean-Paul Watson	Sandia National Labs, USA
David Woodruff	University of California, Davis, USA
Mutsunori Yagiura	Nagoya University, Japan

Local Arrangements

Saifullah bin Hussin,	Renaud Lenne
Manuel López-Ibáñez	Sabrina Oliveira
Zhi Yuan	

Additional Referees

Marco A. Montes de Oca	Lin Xu

Sponsoring Institutions

National Funds for Scientific Research, Belgium
  http://www.fnrs.be

French Community of Belgium (through the research project META-X)
  http://www.cfwb.be

Table of Contents

Short Papers

High-Performance Local Search for Task Scheduling with Human Resource Allocation

Bertrand Estellon[1], Frédéric Gardi[2], and Karim Nouioua[1]

[1] Laboratoire d'Informatique Fondamentale – CNRS UMR 6166, Faculté des Sciences de Luminy, Université Aix-Marseille II, Marseille, France
[2] Bouygues e-lab, Paris, France
bertrand.estellon@lif.univ-mrs.fr, fgardi@bouygues.com,
karim.nouioua@lif.univ-mrs.fr

Abstract. In this paper, a real-life problem of task scheduling with human resource allocation is addressed. This problem was approached by the authors in the context of the ROADEF 2007 Challenge, which is an international competition organized by the French Operations Research Society. The subject of the contest, proposed by the telecommunications company FRANCE TÉLÉCOM, consists in planning maintenance interventions and teams of technicians needed for their achievements. The addressed combinatorial optimization problem is very hard: it contains several NP-hard subproblems and its scale (hundreds of interventions and technicians) induces a huge combinatorics. An effective and efficient local-search heuristic is described to solve this problem. This algorithm was ranked 2nd of the competition (over the 35 teams who have submitted a solution). Moreover, a methodology is revealed to design and engineer high-performance local-search heuristics for solving practically discrete optimization problems.

1 Presentation of the Problem

The problem proposed by the telecommunications company FRANCE TÉLÉCOM as subject of ROADEF 2007 Challenge [1] (an international competition organized every two years by the French Operations Research Society) can be viewed as a task scheduling problem with resource allocation. Here the tasks to plan are maintenance interventions and their achievement requires human resources, some technicians, each one having a skill level in different domains. The interventions are more or less priority; on the whole, 4 levels of priority are defined. Then, the objective is to minimize a linear function which depends on ending times of latest interventions for each priority.

Formally, the input of the problem is composed of n interventions I_i and of m technicians T_t. To each technician T_t is associated its skill level $C(t, d)$ in the domain d and its availability $P(t, j)$ on day j (1 for available, 0 otherwise). Each intervention has several characteristics too: $D(i)$ its execution time, $R(i, d, l)$ the number of technicians of level l in domain d required for its completion, $Z(i)$ its priority level.

T. Stützle, M. Birattari, and H.H. Hoos (Eds.): SLS 2009, LNCS 5752, pp. 1–15, 2009.

Concerning skills, we precise that the different domains of skill are disjoint, but that the levels of each domain are hierarchically organized. Then, a technician of level l in domain d is able to perform any intervention requiring a smaller skill level ($l' < l$) in the same domain. Consequently, the constants $R(i, d, l)$ are cumulative, in the sense that they specify the number of technicians needed at level at least l in domain d. For example, for an intervention I_i which requires two technicians of level 1 and one technician of level 3 in domain d, we have $R(i, d, 0) = 3$, $R(i, d, 1) = 3$, $R(i, d, 2) = 1$, $R(i, d, 3) = 1$ and $R(i, d, l) = 0$ for all $l \geq 4$. Such a definition implies that the $R(i, d, l)$ are non-increasing according to the index l: $R(i, d, l) \geq R(i, d, l')$ for all $l \leq l'$.

Then, the notion of team arises. Daily, the (available) technicians must be grouped into teams (even if a team may be composed of only one technician). We insist on the fact that a team is formed for the entire day (for practical reasons). Then, the problem is to partition daily the technicians into teams and to assign them a set of interventions, in order to minimize an objective function depending on the ending dates of the interventions. Two constraints lie on this assignment: the sum of the lengths of interventions (which are completed sequentially) can not exceed the length of a working day fixed to $H = 120$ and the skills of the team must cover the skills required by the set of tasks in each domain. Finally, a solution of the problem is given as follows: for each day j, the team $E_{j,e}$ to which belongs the technician T_t (the team $E_{j,0}$ contains all the technicians not available on this day); for each intervention I_i, the day j_i and the starting time h_i of its execution as well as the team $E_{j,e}$ in charge of its execution.

The objective of the planning is to minimize the following cost function: $28t_1 + 14t_2 + 4t_3 + f$, where t_k denotes the ending date among those of the latest interventions of priority k and f denotes the ending date of all interventions. The starting date d_i (resp. ending date f_i) of an intervention I_i is obtained as $j_i \cdot H + h_i$ (resp. $j_i \cdot H + h_i + D(i)$), the days being numbered from 0. Initially, this objective function was supposed to imply the minimization of the t_k's in lexicographic order ($t_1 \succ t_2 \succ t_3 \succ f$). However, compensations between the four terms of the objective function were allowed during the competition (impacting gravely our approach as it will be seen later).

Finally, the scope of the problem may be extended in two ways. The first is to introduce precedence relations between interventions: for all intervention I_i, one can define a set $P(i)$ of interventions which must be completed before starting I_i (that is to say, any intervention $I_{i'} \in P(i)$ must satisfy the inequality $f_{i'} \leq d_i$). Note that the natural lapses of time between interventions (travel, breaks, etc.) are here considered as null. The second extension is to define a budget B allowing to subcontract a number of interventions. Then, a cost $S(i)$ is given for any intervention I_i and the sum of the cost $S(i)$ of all abandoned interventions must not exceed the budget B. In order to ensure the respect of precedences in this case, any abandoned intervention I_i leads to recursively abandon any intervention $I_{i'}$ such that $I_i \in P(i')$.

2   Contributions

To the best of our knowledge, this problem was never addressed in these terms in the literature, both from fundamental and experimental points of view. Because of its large definition, the problem contains several NP-hard subproblems. For any partition of technicians into teams a given day, determining if a set of interventions is assignable to these teams while respecting the working duration H, the precedence constraints and the skill constraints is NP-complete, even if the execution time of all interventions is unit (all interventions have equal execution time), the number of teams is fixed to two and the precedence graph is isomorphic to a set of vertex-disjoint paths [2]. In the case of arbitrary precedence constraints, the problem remains NP-complete, even if the execution time of all interventions is unit and the skill constraints are omitted (any intervention can be performed by any team) [3]. Minimizing the number of days to plan all interventions is NP-hard in the strong sense, even if the interventions are performed by one sole team each day (containing all available technicians), without precedence and skill constraints. Indeed, this subproblem corresponds to a bin-packing problem [3] when the length H is given as an input of the problem. Finally, maximizing the sum of lengths of the set of abandoned interventions is equivalent to a knapsack problem (with precedence constraints) [3].

Because of its hardness and large scale (hundreds of interventions and technicians), such a problem is typical of real-life discrete optimisation problems encountered in business and industry. In this paper, an effective and efficient local-search heuristic is described to solve this problem. Our algorithm was ranked 2nd of the ROADEF 2007 Challenge (over the 35 teams who have submitted a solution). The victorious algorithm, due to Hurkens [4], can be viewed as a local-search heuristic where large neighborhoods [5] are explored by integer linear programming (using ILOG CPLEX 10.0 solver); the team Cordeau-Laporte-Pasin-Ropke [6], ranked 2nd ex æquo, have also developed a large neighborhood search approach, but based on destroy and repair moves. Before describing our algorithm, we outline the methodology followed to design and implement it. This methodology, already used at our winning participation to the ROADEF 2005 Challenge [7,8,9], is a simple and clear recipe to engineer high-performance local-search heuristics for solving practically discrete optimization problems. Another successful application of this methodology for solving real-life inventory routing problems is presented in a companion paper [10].

For more details on high-performance algorithm engineering, the reader is referred to the papers by Moret et al. [11,12] and, as an example, to the outstanding works of Helsgaun [13,14,15] on the traveling salesman problem.

3   Methodology: Three-Layers Design

Several papers have been published describing methodologies for engineering local-search heuristics (see for example the survey edited by Aarts and Lenstra [16]). But many of these methodological papers are essentially concentrating on

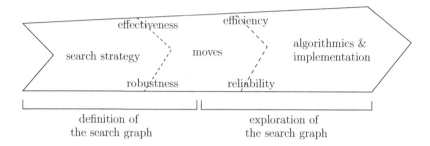

Fig. 1. The three layers of the methodology

search strategies and more particularly metaheuristics (see for example [17,18,19]). In this paper, we suggest to approach the engineering of local-search heuristics according to the following abc framework: a) search strategy, b) moves, c) algorithmics & implementation. We claim that the performance of local-search heuristics depends *equally* on the good treatment of each of these three layers. In fact, each one covers a fundamental point of the local-search paradigm: the definition of the search graph and the exploration of this graph. Figure 1 summarizes the key points of the methodology; note that only a few simple concepts are introduced for describing this one.

The *search space* $S = (S, f)$, with S the set of solutions of the problem and $f : S \mapsto \mathcal{R}$ the objective function to minimize over this set, is defined as the discrete space into which local search walks. The search strategy, dedicated to the problem (or even to instances of the problem), allows to redefine the search space S if necessary. Indeed, the design of the search strategy may lead to redefine the original couple (S, f) into a surrogate one, denoted by (S_g, f_g), which supports the convergence of local search towards high-quality local optima. The idea is to increase the density of the search space S (more solutions in S_g). A way to do that is to relax some constraints of the problem by switching them into the objective function (similarly to Lagrangian relaxations in mathematical programming [20, pp. 349–368]). The idea is to relax only business constraints, and not physical constraints inducing the intrinsic combinatorial structure of the problem (matching, partial ordering, etc.). Indeed, relaxing constraints which strongly structure the solutions of the problem enables a wider diversification, but makes more difficult the convergence toward a new admissible solution.

Then, the *search graph* $\mathcal{G} = (S_g, f_g, A)$, associated to a local-search algorithm, is defined as the directed graph obtained by adding an arc $a \in A$ from $s \in S_g$ to $s' \in S_g$ if a move allows to reach the solution s' from s. Vertices of $S \subseteq S_g$ are green, whereas vertices in $S_g \setminus S$ are red. In the same way, the set A of arcs is partitioned such that $(s, s') \in A$ is green if $f_g(s') \leq f_g(s)$, or red otherwise. Then, the iterations of a local-search algorithm (that is, all the solutions visited during its walk) draw a subgraph in its associated search graph $\mathcal{G}$, inducing a green-arc path. Thus, the red points of the space serve as bridging points to reach better admissible solutions, that is, green points having a better cost in the sense of f.

The *moves* (also called *transformations*) play a central role because they induce the connectivity of the search graph, which is decisive for convergence. Then the idea is to increase the density of the search graph $\mathcal{G}$ (more arcs in A) by defining a lot of moves, more or less orthogonal, more or less large, more or less specialized. This latter notion consists in increasing the success probability of a move (the number of red arcs visited before finding a green one) by using structural properties specific to the problem or even to the instances (see for example the work of Helsgaun [13,14,15] on travelling salesman problems or the works of the authors [8,9] on car sequencing problems). Note that the idea which consists in using systematically a large pool of moves (i.e., of neighborhoods) appears at the root of well-known metaheuristics like Iterated Local Search or Variable Neighborhood Search (see [21] for more details).

This is at these levels – search strategy and moves – that some fragments of metaheuristics can be incorporated (thresholds, tabu lists). However, from our point of view, the diversification of the search must be firstly attained through the (re)definition of the search space (*density*) and the definition of moves (*connectivity*), and not only through a meta-strategy. The main reason is that such a diversification is guided and controlled via the surrogate objective function, unlike traditional metaheuristics. This is why we prefer, at least for starting, implementing a basic first-improvement descent strategy [16] with stochastic choice of moves. In this case, the diversification is realized by accepting to move to solutions with equal cost. Note that the introduction of stochastic elements in every choice made during the search is shown to improve the diversification, in particular by naturally avoiding cycling phenomena (nevertheless, stochastic does not mean uniform).

Finally, *algorithmics*, in particular those related to the evaluation of moves (that is, the exploration of neighborhoods), is crucial for *efficiency*. Since local search is an incomplete search technique, its effectiveness is closely linked to the number of solutions visited before the time limit. In this way, algorithmics forms the engine of the search. Incremental algorithms, exploiting invariants in discrete structures, help to speed up the convergence of local search by several orders of magnitude (see for example the works of Katriel et al. [22] in the context of the Comet software [23]). Then, careful implementations, aware of the locality principle ruling the cache memory allocation and optimized by code profiling, still helps to accelerate local search (see for example the works done on SAT solvers [24]). From experience, it is not surprising to observe an order of 10 between the times of convergence of two local-search heuristics, apparently based on the same principles.

Linked to algorithmics, software and implementation aspects like *reliability* are no less crucial than efficiency. Because relying on complex incremental algorithmics and data structures, engineering local search requires larger efforts for verifying and testing than in traditional (business) software engineering. Hence, the verification process of local-search softwares must be systematic. The first step is to program with assertions [25] (by verifying preconditions, postconditions, invariants all along the program); in particular, one must check at each iteration of the local search (in debugging mode) that the current solution satisfies the constraints of the problem and that its objective value is correct. But one step beyond, the consistency of all dynamic data structures must be checked (in debugging mode) after each iteration of the local search by recomputing them from scratch (with naive algorithms independent from the local-search code). Consequently, a large part of the source code (and of the time spent to implement) in local-search engineering projects must be dedicated to verification and testing: from experience, code checkers represent from 10 to 20 % of the whole source code. Reliability aspects (as well as maintainability and portability issues) must be imperatively taken into account for costing tightly local-search engineering projects.

Once these three levels have been completed, the resulting algorithm can be evaluated by computing statistics on target instances: success rate (number of acceptations over the number of attempts) and improvement rate (number of improvements in the sense of f over the number of attempts) for each move, number of iterations and time to reach best solutions. From experience, the quest for high performance requires many stepwise refinements, following the 80-20 rule (the last 20 % of improvement takes 80 % of the engineering time).

4 Description of the Algorithm

4.1 The Overall Heuristic

The general heuristic is divided into four successive phases, each phase k consisting in planning interventions of priority k. The objective of one phase k is to minimize the ending date t_k of interventions with priority k, without degrading ending dates of interventions with priority $k' < k$. For this, a greedy algorithm completes the feasible solution inherited from the previous phase with interventions of priority k. Then, this solution is modified by local search in order to decrease t_k while maintaining ending dates $t_{k'}$ for each priority $k' < k$. Local search, which is used to pack a set of interventions of a given priority, is the critical routine of the overall heuristic.

More precisely, the local-search step for minimizing the ending date t_k is done as follows. Given one feasible solution with ending dates $t_1, t_2, \ldots, t_k$, a new feasible solution with ending dates $t_1, t_2, \ldots, t_k - 1$ is searched. During the search, an intervention is called infeasible if it is not completed before the ending date $t_k - 1$ or if the team of technicians to which this one is assigned does not own enough skills to complete it. In this way, the surrogate objective of local search is to minimize the number of infeasible interventions. When all are feasible, a new feasible solution is obtained and the process is iterated. This is an example of search strategy increasing density of the search space through constraint relaxation, as described in the methodology section.

A preprocessing phase was added (during the last days of the competition) to the overall heuristic in order to deal with compensations between the four terms of the original objective function (originally assumed to be unlikely according to FRANCE TÉLÉCOM organizers). Indeed, scheduling interventions of priority k

before interventions of priority $k' < k$ may be advantageous according to the global objective function, due to the weakly discriminating coefficients (28, 14, 4, 1). This paradox induces an additional difficulty for which our heuristic was not prepared: to determine in which order the four priorities must be scheduled. Thus, a preprocessing phase was designed to "guess" this order. For this, interventions of each priority k are scheduled separately to determine an upper bound of their completion time c_k; concretely, this is done by the local-search routine in a short execution time (15 seconds for each priority, 1 minute on the whole). Then, the order kept to schedule priorities is the one which minimizes the original objective function, with ending dates t_k obtained by summing durations c_k. For example, assume that one have $c_1 = 1200$, $c_2 = 120$, $c_3 = 600$. The natural ordering of priorities induces the ending dates $t_1 = 1200$, $t_2 = 1320$, $t_3 = 1920$, which implies a cost of 59760. But, by inverting priorities 1 and 2, we obtain $t_1 = 1320$, $t_2 = 120$, $t_3 = 1920$, which implies a cost of 46320. Consequently, the order kept for the application of the overall heuristic will be: 2, 1, 3, 4. The experimental study presented at the end of the paper shows that the optimal ordering of priorities differs from the natural ordering $1, 2, 3, 4$ for more than the half of all instances. However, we do not linger more on this aspect of the problem, since our work was focused on the local-search routine.

4.2 The Transformations

The local-search routine, employed to pack interventions of each priority, consists in applying stochastically some transformations to modify the current solution. We have defined two kinds of transformations, namely moves and swaps, applied on two kinds of objects, namely technicians or interventions. A transformation is accepted if the new solution respects the precedence constraints between interventions, the maximal working duration H in a day, and if the number of infeasible interventions is not increased.

Eight core transformations have been defined, which forms the engine of the local search:

- `MoveTechnician, SwapTechnicians`
- `MoveInterventionInterDays, SwapInterventionsInterDays`
- `MoveInterventionIntraDay, SwapInterventionsIntraDay`
- `MoveInterventionIntraTeam, SwapInterventionsIntraTeam`

The transformations applied to technicians consist in moving or swapping some technicians into a given day of the planning. The transformations applied to interventions consist in moving or swapping interventions of the planning; the suffixes `InterDays` (resp. `IntraDay`, `IntraTeam`) mean that interventions are moved or swapped between different days (resp. into a same day, into a same team). Then, these 8 transformations have been specialized in order to increase their probability of success (it can be viewed as a refinement of neighborhoods which are explored). For each transformation, the three following declinations are defined:

- **Generic**: choose technicians (resp. interventions) randomly;
- **InfeasibleDay**: choose randomly a day among the ones containing an infeasible intervention and pick technicians working this day (resp. interventions performed this day) randomly;
- **InfeasibleTeam**: choose randomly a team among the ones containing an infeasible intervention and pick technicians working in this team (resp. interventions performed by this team) randomly.

Finally, additional transformations have been introduced to tackle the two possible extensions of the problem; namely, adding precedences between interventions, and allowing to abandon interventions within the limit of a budget.

- **AbandonInterventionBudget**: abandon an intervention of the planning (declined into **Generic** and **InfeasibleDay**);
- **SwapInterventionsBudget**: swap an abandoned intervention with a planned one (declined into **Generic** and **InfeasibleDay**);
- **ReinsertInterventionBudget**: reinsert an abandoned intervention into the planning;
- **SwapInterventionsPrecedences**: swap two interventions $I_i, I_{i'}$ such that $d_i \leq d_{i'}$ and the number of descendants of $I_{i'}$ in the precedence graph is greater than or equal to the one of I_i (declined into **InterDays** and **IntraDay**).

On the whole, a pool of 31 transformations is used. At each iteration of the heuristic, a transformation is picked randomly following a certain distribution. Here the convergence speed of the local search depends strongly of the utilization rate of each transformation. These rates have been fixed by hand after experimentations done with the first 20 benchmarks provided by FRANCE TÉLÉCOM. Here is the outline of the distribution: (i) 25 % of **MoveInterventionInterDays** declined into **InfeasibleDay**, (ii) 25 % of **MoveTechnician** declined into **InfeasibleTeam**, (iii) 15 % of **SwapTechnicians** declined into **InfeasibleTeam**, and from 5 % to 1 % for the 28 other moves (if no budget is available, no budget-specific transformation is used; idem for precedences). The prominence of transformations (i), (ii), (iii) in the distribution is sensible: (i) is in charge of reinserting interventions making a day infeasible into another ones, whereas (ii) and (iii) are supposed to solve the infeasibility generated by lack of skills in teams. Note that, despite their low utilization rate, the 28 other moves participate to the diversification of the search.

4.3   Algorithmics and Implementation

Applying a transformation follows this scheme: if the evaluation of the move is positive (evaluate), then the move is performed and all the incremental data structures are updated (commit), else the incremental data structures are initialized (rollback). Since the number of attempted moves is generally much higher than the number of accepted moves, evaluate and rollback procedures are critical for the efficiency of the local search. The evaluation procedure is staged in order to stop early in case of rejection of the move; the different tests which are part of it are ordered according to their time complexity and their propensity to fail. For example, since the precedence constraints are considered as inviolable, all tests related to precedences in the evaluation process of moves `MoveIntervention` and `SwapInterventions` are done first. Since the evaluation process cannot be detailed for each of the 8 core transformations, we will only insist on two main points: the evaluation related to skills and the evaluation related to precedences.

Evaluation of Skills. Any move which impacts the technicians or the interventions of a team calls for an evaluation of the adequation between skills provided by the technicians and skills required by the interventions of this team. To realize this evaluation, to each team of technicians is associated a matrix C_e of skills giving for each domain d and level l, the number of technicians of level at least l in the domain d. Then, an intervention I_i assigned to the team E_e is infeasible (according to skills) if a pair (d, l) exists such that $C_i(d, l) > C_e(d, l)$. Since the number of domains and levels is not bounded (for example, the instance B4 of benchmarks provided by FRANCE TÉLÉCOM includes 40 domains), it is difficult to design a data structure more efficient than this matrix domain/level to evaluate skills. Consequently, evaluating the impact of a move on skills becomes time expensive in the worst case, because in $O(dl)$ time.

Fortunately, the number of cells of this matrix which are necessary to scan can be drastically reduced in practice. For example, the scan can be restricted to the useful domains of the matrix of skills required by the intervention, that is, the domains for which at least one technician is required. Then, for each useful domain d, the scan can be reduced to an interval of levels. Remind that our skill matrices are built cumulatively: for each domain, the number of technicians is non-increasing according to levels. Thus, the evaluation can start at the higher level l_{inf} such that $C_i(d, l_{inf}) = C_i(d, l)$ for all $l \leq l_{inf}$ and stop at the lower level l_{sup} such that $C_i(d, l_{sup}) = 0$.

Finally, a heuristic test with a lower time-complexity can be done before the scan of the matrix, in order to stop earlier in case of negative evaluation. For each domain d, define $C_e(d) = \sum_l C_e(d, l)$ and symmetrically $C_i(d) = \sum_l C_i(d, l)$. Then, the following necessary condition holds: if one domain d exists such that $C_i(d) > C_e(d)$, then I_i is infeasible (note that the reciprocal is trivially false). Such a test located upstream enables to determine in only $O(d)$ time the infeasible status of the intervention. In the same way, it is appropriate to place even before another test verifying if $C_i = \sum_d C_i(d)$ is strictly greater than $C_e = \sum_d C_e(d)$. Finally, the evaluation of skills is composed of three successive tests, respectively in $O(1)$ time, in $O(d)$ time, and in $O(dl)$ time, each one allowing to conclude in case of failure. Of course, all the structures involved in these tests must be maintained incrementally during the search.

Maintaining Precedences. The second point concerns the evaluation of the ending dates $t_1, t_2, \ldots, t_k-1$, and more generally the evaluation of the completion dates of the set of interventions assigned to each team. The computation of these values are complicated by precedences between interventions, because requiring to compute longest paths in a directed acyclic graph (DAG). For this, a DAG is attached to each day of the planning. Each DAG contains a source node representing the start of the day and a destination node representing its end. Then, to each intervention planned into the day is associated one node in the DAG. These nodes are linked by two kinds of precedences: blue arcs which induce the order of the interventions assigned to each team of technicians into the day, and red arcs which represent the precedences given in input. The length $l(i, i')$ of the arc connecting the nodes corresponding two interventions $I_i \prec I_{i'}$ is given by the duration $D(i)$ of the intervention I_i. In this way, the earliest starting date of one intervention is determined by the length of a longest path from the source node to its node into the DAG. This date, stored at each node, allows to verify if the maximal working duration H is respected for all teams, and to compute the ending dates $t_1, t_2, \ldots, t_k - 1$.

Thus, any transformation `MoveIntervention` or `SwapIntervention` implies a cascade of insertion/suppression of arcs into the DAG of impacted days, needing a (temporary) update of the longest paths in order to evaluate the impact of the transformation. Since the interventions of each team are completed sequentially, each node has only one blue predecessor and only one blue successor. The red predecessors and successors are stored as unordered lists into the data structure of the node. These lists, implemented as arrays, are designed to support basic routines (find, insert, delete, clear) in $O(1)$ time. Such a representation was motivated by the sparsity of the precedence graph on benchmarks A and B (where the number of red arcs is lower than the number n of interventions).

The temporary update of longest paths is done by a recursive bread-first propagation from the inserted/suppressed node. The new longest path at a node is computed by scanning its predecessors: if the new longest path is different from the old one, then the successors of the node are placed into a queue in order to be examined recursively. This propagation also enables to detect the creation of cycles, which makes the transformation rejected. When the maximum degree of the DAG remains in $O(1)$, which is the case here, our incremental algorithm (evaluate, commit and rollback procedures) runs in optimal time and space $O(a)$ with a the number of affected nodes (that is, having a modified longest path). The interested reader can consult the works of Katriel et al. [22] on the subject, which give an incremental algorithm whose complexity becomes advantageous when the maximum in-degree of a node is large.

An Implementation Detail. As claimed in introduction, every choice made during the search follows stochastic rules, in order to avoid bias and to enforce diversification. Then, a number of choices are made before applying each single move. On average, the function `MyRand(n)`, which returns a pseudo-random integer value between 0 and $n-1$, is called 5 times per attempted move. For example, the transformation `MoveInterventionInterDays` declined into `InfeasibleDay` (which represents 25 % of attempted moves) uses it 6 times. `MyRand` is in fact the portion of code which is the most called into our program (more than 10 billion of calls over 20 minutes of running time).

A direct implementation (in ISO C programming language) of `MyRand(n)` is `n * rand() / (RAND_MAX + 1.0)` [26, p. 277], where `rand()` is a function of the `stdlib` library returning a pseudo-random integer between 0 and the largest positive `int`-type number. Although providing pseudo-random integer sequences of sufficient quality for our application, a profiling of our program with *gprof* [27] pointed `MyRand` as the main bottleneck for running time. Inspired by the Knuth-Lewis generator [26, pp. 283–286], we have engineered a quick `MyRand(n)` function dedicated to our needs: `(n * ((seed = 1664525 * seed + 1013904223) >> 16)) >> 16`, which is correct if n is between 0 and $2^{16} - 1 = 65535$ and if the `int` type is encoded on 32 bits (the traditional `seed` of the generator is initialized at the beginning of the program).

Experimentations on different computing platforms have shown that this concise implementation is at least 3 times faster than the direct implementation. The period of the generator is of length $2^{32} > 4 \times 10^9$, which is comparable to the one of `rand()` and remains sufficient in this context (from experience, the quality of the pseudo-random number generation is not highly critical for simulating randomness in local search). This enables us to reduce the part of running time spent in `MyRand` from 17 % to 7 %, lowering it to the levels of the other time-consuming functions of the program (the 3 functions appearing just after `MyRand`, which are parts of the evaluation process, consume each one nearly 5 % of the total running time).

5   Experimental Results

The whole algorithm was implemented in C programming language (ISO C99). The resulting program, which includes nearly 12000 lines of code, was compiled and tested on several computing platforms with comparable performance (Red Hat Linux/AMD Athlon 64, Windows XP/Intel Pentium 4, Windows XP/Intel Xeon, Windows Vista/Intel Xeon 64) using the free compiler `GCC 3.4.4` with options `-O3 -pedantic -Wall -W -std=c99`}. Note that nearly 10 % of the source code is dedicated to the verification of the program.

The benchmarks A, B, X provided by FRANCE TÉLÉCOM and used for tests can be downloaded on the web page of the Challenge [1] (the set X, used to rank the competitors, was unveiled once the final results proclaimed). On each tested platform, our local-search algorithm *attempts more than 1 million moves per second*, even for large-scale instances (for example instance B8: 800 interventions, 150 technicians, 10 domains and 4 levels for skills, 440 precedences. Over 20 minutes of running time (which is the maximum allowed for the competition), the heuristic *visits more than 1 billion solutions* into the surrogate search space. The average success rate of transformations (that is, the number of accepted transformations divided by the number of attempted ones) varies between 10 and 60 % according to the instances. The memory allocated by the program does not exceed 10 Mo for any instance of the benchmarks (for example, 8 Mo of memory are allocated for B8 instance), allowing a full exploitation of the cache memory. Table 1 reports the results obtained on a computer equipped with a

Table 1. Benchmarks A, B, X: characteristics and results (M = million)

data	n	m	d	l	P	B	FT	EGN	BEST	gap	priority	attempt	accept	improve
A1	5	5	3	2	0	0	2490	2340	2340	0.0 %	1234	8696 M	1260 M	2
A2	5	5	3	2	2	0	4755	4755	4755	0.0 %	1234	4626 M	1530 M	2
A3	20	7	3	2	0	0	15840	11880	11880	0.0 %	2134	4262 M	1178 M	3
A4	20	7	4	3	7	0	14880	14040	13452	4.4 %	1234	4558 M	1047 M	80
A5	50	10	3	2	13	0	41220	29400	28845	2.0 %	2134	5203 M	951 M	273
A6	50	10	5	4	11	0	30090	18795	18795	0.0 %	2134	4861 M	1163 M	225
A7	100	20	5	4	31	0	38580	30540	29690	2.9 %	1234	4968 M	892 M	669
A8	100	20	5	4	21	0	26820	20100	16920	18.8 %	1234	4958 M	1176 M	1014
A9	100	20	5	4	22	0	35600	27440	27440	0.0 %	2134	5081 M	877 M	1166
A10	100	15	5	4	31	0	51720	38460	38296	0.5 %	1234	5689 M	707 M	577
B1	200	20	4	4	47	300	69960	33900	33675	0.7 %	1234	4453 M	1012 M	833
B2	300	30	5	3	143	300	34065	16260	15510	4.9 %	1234	4259 M	945 M	1195
B3	400	40	4	4	57	500	34095	16005	15870	0.9 %	1234	3722 M	825 M	1830
B4	400	30	40	3	112	300	50340	24330	23700	2.7 %	2134	2485 M	604 M	604
B5	500	50	7	4	427	900	150360	88680	87300	1.6 %	1234	3344 M	1520 M	612
B6	500	30	8	3	457	300	47595	27675	27210	1.8 %	2134	4437 M	616 M	1534
B7	500	100	10	5	387	500	56940	36900	33060	11.7 %	1234	2867 M	1544 M	643
B8	800	150	10	4	440	500	51720	36840	32160	14.6 %	1234	2927 M	1513 M	1036
B9	120	60	5	5	55	100	44640	32700	28080	16.5 %	1234	3853 M	1470 M	697
B10	120	40	5	5	55	500	61560	41280	34440	19.9 %	1234	3704 M	1499 M	565
X1	600	60	15	4	195	50	n/a	180240	151140	19.3 %	1234	2622 M	1136 M	546
X2	800	100	6	6	536	500	n/a	8370	7260	15.3 %	1234	2764 M	962 M	2712
X3	300	50	20	3	224	1000	n/a	50760	50040	1.5 %	1234	2458 M	1464 M	888
X4	800	70	15	7	321	150	n/a	68960	65400	5.5 %	2134	3383 M	623 M	2015
X5	600	60	15	4	201	50	n/a	178560	147000	21.5 %	1234	2551 M	1222 M	599
X6	200	20	6	6	128	500	n/a	10440	9480	10.2 %	1234	3573 M	1051 M	487
X7	300	50	20	3	235	1000	n/a	38400	33240	15.6 %	1234	2533 M	1405 M	527
X8	100	30	15	7	40	150	n/a	23800	23640	0.7 %	1234	2712 M	1330 M	327
X9	500	50	15	4	184	50	n/a	154920	134760	15.0 %	1234	2541 M	1156 M	522
X10	500	40	15	4	184	500	n/a	152280	137040	11.2 %	1234	2739 M	1183 M	546
average										7.3 %		3894 M	1129 M	790

Windows XP operating system and a chipset Intel Xeon 3075 (CPU 2.67 GHz, L1 cache 64 Kio, L2 cache 4 Mio, RAM 2 Go). An executable binary file (compiled for the desired computing architecture) is available on request from the authors.

The characteristics of each instance are given on the left part of the table: the number n of interventions, the number m of technicians, the number d of skill domains, the number l of skill levels, the number P of (non transitive) precedences between interventions, the budget B available. For each instance, 5 runs were performed, each one limited to 1200 seconds (20 minutes). In the middle part of the table, the columns "FT", "EGN", "BEST", "% gap", "priority" contain respectively the result obtained by FRANCE TÉLÉCOM's algorithm, the worst result obtained by our algorithm (over the 5 runs), the best result obtained among all the competitors (including the 5 runs of our algorithm), the relative gap (in %) between the values of the two previous columns, and the ordering of priorities used by the EGN algorithm (for example, the value 3214 means that the priorities were scheduled according to the ordering 3, 2, 1, 4). In the right

Table 2. Results with optimal priority ordering (left) or extended time limits (right)

data	EGN	EGN*	BEST	% gap	priority
A5	29700	28845	28845	0.0	3214
A8	20100	16979	16979	0.0	2134
B7	36900	35700	33300	7.3	2134
B9	32700	28080	28080	0.0	2134
B10	41280	34440	34440	0.0	2314
X2	8370	7440	7260	2.5	2134
X6	10440	10140	9480	7.0	2134
X7	38400	32280	32280	0.0	2134
X8	23800	23220	23220	0.0	2134

data	20 min	1 hr	3 hrs	9 hrs
X1	180240	170460	168240	158280
X5	178560	167280	165120	164760
X9	154920	146520	146040	141720
X10	152280	144360	140340	140160

part of the table, the column "attempt" (resp. "accept", "improve") reports the average number of attempted transformations (resp. accepted transformations, strictly improving transformations).

A weak gap is observed between the results of the 5 runs of our algorithm (that is why only the worst result is given here). Note that this gap increases with the number of planned days. Thus, gaps greater than 1 % between runs are observed for the following instances: X1 (57 days), X5 (52 days), X9 (50 days), X10 (49 days). Then, the relative gap between the results of our algorithm and the best results of the Challenge shows that this one is very competitive. On average, EGN algorithm reduces by 30 % the cost of the solutions proposed by FRANCE TÉLÉCOM (and by 41 % for the sole benchmark B). On the other hand, the gap between our solutions and the best solutions obtained among all competitors is of 7.3 % on average (with a standard deviation of 7.5 %). On the 30 instances, our algorithm obtains the best solution for 13 ones (7 for A, 6 for B, 3 for X) and obtains a solution having a cost lower than 6 % of the cost of the best solution for 18 instances (9 for A, 6 for B, 3 for X).

Besides, we are able to explain why EGN algorithm fails to find the best solution for the 17 remaining instances. The main reason is that the ordering of priorities computed in the preprocessing stage is not the most appropriate. The table on the left part of Table 2 shows the cost obtained by our algorithm assuming that the optimal ordering is known. This cost appears in the column named "EGN*" and the optimal ordering appears in the column named "priority". In this case, one can observe that for 6 more instances we obtain the best solution. The second reason is still due to the multi-objective nature of the cost function. For example, for instance A4, EGN algorithm obtains the following solution: $t_1 = 315$, $t_2 = 540$ and $t_3 = 660$ with global cost 14040. Now, relaxing slightly the ending date of interventions with priority 1 allows to improve the global cost thanks to the compensation of the two first terms of the objective function: $t_1 = 324$, $t_2 = 480$ and $t_3 = 660$ with global cost 13452 (best known solution).

However, our local-search approach is overcome on instances X1, X5, X9, X10 by large neighborhood search approaches of Hurkens [4], winner of the Challenge, and to a lesser extend, of Cordeau et al. [6] ranked second ex æquo. In fact, these instances contain in majority long interventions (of length 60 or

120) requiring many technicians, which reduces considerably the combinatorics induced by the assignment of interventions to teams and then allows integer programming approaches for tackling subproblems. To make up for this weakness, it seems therefore appropriate to add some moves with larger neighborhoods to our pool of transformations (as done in [8] for car sequencing problems). A first simple idea is to implement (k, l)-swap transformations, consisting in exchanging k interventions with l other ones (here only $(1, 1)$-swaps are done). The table on the right part of Table 2 gives results obtained for these 4 instances with extended time limits, showing that our algorithm converges toward a solution of quality near from the ones of Hurkens and Cordeau et al. [1].

References

1. ROADEF Challenge (2007): http://www.g-scop.fr/ChallengeROADEF2007/
2. Jansen, K., Woeginger, G., Yu, Z.: UET-scheduling with chain-type precedence constraints. Computers and Operations Research 22(9), 915–920 (1995)
3. Garey, M., Johnson, D.: Computer and Intractability: a Guide to the Theory of NP-Completeness. W.H. Freeman & Co., New York (1979)
4. Hurkens, C.: Incorporating the strength of MIP modeling in schedule construction. In: ROADEF 2007, le 8ème Congrès de la Société Française de Recherche Opérationnelle et d'Aide à la Décision, Grenoble, France (2007) (in French)
5. Ahuja, R., Ergun, Ö., Orlin, J., Punnen, A.: A survey of very large-scale neighborhood search techniques. Discrete Applied Mathematics 123, 75–102 (2002)
6. Cordeau, J.F., Laporte, G., Pasin, F., Ropke, S.: ROADEF 2007 challenge: scheduling of technicians and interventions in a telecommunications company. In: ROADEF 2007, le 8ème Congrès de la Société Française de Recherche Opérationnelle et d'Aide à la Décision, Grenoble, France (2007) (in French)
7. ROADEF Challenge 2005:
   http://www.prism.uvsq.fr/~vdc/ROADEF/CHALLENGES/2005/
8. Estellon, B., Gardi, F., Nouioua, K.: A survey of very large-scale neighborhood search techniques. RAIRO Operations Research 40(4), 355–379 (2006)
9. Estellon, B., Gardi, F., Nouioua, K.: Two local search approaches for solving real-life car sequencing problems. European Journal of Operational Research 191(3), 928–944 (2008)
10. Benoist, T., Estellon, B., Gardi, F., Jeanjean, A.: High-performance local search for solving inventory routing problems. In: Stützle, T., Birattari, M., Hoos, H.H. (eds.) SLS 2009. LNCS, vol. 5752, pp. 105–109. Springer, Heidelberg (2009)
11. Moret, B.: Towards a discipline of experimental algorithmics. In: Goldwasser, M., Johnson, D., McGeoch, C. (eds.) Data Structures, Near Neighbor Searches, and Methodology: 5th and 6th DIMACS Implementation Challenges. DIMACS Monographs, vol. 59, pp. 197–213. American Mathematical Society, Providence (2002)
12. Moret, B., Bader, D., Warnow, T.: High-performance algorithm engineering for computational phylogenetics. Journal of Supercomputing 22(1), 99–111 (2002)
13. Helsgaun, K.: An effective implementation of the Lin-Kernighan traveling salesman heuristic. Datalogiske Skrifter (Writings on Computer Science) 81, Roskilde University, Denmark (1998)
14. Helsgaun, K.: An effective implementation of the Lin-Kernighan traveling salesman heuristic. European Journal of Operational Research 126(1), 106–130 (2000)

15. Helsgaun, K.: An effective implementation of k-opt moves for the Lin-Kernighan tsp heuristic. Datalogiske Skrifter (Writings on Computer Science) 109, Roskilde University, Denmark (2006)
16. Aarts, E., Lenstra, J. (eds.): Local Search in Combinatorial Optimization. Wiley-Interscience Series in Discrete Mathematics and Optimization. John Wiley & Sons, Chichester (1997)
17. Hansen, P., Mladenović, N., Pérez, J.M.: Variable neighborhood search: methods and applications. 4OR 6(4), 319–360 (2008)
18. Løkketangen, A.: The importance of being careful. In: Stützle, T., Birattari, M., Hoos, H.H. (eds.) SLS 2007. LNCS, vol. 4638, pp. 1–15. Springer, Heidelberg (2007)
19. Pellegrini, P., Birattari, M.: Implementation effort and performance. In: Stützle, T., Birattari, M., Hoos, H.H. (eds.) SLS 2007. LNCS, vol. 4638, pp. 31–45. Springer, Heidelberg (2007)
20. Minoux, M.: Programmation Mathématique: Théorie et Algorithmes. Éditions Tec & Doc, Lavoisier, 2nd edn. (2008) (in French)
21. Glover, F., Kochenberger, G. (eds.): Handbook of Metaheuristics. International Series in Operations Research and Management Science, vol. 57. Kluwer Academic Publishers, Dordrecht (2002)
22. Katriel, I., Michel, L., Hentenryck, P.V.: Maintaining longest paths incrementally. Constraints 10(2), 159–183 (2005)
23. Michel, L., Hentenryck, P.V.: A constraint-based architecture for local search. In: Proceedings of OOPSLA 2002, the 2002 ACM SIGPLAN Conference on Object-Oriented Programming Systems, Languages and Applications. SIGPLAN Notices, vol. 37, pp. 83–100. ACM Press, New York (2002)
24. Zhang, L., Malik, S.: Cache performance of SAT solvers: a case study for efficient implementation of algorithms. In: Giunchiglia, E., Tacchella, A. (eds.) SAT 2003. LNCS, vol. 2919, pp. 287–298. Springer, Heidelberg (2004)
25. Rosenblum, D.: Towards a method of programming with assertions. In: Proceedings of ICSE 1992, the 14th International Conference on Software Engineering, pp. 92–104. ACM Press, New York (1992)
26. Press, W., Tenkolsky, S., Vetterling, W., Flannery, B.: Numerical Recipes in C: the Art of Scientific Computing, 2nd edn. Cambridge University Press, Cambridge (1995)
27. Fenlason, J., Stallman, R.: GNU gprof: the GNU profiler (1998), http://www.gnu.org/software/binutils/

On the Use of Run Time Distributions to Evaluate and Compare Stochastic Local Search Algorithms

Celso C. Ribeiro[1], Isabel Rosseti[2], and Reinaldo Vallejos[3]

[1] Department of Computer Science, Universidade Federal Fluminense, Niterói, Brazil
[2] Department of Science and Technology, Universidade Federal Fluminense,
Rio das Ostras, Brazil
[3] Telematics Group, Department of Electronic Engineering, Universidad Técnica
Federico Santa María, Valparaíso, Chile
{celso,rosseti}@ic.uff.br, reinaldo.vallejos@usm.cl

Abstract. Run time distributions or time-to-target plots are very useful tools to characterize the running times of stochastic algorithms for combinatorial optimization. We further explore run time distributions and describe a new tool to compare two algorithms based on stochastic local search. For the case where the running times of both algorithms fit exponential distributions, we derive a closed form index that gives the probability that one of them finds a solution at least as good as a given target value in a smaller computation time than the other. This result is extended to the case of general run time distributions and a numerical iterative procedure is described for the computation of the above probability value. Numerical examples illustrate the application of this tool in the comparison of different algorithms for three different problems.

1 Motivation

Run time distributions or time-to-target plots display on the ordinate axis the probability that an algorithm will find a solution at least as good as a given target value within a given running time, shown on the abscissa axis. Time-to-target plots were first used by Feo et al. [1]. Run time distributions have been advocated also by Hoos and Stützle [2,3] as a way to characterize the running times of stochastic algorithms for combinatorial optimization.

It has been observed that in many implementations of local search heuristics for combinatorial optimization problems, such as simulated annealing, genetic algorithms, iterated local search, tabu search, and GRASP [4,5,6,7,8,9,10,11,12], the random variable *time to target value* fits an exponential (or a shifted exponential) distribution. Hoos and Stützle [13,8] conjecture that this is true for all local search methods for combinatorial optimization.

Aiex et al. [14] describe a perl program to create time-to-target plots for measured times that are assumed to fit a shifted exponential distribution, following [4]. Such plots are very useful in the comparison of different algorithms for solving a given problem and have been widely used as a tool for algorithm design and comparison.

T. Stützle, M. Birattari, and H.H. Hoos (Eds.): SLS 2009, LNCS 5752, pp. 16–30, 2009.

In this work, we further explore run time distributions to evaluate stochastic local search algorithms. We describe a new tool to compare any pair of different stochastic local search algorithms and we use it in the investigation of different applications. Under the assumption that the running times of the two algorithms follow exponential (or shifted exponential) distributions, we develop in Section 2 a closed form index that gives the probability that one of the algorithms finds a target solution value in a smaller computation time than the other. In Section 3, this result is extended to the case of general run time distributions and a numerical iterative procedure is described for the computation of such probability. Applications illustrating the comparison of different algorithms for the same problem appear in Section 4. Concluding remarks are made in the last section.

2 Comparing Exponential-Time Algorithms

We assume the existence of two stochastic local search algorithms A_1 and A_2 for some combinatorial optimization problem. Furthermore, we assume that their running times fit exponential (or shifted exponential) distributions. We denote by X_1 (resp. X_2) the continuous random variable representing the time needed by algorithm A_1 (resp. A_2) to find a solution as good as a given target value:

$$X_1 \mapsto \begin{cases} 0, & \tau < T_1 \\ \lambda_1 e^{-\lambda_1(\tau-T_1)}, & \tau \geq T_1 \end{cases}$$

and

$$X_2 \mapsto \begin{cases} 0, & \tau < T_2 \\ \lambda_2 e^{-\lambda_2(\tau-T_2)}, & \tau \geq T_2 \end{cases}$$

where T_1, λ_1, T_2, and λ_2 are parameters. The cumulative probability distribution and the probability density function of X_1 are depicted in Figure 1.

Since both algorithms stop when they find a solution at least as good as the target, we may say that algorithm A_1 performs better than A_2 if the former stops before the latter. Therefore, we must evaluate the probability that X_1 takes a value smaller than or equal to X_2, i.e. we compute $Pr(X_1 \leq X_2)$. Conditioning on the value of X_2 and applying the total probability theorem, we obtain:

$$Pr(X_1 \leq X_2) = \int_{-\infty}^{\infty} Pr(X_1 \leq X_2 | X_2 = \tau) f_{X_2}(\tau) d\tau =$$

$$= \int_{T_2}^{\infty} Pr(X_1 \leq X_2 | X_2 = \tau) \lambda_2 e^{-\lambda_2(\tau-T_2)} d\tau = \int_{T_2}^{\infty} Pr(X_1 \leq \tau) \lambda_2 e^{-\lambda_2(\tau-T_2)} d\tau.$$

Let $\nu = \tau - T_2$. Then, $d\nu = d\tau$ and

$$Pr(X_1 \leq X_2) = \int_0^{\infty} Pr[X_1 \leq (\nu + T_2)] \lambda_2 e^{-\lambda_2 \nu} d\nu. \tag{1}$$

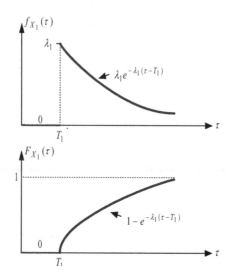

Fig. 1. Probability density function and cumulative probability distribution of X_1

To solve the above integral, one first has to compute

$$Pr[X_1 \leq (\nu + T_2)] = \int_{-\infty}^{\nu+T_2} f_{X_1}(\tau)d\tau.$$

Assuming that $T_2 \geq T_1$, without loss of generality, we have that:

$$Pr[X_1 \leq (\nu + T_2)] = \int_{T_1}^{\nu+T_2} \lambda_1 e^{-\lambda_1(\tau-T_1)}d\tau.$$

Now, let $w = \tau - T_1$. Then, $dw = d\tau$ and

$$Pr[X_1 \leq (\nu + T_2)] = \int_{0}^{\nu+T_2-T_1} \lambda_1 e^{-\lambda_1 w}dw = 1 - e^{-\lambda_1(\nu+T_2-T_1)}. \qquad (2)$$

Replacing (2) in equation (1), we obtain

$$Pr(X_1 \leq X_2) = \int_{0}^{\infty} [1 - e^{-\lambda_1(\nu+T_2-T_1)}]\lambda_2 e^{-\lambda_2\nu}d\nu =$$

$$= 1 - e^{-\lambda_1(T_2-T_1)} \int_{0}^{\infty} e^{-\nu(\lambda_1+\lambda_2)}d\nu = 1 + e^{-\lambda_1(T_2-T_1)}\lambda_2 \frac{e^{-\nu(\lambda_1+\lambda_2)}}{\lambda_1 + \lambda_2} \Bigg|_{\nu=0}^{\nu=\infty}.$$

Finally,

$$Pr(X_1 \leq X_2) = 1 - e^{-\lambda_1(T_2-T_1)}\frac{\lambda_2}{\lambda_1 + \lambda_2}. \qquad (3)$$

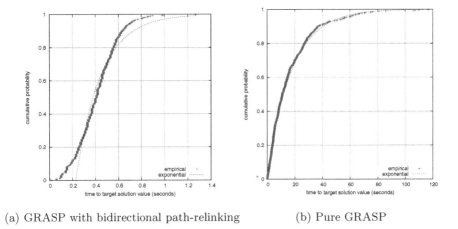

(a) GRASP with bidirectional path-relinking   (b) Pure GRASP

Fig. 2. Run time distributions on an instance of the 2-path network design problem with 80 nodes and 800 origin-destination pairs, with target value set at 588

This result can be better interpreted by rewriting expression (3) as:

$$Pr(X_1 \leq X_2) = (1 - e^{-\lambda_1(T_2 - T_1)}) + e^{-\lambda_1(T_2 - T_1)}\frac{\lambda_1}{\lambda_1 + \lambda_2}. \tag{4}$$

The first term of the right-hand side of equation (4) is the probability that $0 \leq X_1 \leq T_2$, in which case X_1 is clearly less than or equal to X_2. The second term of (4) is the probability that X_1 be greater than T_2 and less than or equal to X_2, given that $X_1 \geq T_2$, which completes the interpretation.

To illustrate the above result, we consider two algorithms described in [15] for solving the 2-path network design problem. Algorithm A_1 is an implementation of GRASP with bidirectional path-relinking, while algorithm A_2 is a pure GRASP heuristic. Figure 2 depicts the run time distributions obtained after 500 runs with different seeds on an instance with 80 nodes and 800 origin-destination pairs, with the target value set at 588. The plots have been obtained with the perl tool provided in [14], which also computed the parameters of the two distributions: $\lambda_1 = 0.218988$, $T_1 = 0.01$, $\lambda_2 = 17.829236$, and $T_2 = 0.01$. Applying expression (3), we get $Pr(X_1 \leq X_2) = 0.943516$. This probability is consistent with Figure 3, in which the run time distribution of GRASP with bidirectional path-relinking is much to the left of that of pure GRASP for the same instance.

Aiex et al. [4] have shown experimentally that the time taken by a GRASP heuristic to find a solution at least as good as a given target value fits an exponential distribution. If the setup times are not negligible, it fits a two-parameter shifted exponential distribution. The experiments involved 2,400 runs of five problems: maximum stable set [1], quadratic assignment [16], graph planarization [17], maximum weighted satisfiability [18], and maximum covering [19].

However, if path-relinking is applied as an intensification step at the end of each iteration [20,21,15], then the iterations are no longer independent and the

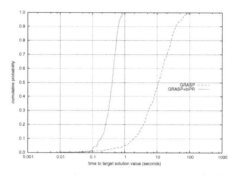

Fig. 3. Superimposed run time distributions of GRASP with bidirectional path-relinking and pure GRASP

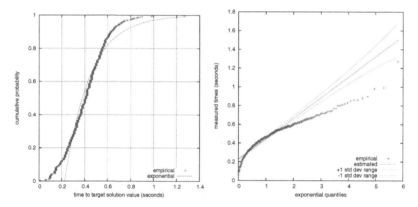

Fig. 4. Run time distribution and quantile-quantile plot for GRASP with bidirectional path-relinking on an instance of the 2-path network design problem with 80 nodes and 800 origin-destination pairs, with target set to 588

memoryless characteristic of GRASP is destroyed. Consequently, the time-to-target random variable may not fit an exponential distribution.

This claim is illustrated by two implementations of GRASP with path-relinking. The first is an application to the 2-path network design problem [15]. The run time distribution and the quantile-quantile plot for an instance with 80 nodes and 800 origin-destination pairs are depicted in Figure 4. The second is an application to the three-index assignment problem [22]. Run time distributions and quantile-quantile plots for Balas and Saltzman problems 22.1 (target set to 8) and 24.1 (target set to 7) are shown in Figures 5 and 6, respectively. We observe that points steadily deviate by more than one standard deviation from the estimate for the upper quantiles in the quantile-quantile plots (i.e., many points associated with large computation times fall outside the plus or minus one standard deviation bounds). Therefore, we may say that these run time distributions are not exponential.

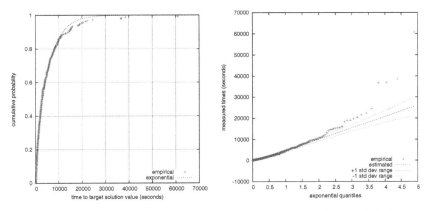

Fig. 5. Run time distribution and quantile-quantile plot for GRASP with bidirectional path-relinking on Balas and Saltzman problem 22.1, with target set to 8

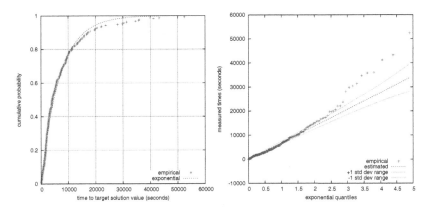

Fig. 6. Run time distribution and quantile-quantile plot for GRASP with bidirectional path-relinking on Balas and Saltzman problem 24.1, with target value to 7

If the running times do not fit exponential distributions, then the result established by expression (3) does not hold. Therefore, this approach is extended to general run time distributions in the next section.

3   General Run Time Distributions

Let X_1 and X_2 be continuous random variables, with cumulative probability distributions $F_{X_1}(\tau)$ and $F_{X_2}(\tau)$ and probability density functions $f_{X_1}(\tau)$ and $f_{X_2}(\tau)$. Then,

$$Pr(X_1 \leq X_2) = \int_{-\infty}^{\infty} Pr(X_1 \leq \tau)f_{X_2}(\tau)d\tau = \int_{0}^{\infty} Pr(X_1 \leq \tau)f_{X_2}(\tau)d\tau,$$

since $f_{X_1}(\tau) = f_{X_2}(\tau) = 0$ for any $\tau < 0$. For an arbitrary small real number ε, the above expression can be rewritten as

$$Pr(X_1 \leq X_2) = \sum_{i=0}^{\infty} \int_{i\varepsilon}^{(i+1)\varepsilon} Pr(X_1 \leq \tau) f_{X_2}(\tau) d\tau. \tag{5}$$

Since $Pr(X_1 \leq i\varepsilon) \leq Pr(X_1 \leq \tau) \leq Pr(X_1 \leq (i+1)\varepsilon)$ for $i\varepsilon \leq \tau \leq (i+1)\varepsilon$, replacing $Pr(X_1 \leq \tau)$ by $Pr(X_1 \leq i\varepsilon)$ and by $Pr(X_1 \leq (i+1)\varepsilon)$ in (5) leads to

$$\sum_{i=0}^{\infty} F_{X_1}(i\varepsilon) \int_{i\varepsilon}^{(i+1)\varepsilon} f_{X_2}(\tau)d\tau \leq Pr(X_1 \leq X_2) \leq \sum_{i=0}^{\infty} F_{X_1}((i+1)\varepsilon) \int_{i\varepsilon}^{(i+1)\varepsilon} f_{X_2}(\tau)d\tau.$$

Let $L(\varepsilon)$ and $R(\varepsilon)$ be the value of the left and right hand sides of the above expression, respectively, with $\Delta(\varepsilon) = R(\varepsilon) - L(\varepsilon)$ being the difference between the upper and lower bounds of $Pr(X_1 \leq X_2)$. Then,

$$\Delta(\varepsilon) = \sum_{i=0}^{\infty} [F_{X_1}((i+1)\varepsilon) - F_{X_1}(i\varepsilon)] \int_{i\varepsilon}^{(i+1)\varepsilon} f_{X_2}(\tau)d\tau.$$

Let $\delta = \max_{\tau \geq 0}\{f_{X_1}(\tau)\}$. Since $|F_{X_1}((i+1)\varepsilon) - F_{X_1}(i\varepsilon)| \leq \delta\varepsilon$ for $i \geq 0$,

$$\Delta(\varepsilon) \leq \sum_{i=0}^{\infty} \delta\varepsilon \int_{i\varepsilon}^{(i+1)\varepsilon} f_{X_2}(\tau)d\tau = \delta\varepsilon \int_{0}^{\infty} f_{X_2}(\tau)d\tau = \delta\varepsilon.$$

In order to evaluate a good approximation to $Pr(X_1 \leq X_2)$, we select the appropriate value of ε such that the resulting approximation error $\Delta(\varepsilon)$ is sufficiently small. Next, we compute $L(\varepsilon)$ and $R(\varepsilon)$ to obtain the approximation

$$Pr(X_1 \leq X_2) \approx \frac{L(\varepsilon) + R(\varepsilon)}{2}. \tag{6}$$

In practice, the probability distributions are unknown. Instead of them, all the information available is a large number N of observations of the random variables X_1 and X_2. Since $\delta = \max_{\tau \geq 0}\{f_{X_1}(\tau)\}$ is unknown, the value of ε cannot be estimated. Then, we proceed iteratively as follows.

Let $t_1(j)$ (resp. $t_2(j)$) be the value of the j-th smallest observation of X_1 (resp. X_2), for $j = 1, \ldots, N$. We set the bounds $a = \min\{t_1(1), t_2(1)\}$ and $b = \max\{t_1(N), t_2(N)\}$ and choose an arbitrary number h of integration intervals to compute an initial value for the integration interval $\varepsilon = (b - a)/h$. For small values of ε, the probability density function $f_{X_1}(\tau)$ in the interval $[i\varepsilon, (i+1)\varepsilon]$ can be approximated by $\hat{f}_{X_1}(\tau) = (\hat{F}_{X_1}((i+1)\varepsilon) - \hat{F}_{X_1}(i\varepsilon))/\varepsilon$, where

$$\hat{F}_{X_1}(i\varepsilon) = |\{t_1(j), j = 1, \ldots, N : t_1(j) \leq i\varepsilon\}|.$$

The same approximations hold for random variable X_2.

Finally, the value of $Pr(X_1 \leq X_2)$ can be computed as in (6), using the estimates $\hat{f}_{X_1}(\tau)$ and $\hat{f}_{X_2}(\tau)$ in the computation of $L(\varepsilon)$ and $R(\varepsilon)$. If the approximation error $\Delta(\varepsilon) = R(\varepsilon) - L(\varepsilon)$ is sufficiently small, then the procedure stops. Otherwise, the value of ε is halved and the above steps are repeated.

4   Numerical Applications

We apply the tool described in the previous section to compare pairs of stochastic local search algorithms running on the same instance of three different test problems: server replication for reliable multicast, routing and wavelength assignment, and 2-path network design.

4.1   DM-D5 and GRASP Algorithms for Server Replication

Current multicast services use a delivery tree, whose root represents the sender, leaves represent the receivers, and internal nodes represent relaying servers. Transmission is performed by creating copies of the data at split points of the tree. A successful technique to provide a reliable multicast service is the server replication approach, in which data is replicated at some multicast-capable relaying servers and each of them is responsible for the retransmission of packets to receivers in its group. The problem consists of selecting the best multicast-capable relaying hosts to act as replicated servers in a multicast scenario.

DM-GRASP is a hybrid version of the GRASP metaheuristic that incorporates a data-mining process [23]. Its basic principle consists of mining for patterns found in good-quality solutions to guide the construction of new solutions. We compare two different heuristics for the server replication problem: algorithm A_1 is an implementation of the DM-D5 version [24] of DM-GRASP, in which the mining algorithm is periodically applied, while A_2 is a pure GRASP heuristic. We present illustrative results for two instances using the same network scenario, with $m = 25$ and $m = 50$ replication servers.

Each algorithm was run 200 times with different seeds. The target was set at 2,818.925 for the instance with $m = 25$ and at 2,299.07 for that with $m = 50$. Figures 7 and 8 depict run time distributions and quantile-quantile plots for DM-D5. Running times of the latter did not fit exponential distributions for

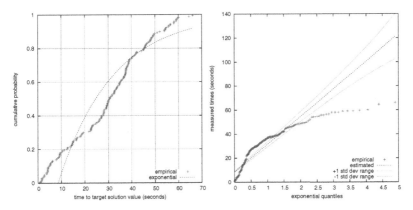

Fig. 7. Run time distribution and quantile-quantile plot for DM-D5 algorithm on the instance with $m = 25$ and target value set at 2,818.925

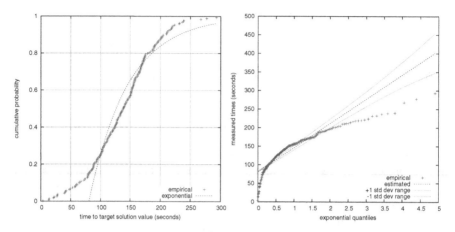

Fig. 8. Run time distribution and quantile-quantile plot for DM-D5 algorithm on the instance with $m = 50$ and target value set at 2,299.07

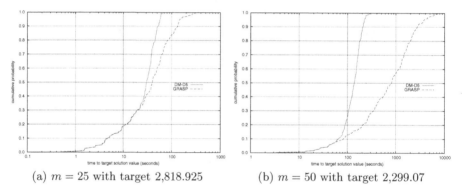

(a) $m = 25$ with target 2,818.925   (b) $m = 50$ with target 2,299.07

Fig. 9. Superimposed run time distributions of DM-D5 and GRASP: (a) $Pr(X_1 \leq X_2) = 0.614775$, and (b) $Pr(X_1 \leq X_2) = 0.849163$

any of the instances. GRASP running times were exponential for both. The run time distributions of DM-D5 and GRASP are superimposed in Figure 9. Algorithm DM-D5 outperformed GRASP, since the run-time distribution of the first is slightly to the left of that of the second for the instance with $m = 25$, and much more clearly for $m = 50$. Consistently, the computations show that $Pr(X_1 \leq X_2) = 0.614775$ and $Pr(X_1 \leq X_2) = 0.849163$ for the instances with $m = 25$ and $m = 50$, respectively.

4.2   Multistart and Tabu Search Algorithms for Routing and Wavelength Assignment

A point-to-point connection between two endnodes of an optical network is called a lightpath. Two lightpaths may use the same wavelength, provided they do

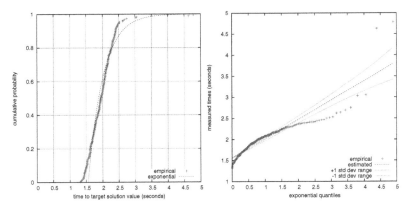

Fig. 10. Run time distribution and quantile-quantile plot for tabu search on Brazil instance with target value set at 24

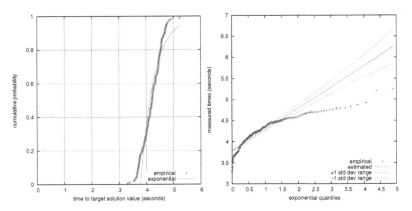

Fig. 11. Run time distribution and quantile-quantile plot for tabu search on Finland instance with target value set at 50

not share any common link. The routing and wavelength assignment problem is that of routing a set of lightpaths and assigning a wavelength to each of them, minimizing the number of wavelengths needed. Noronha and Ribeiro [25] proposed a decomposition heuristic for this problem. First, a set of routes is precomputed for each lightpath. Next, one of them and a wavelength are assigned to each lightpath by a tabu search heuristic solving a partition coloring problem.

We compare this decomposition strategy with the multistart greedy heuristic of Manohar et al. [26]. Two networks are used for benchmarking. The first has 27 nodes representing the capital cities in Brazil, with 70 links connecting them. There are 702 lightpaths to be routed. Instance [27] Finland is formed by 31 nodes and 51 links, with 930 lightpaths to be routed.

Each algorithm was run 200 times with different seeds. The target was set at 24 for instance Brazil and at 50 for instance Finland. Algorithm A_1 is the

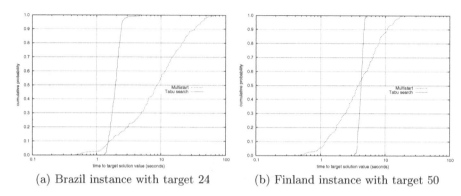

(a) Brazil instance with target 24   (b) Finland instance with target 50

Fig. 12. Superimposed run time distributions of multistart and tabu search: (a) $Pr(X_1 \leq X_2) = 0.106766$, and (b) $Pr(X_1 \leq X_2) = 0.545619$

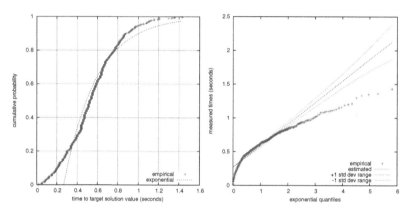

Fig. 13. Run time distribution and quantile-quantile plot for GRASP with forward path-relinking on 90-node instance with target 673

multistart heuristic, while A_2 is the tabu search decomposition scheme. The multistart running times fit exponential distributions for both instances. Figures 10 and 11 display run time distributions and quantile-quantile plots for instances Brazil and Finland, respectively. The run time distributions of the decomposition and multistart strategies are superimposed in Figure 12. The direct comparison of the two approaches shows that decomposition clearly outperformed the multistart strategy for instance Brazil, since $Pr(X_1 \leq X_2) = 0.106766$ in this case. However, the situation changes for instance Finland. Although both algorithms have similar performances, multistart is slightly better with respect to the measure proposed in this work, since $Pr(X_1 \leq X_2) = 0.545619$.

4.3   GRASP Algorithms for 2-Path Network Design

Given a connected undirected graph with non-negative weights associated with its edges, together with a set of origin-destination nodes, the 2-path network

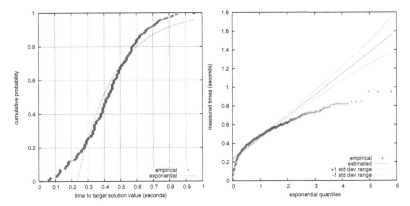

Fig. 14. Run time distribution and quantile-quantile plot for GRASP with bidirectional path-relinking on 90-node instance with target 673

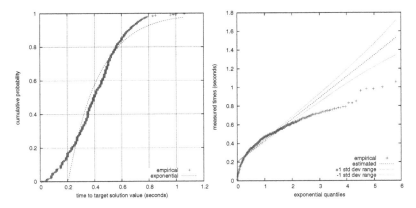

Fig. 15. Run time distribution and quantile-quantile plot for GRASP with backward path-relinking on 90-node instance with target 673

design problem consists of finding a minimum weighted subset of edges containing a path formed by at most two edges between every origin-destination pair. Applications can be found in the design of communication networks, in which paths with few edges are sought to enforce high reliability and small delays. Its decision version was proved to be NP-complete by Dahl and Johannessen [28].

We compare different heuristics [15] for approximately solving this problem. The first is a pure GRASP algorithm (algorithm A_1). The others integrate different path-relinking strategies for search intensification at the end of each GRASP iteration: forward (algorithm A_2), bidirectional (algorithm A_3), and backward (algorithm A_4) [29,21].

Each algorithm was run 500 independent times. The experiments are summarized by the results obtained on a benchmarking instance with 90 nodes and

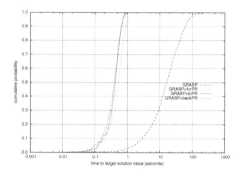

Fig. 16. Superimposed run time distributions of pure GRASP and three versions of GRASP with path-relinking

900 origin-destination pairs, with the target value set at 673. Run time distributions and quantile-quantile plots for the different versions of GRASP with path-relinking are illustrated in Figures 13 to 15. The run time distributions of the four algorithms are superimposed in Figure 16. Algorithm A_2 (as well as A_3 and A_4) performs much better than A_1, since $Pr(X_2 \leq X_1) = 0.984470$. Algorithm A_3 outperforms A_2, as illustrated by the fact that $Pr(X_3 \leq X_2) = 0.634002$. Finally, we observe that algorithms A_3 and A_4 behave very similarly, although A_4 performs slightly better for this instance with respect to the measure proposed in this work, since $Pr(X_4 \leq X_3) = 0.536016$.

5   Concluding Remarks

Run time distributions are very useful tools to characterize the running times of stochastic algorithms for combinatorial optimization. In this work, we extended previous tools for plotting and evaluating run time distributions.

Under the assumption that running times of two stochastic local search algorithms follow exponential distributions, we derived a closed form index to compute the probability that one of them finds a target solution value in a smaller computation time than the other. A numerical iterative procedure was described for the computation of such index in the case of general run time distributions.

This new tool and the resulting probability index revealed themselves as very promising and provide a new, additional measure for comparing the performance of stochastic local search algorithms or different versions of the same algorithm. They can also be used for setting the best parameters of a given algorithm. Numerical applications to different algorithm paradigms, problem types, and test instances illustrated the applicability of the tool.

In another context, they can also be used in the evaluation of parallel implementations of local search algorithms, providing a numerical indicator to evaluate the trade-offs between computation times and the number of processors.

References

1. Feo, T., Resende, M., Smith, S.: A greedy randomized adaptive search procedure for maximum independent set. Operations Research 42, 860–878 (1994)
2. Hoos, H., Stützle, T.: On the empirical evaluation of Las Vegas algorithms - Position paper. Technical report, Computer Science Department, University of British Columbia (1998)
3. Hoos, H., Stützle, T.: Evaluation of Las Vegas algorithms - Pitfalls and remedies. In: Proceedings of the 14th Conference on Uncertainty in Artificial Intelligence, pp. 238–245 (1998)
4. Aiex, R., Resende, M., Ribeiro, C.: Probability distribution of solution time in GRASP: An experimental investigation. Journal of Heuristics 8, 343–373 (2002)
5. Dodd, N.: Slow annealing versus multiple fast annealing runs: An empirical investigation. Parallel Computing 16, 269–272 (1990)
6. Eikelder, H.T., Verhoeven, M., Vossen, T., Aarts, E.: A probabilistic analysis of local search. In: Osman, I., Kelly, J. (eds.) Metaheuristics: Theory and Applications, pp. 605–618. Kluwer, Dordrecht (1996)
7. Hoos, H.: On the run-time behaviour of stochastic local search algorithms for SAT. In: Proc. AAAI 1999, pp. 661–666. MIT Press, Cambridge (1999)
8. Hoos, H., Stützle, T.: Towards a characterisation of the behaviour of stochastic local search algorithms for SAT. Artificial Intelligence 112, 213–232 (1999)
9. Osborne, L., Gillett, B.: A comparison of two simulated annealing algorithms applied to the directed Steiner problem on networks. ORSA Journal on Computing 3, 213–225 (1991)
10. Selman, B., Kautz, H., Cohen, B.: Noise strategies for improving local search. In: Proceedings of the AAAI 1994, pp. 337–343. MIT Press, Cambridge (1994)
11. Taillard, E.: Robust taboo search for the quadratic assignment problem. Parallel Computing 17, 443–455 (1991)
12. Verhoeven, M., Aarts, E.: Parallel local search. Journal of Heuristics 1, 43–66 (1995)
13. Hoos, H., Stützle, T.: Some surprising regularities in the behaviour of stochastic local search. In: Maher, M.J., Puget, J.-F. (eds.) CP 1998. LNCS, vol. 1520, p. 470. Springer, Heidelberg (1998)
14. Aiex, R., Resende, M., Ribeiro, C.: TTTPLOTS: A perl program to create time-to-target plots. Optimization Letters 1, 355–366 (2007)
15. Ribeiro, C., Rosseti, I.: Efficient parallel cooperative implementations of GRASP heuristics. Parallel Computing 33, 21–35 (2007)
16. Li, Y., Pardalos, P., Resende, M.: A greedy randomized adaptive search procedure for the quadratic assignment problem. In: Pardalos, P., Wolkowicz, H. (eds.) Quadratic Assignment and Related Problems. DIMACS Series on Discrete Mathematics and Theoretical Computer Science, vol. 16, pp. 237–261. American Mathematical Society, Providence (1994)
17. Resende, M., Ribeiro, C.: A GRASP for graph planarization. Networks 29, 173–189 (1997)
18. Resende, M., Pitsoulis, L., Pardalos, P.: Fortran subroutines for computing approximate solutions of MAX-SAT problems using GRASP. Discrete Applied Mathematics 100, 95–113 (2000)
19. Resende, M.: Computing approximate solutions of the maximum covering problem using GRASP. Journal of Heuristics 4, 161–171 (1998)
20. Canuto, S., Resende, M., Ribeiro, C.: Local search with perturbations for the prize-collecting Steiner tree problem in graphs. Networks 38, 50–58 (2001)

21. Resende, M., Ribeiro, C.: GRASP with path-relinking: Recent advances and applications. In: Ibaraki, T., Nonobe, K., Yagiura, M. (eds.) Metaheuristics: Progress as Real Problem Solvers, pp. 29–63. Springer, Heidelberg (2005)
22. Aiex, R., Pardalos, P., Resende, M., Toraldo, G.: GRASP with path relinking for three-index assignment. INFORMS Journal on Computing 17, 224–247 (2005)
23. Santos, L., Martins, S., Plastino, A.: Applications of the DM-GRASP heuristic: A survey. International Transactions in Operational Research 15, 387–416 (2008)
24. Fonseca, E., Fuchsuber, R., Santos, L., Plastino, A., Martins, S.: Exploring the hybrid metaheuristic DM-GRASP for efficient server replication for reliable multicast. In: International Conference on Metaheuristics and Nature Inspired Computing, Hammamet (2008)
25. Noronha, T., Ribeiro, C.: Routing and wavelength assignment by partition coloring. European Journal of Operational Research 171, 797–810 (2006)
26. Manohar, P., Manjunath, D., Shevgaonkar, R.: Routing and wavelength assignment in optical networks from edge disjoint path algorithms. IEEE Communications Letters 5, 211–213 (2002)
27. Hyytiä, E., Virtamo, J.: Wavelength assignment and routing in WDM networks. In: Nordic Teletraffic Seminar 14, pp. 31–40 (1998)
28. Dahl, G., Johannessen, B.: The 2-path network problem. Networks 43, 190–199 (2004)
29. Resende, M., Ribeiro, C.: Greedy randomized adaptive search procedures. In: Glover, F., Kochenberger, G. (eds.) Handbook of Metaheuristics, pp. 219–249. Kluwer, Dordrecht (2003)

Estimating Bounds on Expected Plateau Size in MAXSAT Problems*

Andrew M. Sutton, Adele E. Howe, and L. Darrell Whitley

Department of Computer Science, Colorado State University,
Fort Collins CO, USA
{sutton,howe,whitley}@cs.colostate.edu

Abstract. Stochastic local search algorithms can now successfully solve MAXSAT problems with thousands of variables or more. A key to this success is how effectively the search can navigate and escape plateau regions. Furthermore, the solubility of a problem depends on the size and exit density of plateaus, especially those closest to the optimal solution. In this paper we model the plateau phenomenon as a percolation process on hypercube graphs. We develop two models for estimating bounds on the size of plateaus and prove that one is a lower bound and the other an upper bound on the expected size of plateaus at a given level. The models' accuracy is demonstrated on controlled random hypercube landscapes. We apply the models to MAXSAT through analogy to hypercube graphs and by introducing an approach to estimating, through sampling, a key parameter of the models. Using this approach, we assess the accuracy of our bound estimations on uniform random and structured benchmarks. Surprisingly, we find similar trends in accuracy across random and structured problem instances. Less surprisingly, we find a high accuracy on smaller plateaus with systematic divergence as plateaus increase in size.

1 Introduction

The success of stochastic local search algorithms on satisfiability problems is attributed in part to their exploitation of equal or "sideways" moves in the search neighborhood [1]. In many cases, this strategy results in an empirical improvement in generated solutions [2] and a theoretical improvement in the approximation ratio on special cases [3]. Accepting equal moves can result in "plateau behavior" of search [4]: potentially long epochs during which any discrete "gradient" information is absent, and search algorithms must either perform a random walk on the plateau or attempt to search it systematically until an improving move is found.

---

* This research was sponsored by the Air Force Office of Scientific Research, Air Force Materiel Command, USAF, under grant number FA9550-08-1-0422. The U.S. Government is authorized to reproduce and distribute reprints for Governmental purposes notwithstanding any copyright notation thereon.

T. Stützle, M. Birattari, and H.H. Hoos (Eds.): SLS 2009, LNCS 5752, pp. 31–45, 2009.

The two characteristics that determine the hardness of escaping a plateau are its *exit density*: the number of strictly improving moves incident to plateau solutions, and its *size*: the number of solutions belonging to the plateau. Since the progress of a stochastic local search algorithm is ultimately connected to how well it can escape plateaus, plateau characteristics are intimately related to problem difficulty for local search [4,5,6].

Not all plateaus contain exits. In the worst case, the entire plateau must be expanded before determining whether it is escapable or not. On a MAXSAT problem with n variables and m clauses there must exist a set of equal value solutions (not necessarily connected) that has cardinality $\Omega\left(\frac{2^n}{m}\right)$. This means that plateaus tend to be intractable to enumerate on average. Methods to determine plateau size need to be extremely efficient and not rely on enumeration.

In this paper we take a first step in predicting plateau characteristics for problem instances by focusing on plateau size. We develop methods for estimating upper and lower bounds on the expected plateau size in MAXSAT problems. Such bounds can benefit search algorithms in two ways: first by providing an estimate of how hard a problem instance is likely to be for stochastic local search, and second by predicting when the expected size of a plateau is likely to be too large to systematically search.

Under some simplifying assumptions on the distribution of equal valued solutions in the search space, we construct a correspondence between *plateaus* in MAXSAT problems and *percolation clusters* in hypercube graphs. We present models for bounding the expected size of plateaus from above and below. Furthermore, we introduce a method for estimating the probability that nearby points belong to the same level set by locally sampling the region of a point.

We find that the trends in accuracy for prediction are surprisingly uniform across random and structured problem sets. As we expected, the lower bound diverges in a consistent manner with respect to plateau size due to an approximation term in the prediction expression.

1.1 Related Work

Hampson and Kibler [5] empirically investigated the plateau behavior of local search on satisfiability problems. They discovered that many plateaus at high evaluation levels were intractably large and restarting was more beneficial than extensive plateau search in some cases. They found the exit density of plateaus is inversely proportional to the number of variables, and conjectured that the expected time to search these plateaus would increase linearly in the problem size. Most importantly, they found that the size of plateaus increased exponentially in the number of variables.

Frank et al. [4] studied the properties of plateau regions across several classes of MAXSAT problem. They used GSAT to locate solutions at the top evaluation levels and performed breadth-first search to exhaustively expand the plateaus to which each solution belonged. They collected statistics on the distribution of plateaus with and without exits. They found that different problem classes may be harder for local search because plateau characteristics differ across such classes.

In a more general setting, Hoos and Stützle [7] extended the plateau concept to general combinatorial search spaces and defined metrics for plateau characteristics (e.g., width). They developed plateau connection graphs: directed acyclic graphs that capture connectivity between plateau regions and associated transition probabilities.

Smyth [8] examined plateau characteristics for uniform random 3-SAT instances. He found that solutions on lower level sets tended to cluster together in one common large plateau where solutions on better level sets belonged to many smaller plateaus. He also studied the internal structure of plateau regions, finding that the graphs had very low branching factors and diameter greater than or equal to the number of variables.

Plateaus emerge in the presence of *neutrality*: the existence of neighboring states with equal evaluation. Reidys and Stadler [9] studied the nature of neutrality and developed an additive random model on which neutrality can be expressed as a random variable. They derived a probability mass function for the length of *neutral walks*: monotonic random paths of equal valued states which we will employ in this paper. Reidys and Stadler extended work originally done on RNA landscapes [10] where *neutral networks*, induced subgraphs of a landscape, are studied using the theory of random graphs.

2   Size Prediction

A combinatorial search problem is defined as a set X of candidate solutions and an objective function $f : X \to \mathbb{R}$ that assigns some value to each element of X. The solution set X for satisfiability problems is the set of true/false assignments to n variables which can be characterized as the set of strings $\{0,1\}^n$. For MAXSAT, the objective function f counts the number of satisfied clauses given by a particular solution x.

A local search algorithm defines some computationally tractable neighborhood function $N : X \to 2^X$ and, starting from an independently generated initial candidate solution, walks along the graph induced by the neighborhood function. That is, if $x \in X$ is the current candidate solution, in each iteration a new element $y \in N(x)$ is selected to become the new candidate solution according to a pivot rule. The behavior of local search can be characterized as a biased walk on the neighborhood graph $G(X, E)$ induced by N, that is, $(x, y) \in E \iff y \in N(x)$.

For MAXSAT problems, the seemingly most natural neighborhood N maps solutions to their set of Hamming neighbors: solutions that differ in exactly one variable. Thus $G(X, E)$ is isomorphic to a hypercube graph of order n. Since we are concerned only with the MAXSAT domain in this paper, we hereafter work only with this graph. The Hamming distance between two solutions x and y is denoted as $d(x, y)$ and represents the minimal distance between x and y on the hypercube.

Let $L \subseteq X$ be a maximal set of solutions such that $\forall x \in L, f(x) = \ell$. We refer to L as the *level set* at level ℓ. A neutral path $\mathcal{N}(x, y)$ in G is a sequence of distinct solutions $(x = x_1, x_2, \ldots, x_k = y)$ such that, for all $i \in \{1, \ldots, k-1\}$, the following conditions hold.

1. $x_{i+1} \in N(x_i)$
2. $f(x_i) = f(x_{i+1})$

A plateau is a *maximal* set P such that for all $x, y \in P$, $\exists\, \mathcal{N}(x, y)$. Thus a plateau is simply a connected component of the subgraph of the neighborhood graph G induced by a level set, and the set of all plateaus form a partition of G. The *size* of a plateau P is defined as its cardinality $|P|$. Note that our definition allows for $|P| = 1$. In other words, the set of all plateaus partition the search space X, and a vertex with no equal neighbors is a degenerate plateau. This definition is analogous to that in other studies, e.g., [4,7,8].

2.1   Estimating a Lower Bound: Hamming Path Set

We define a neutral Hamming path $\mathcal{N}_\mathcal{H}(x, y)$ in G between two solutions x and y is a particular case of a neutral path $\mathcal{N}(x, y) = (x = x_1, \ldots, x_k = y)$ with the added monotonicity constraint that $d(x, x_{i+1}) = d(x, x_i) + 1$ for all $i \in \{1, \ldots, k-1\}$.

Let x be an arbitrary solution in a plateau P. We define the Hamming path set H_x associated with x as

$$H_x = \{y \in P : \exists\, \mathcal{N}_\mathcal{H}(x, y)\}$$

Clearly, $H_x \subseteq P$ and thus $|H_x| \leq |P|$.

On a particular problem instance, we can consider H_x taken over all randomly selected $x \in X$. We can thus characterize $|H_x|$ as a random variable. Denote as $\mathbb{E}[|H_x|]$ its *expected value*. By linearity of expectation we have

$$\mathbb{E}[|H_x \cup (P \setminus H_x)|] = \mathbb{E}[|P|]$$
$$\mathbb{E}[|H_x|] \leq \mathbb{E}[|P|]$$

In practice, the magnitude of the difference between the left hand and right hand side of the above relation will ultimately depend on our choice of $x \in P$.

Under a simplifying assumption which we will make in the following section, we will find that the probability that a solution belongs to H_x depends only on its distance from x. Denote as

$$h_x(r) = \Pr\{y \in H_x\} \text{ for any } y : d(x, y) = r$$

the probability that a solution y at distance r from x belongs to H_x. On the hypercube of order n, there are $\binom{n}{r}$ solutions at distance r from an arbitrary vertex. Thus we derive the expected size of the Hamming path set (and therefore our lower bound on plateau size) as

$$\mathbb{E}[|H_x|] = \sum_{r=0}^{n} \binom{n}{r} h_x(r) \tag{1}$$

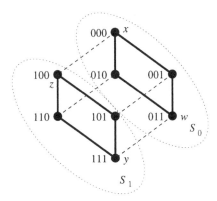

Fig. 1. Partitioning of a hypercube into S_0 and S_1

We develop an estimate of $h_x(r)$ (and so $\mathbb{E}[\|H_x\|]$) using a percolation approach. Let C_n be a hypercube graph of order n. Each vertex in C_n corresponds to a string $\{0,1\}^n$. Let $x = (000\ldots 0)$ and $y = (111\ldots 1)$. We refer to x and y as the *corner* vertices. A vertex is *active* if it belongs to the same level set as x. We define the *concentration* as the probability p that a vertex is on the same level set as x, and thus active. We assume this probability is constant and independent across all vertices. In other words, p depends only on the level set under consideration. Note that x is a *fixed active* vertex since it trivially belongs to its own level set. We say the cube *percolates from y to x* if there is a monotonic path $(y = x_1, x_2, \ldots, x_k = x)$ such that all x_i are active.

Let $c(n, p)$ denote the probability that C_n percolates with concentration p from y to the fixed active vertex x.

Proposition 1. *For some real number* $0 \le g(n) \le 1$

$$c(n, p) = p \cdot \left(2 \cdot c(n - 1, p) - c(n - 1, p)^2 \right) + g(n)$$

Proof. We partition the vertices C_n into two disjoint sets S_0 and S_1. S_0 consists of the vertices represented by the strings $(0 * * \ldots *)$. S_1 consists of the vertices represented by the strings $(1 * * \ldots *)$.

Note that S_0 and S_1 form hypercubes (see Figure 1). Each subcube shares one of its corner vertices with C_n. In the case of S_0, one of its corner vertices is x, while the opposite corner is a vertex $w = (0, 1, 1, \ldots, 1)$. In the case of S_1, one of its corner vertices is y and the opposite corner is a vertex $z = (1, 0, 0, \ldots, 0)$.

All percolating paths from y to x must pass from S_1 to S_0 exactly once and cannot pass back from S_0 to S_1 (since at each step of the path, the number of ones in the bitstring must decrease by exactly one).

We refer to paths that pass from S_1 to S_0 through edges (y, w) or (z, x) as *external crossing paths*. We refer to the remaining paths as *internal crossing paths*. Let E_{ex} be the event that at least one external crossing path percolates from y to x. Let E_{in} be the event that at least one internal crossing path percolates.

If y is inactive, then C_n does not percolate from y to x. Now suppose y is active. The probability that S_0 percolates from w to the fixed active vertex x is $c(n-1, p)$. Now we consider S_1. Note that $x \notin S_1$, but y takes the role of the fixed active vertex (since we have assumed it is active). The probability of S_1 percolating from z to y is $c(n-1, p)$.

Percolation is direction invariant. Thus if S_1 percolates from z to y, there is a percolating external crossing path from y to x through the edge (z, x), and thus C_n percolates. Similarly, if S_0 percolates from w to x, since we have assumed y is active there is a percolating external crossing path from y to x through the edge (y, w). Thus if either S_0 or S_1 percolate, then C_n must percolate. These events are not mutually exclusive, so the probability that there is a percolating external crossing path through either subcube is $2 \cdot c(n-1, p) - c(n-1, p)^2$. We multiply this expression by p, the probability that y is active, to obtain the probability that C_n percolates via an external crossing path.

$$\Pr(E_{ex}) = p \cdot \left(2 \cdot c(n-1, p) - c(n-1, p)^2\right) \tag{2}$$

Now consider the internal crossing paths. Clearly we have,

$$\Pr(E_{in}) - \Pr(E_{ex} \cap E_{in}) = g(n) \tag{3}$$

where $0 \leq g(n) \leq 1$ is a real number that depends on n. The probability that C_n percolates can be expressed as $\Pr(E_{ex}) + \Pr(E_{in}) - \Pr(E_{ex} \cap E_{in})$. Substituting Equations (2) and (3) gives the result. $\qquad\square$

We thus ignore the internal crossing paths and bound the percolation probability.

Corollary 1. *Since $0 \leq g(n) \leq 1$, $c(n, p) \geq p \cdot \left(2 \cdot c(n-1, p) - c(n-1, p)^2\right)$*

We define $\hat{c}(n, p)$ as the lower bound on $c(n, p)$:

$$\hat{c}(1, p) = p$$
$$\hat{c}(n, p) = p \cdot \left(2 \cdot \hat{c}(n-1, p) - \hat{c}(n-1, p)^2\right) \tag{4}$$

The above result allows us to place a lower bound on $\mathbb{E}[H_x]$.

Proposition 2. *Let x be an arbitrary solution in X. Suppose that for each element $y \in X$, $\Pr\{f(y) = f(x)\} = p$. Then $h_x(d(x, y)) = c(d(x, y), p)$.*

Proof. This follows directly from the definition of $c(n, p)$. Note that a vertex in a Hamming path from y to x must lie in the subcube of order $d(x, y)$ between x and y. If a vertex in the subcube is on the same level set as x, it is considered active. Since each vertex is active with probability p, a neutral Hamming path is simply a percolating path in the subcube of order $d(x, y)$. $\qquad\square$

Thus, we have

$$\mathbb{E}[|H_x|] \geq \sum_{r=0}^{n} \binom{n}{r} \hat{c}(r, p) \tag{5}$$

If we know p for a particular level set, then we can bound the expected plateau size. Note that our premise that the concentration parameter p is independent across a given level set is a rather heavy simplifying assumption. In fact, we would expect in practice that solutions have distinct correlations among them. However, this assumption makes the analysis easier.

Finally, the elimination of the $g(n)$ term in the approximation expression will cause the lower bound to diverge as $n \to \infty$ since the approximation loses accuracy for each value of n. Thus, we expect the error to have superlinear growth with n since $g(n)$ is proportional to subcube size.

2.2   Estimating an Upper Bound: Bethe Lattice Approximation

We have characterized plateaus as connected clusters of active sites in the hypercube graph. In this section we will use an exact result from percolation theory to derive an upper limit on the expectation of plateau size for certain values of p. The Bethe lattice (or Cayley tree) of coordination number n is defined as a connected acyclic graph in which each vertex is connected to n neighboring vertices.

For a given concentration p, the expected size of connected clusters of active sites in the Bethe lattice will always be greater than or equal to the expected size of clusters of active sites in the hypercube graph. This can be shown by a simple counting argument. Since the Bethe lattice is acyclic, every site in the cluster rooted at a site b has exactly one path of active vertices to b. Thus the expected number of neighbors of a cluster site that extend the cluster a step further from b is $p \cdot (n-1)$. On the other hand, a vertex in the hypercube graph that belongs to a cluster rooted at some vertex x will have *at least* one path of active vertices to x since cycles are possible. The expected number of neighbors that extend the cluster further is therefore less than or equal to $p \cdot (n-1)$. Thus the expected size of connected active clusters in the Bethe lattice for a particular p is an upper bound on the expected plateau size in the hypercube graph.

The expected cluster size on the Bethe lattice has an exact solution. Let b be an arbitrary active site in the lattice. Let T be the expected size of the clusters rooted at each neighbor of b. By the symmetries of the lattice we have

$$T = p\,(1 + (n-1)T)$$

Solving for T we have $T = \frac{p}{1-(n-1)p}$ and the expected cluster size at arbitrary b is $1 + nT$:

$$\frac{1+p}{1-(n-1)p} \tag{6}$$

Since the Bethe lattice is an infinite system, its value as an approximation of the finite hypercube becomes poorer as p gets larger. In fact, there is a singularity in Equation (6) when $p = \frac{1}{n-1}$. This corresponds to the critical point at which an infinite cluster appears in the lattice and expected cluster size is no longer well-defined. Thus the Bethe lattice approximation is only valid in the subcritical region: values of p strictly less than $\frac{1}{n-1}$. A useful introduction to percolation theory can be found in [11].

2.3   Estimating Concentration: Neutral Walk Method

Except in synthetic cases, the concentration parameter p will not be known *a priori*. Thus we must determine a method to estimate p. One approach might be to simply sample points on the landscape until the proportion of solutions that belong to a particular level set is accurately represented. However, this approach is insufficient for the following reasons.

1. It may take exponential time to obtain an accurate estimate of the true proportion for smaller level sets.
2. The actual concentration p is likely to be correlated with distance. For example, in MAXSAT, solutions at Hamming distance one are more likely to be on the same level set than solutions an arbitrary distance away.

To address these points, we develop a method that uses a *neutral walk*: a polynomial time algorithm that locally samples around a solution. The concept of a neutral walk was introduced by Schuster et al. [12] to measure the extent of plateaus (which they refer to as components of a neutral network) for RNA landscapes. A neutral walk is defined as a random walk of monotonically increasing distance from a reference vertex such that all walk vertices have the same evaluation. On the hypercube, there can be at most n increasing steps, each with a neighborhood size that is $O(n)$ in the worst case. Thus the time to perform a neutral walk is bounded above by $n \sum_{i=1}^{n} i = O(n^3)$.

The probability mass function of neutral walk length $\mathcal{L}$ was derived by Reidys and Stadler [9]. We adopt a specialization for the hypercube. Let p be the probability that a solution belongs to the same level set as the origin of the walk. A vertex at distance r from the walk's origin has $n - r$ neighbors at distance $r + 1$. Thus the probability that a walk can be extended to distance r is $\prod_{i=1}^{r} \left[1 - (1-p)^{n-(i-1)} \right]$. The probability that the vertex at distance r terminates the walk is $(1-p)^{n-r}$. Hence, given concentration p, the probability that a neutral walk is of length r can be written as

$$\Pr\{\mathcal{L} = r\} = (1-p)^{n-r} \prod_{i=1}^{r} \left[1 - (1-p)^{n-(i-1)} \right]$$

We use this result to compute the expected neutral walk length as follows.

$$\mathbb{E}_p[\mathcal{L}] = \sum_{r=1}^{n} r \Pr\{\mathcal{L} = r\} \tag{7}$$

To estimate p for a level set L, we compute the empirical mean neutral walk length $\mathcal{L}_\mu$ by performing a number of neutral walks from sampled points on L. If we assume $\mathcal{L}_\mu$ accurately estimates $\mathbb{E}_p[\mathcal{L}]$, then an estimate of the concentration is simply the root of the monotonic function

$$\mathbb{E}_p[\mathcal{L}] - \mathcal{L}_\mu$$

using Equation (7) parameterized by p. We use a numerical root finding algorithm to solve for p, giving us the estimate.

3 Computational Experiments

We have proved that, given our assumptions, our models provide upper and lower bounds. However, we do not know how well the models perform on actual problems where the concentration is not known. We evaluate the accuracy of our prediction bounds by exhaustively enumerating plateaus on a number of different search landscapes and comparing the actual value with the predictions given by Equations (5) and (6). To assess the accuracy and trends of the prediction we first use synthetic landscapes on which concentration is known, and then both random and structured MAXSAT landscapes on which we predict the concentration using the neutral walk method. Because we need to fully enumerate the plateaus for accuracy, we are limited to small problems in this analysis.

3.1 Concentration-Controlled Random Landscapes

To test the size prediction bounds given known concentrations, we evaluate predictions for random hypercube landscapes on which we explicitly control concentration. In particular, given a hypercube landscape X, we assign each solution an objective function value of 1 with probability p and a value of 0 with probability $1 - p$. We sample solutions at random on the landscape. If the solution is of value 1, we expand its plateau using breadth-first search. We also compute its Hamming path set. We compare the actual cardinalities with the prediction equation and the Bethe lattice approximation for concentrations that lie in the subcritical region.

We generate 100 random landscapes controlling for concentration from $p = 0.01$ to $p = 0.4$. On each landscape we calculate the Hamming path set lower bound and the Bethe upper bound using the known value of p. We sample 100 random points from the level set at value 1 and perform breadth-first search to exhaustively enumerate the plateaus. We also perform a depth-first search from each plateau vertex back to the root to enumerate the Hamming path set. We compare the average plateau and Hamming path set sizes with the prediction bounds.

We report our prediction data in the form of correlation plots. There are three types of data points. "Plateau/HP" is actual plateau size vs. Hamming path prediction. "HP/HP" denotes actual Hamming path set size vs. Hamming path prediction. "Plateau/Bethe" denotes actual plateau size vs. Bethe prediction. A perfect prediction would lie on the diagonal line included in the plots. Data for a 20 dimensional random landscape are plotted in Figure 2. The low number of "plateau/Bethe" points are because the higher concentrations exceed the critical value for the Bethe lattice.

To determine the accuracy of our concentration estimate, we run the above experiments again and estimate p using the neutral walk method. Instead of using

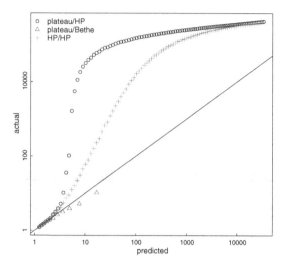

Fig. 2. Log-log plot of predictions on 20 dimensional random landscape

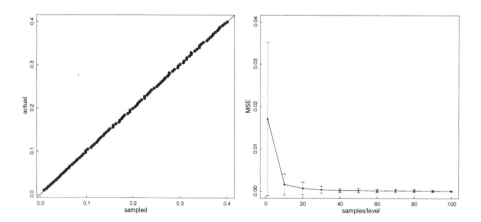

Fig. 3. Actual p vs. estimated p (left). Mean squared error between actual and estimated p vs samples/level set (right).

the known p value for the prediction bounds, we take 10 neutral walks from each of the 100 sampled points and predict the concentration with the resulting walk lengths. We compare the actual p values used to generate the landscape with the values estimated by the neutral walk method. These data are plotted on the left in Figure 3. We find a tight correlation between the predicted and actual concentrations. To determine how much effort needs to be expended to estimate p, we plot the mean squared error between known concentration and estimated concentration with respect to samples per level set on the right in Figure 3. Both plots were generated using data from the 20 dimensional random hypercube.

The high accuracy of the p estimation with low sample size is encouraging because the time to predict the size of the plateau for a *single* solution (including neutral walk sampling) is on the order of 200-5000 microseconds whereas measuring the actual plateau can take several minutes or longer on the relatively small problems we investigated.

3.2   MAXSAT Landscapes

To test how well the bounds transfer to actual problems, we perform experiments on random and structured MAXSAT problems. On MAXSAT the objective function is the number of formula clauses satisfied. On uniform random problems, most solutions belong to a small number of objective function values. This typically results in solutions of average value belonging to vast plateaus. Hampson and Kibler [5] found that, due to their relatively high exit density, plateaus of average value are easy for local search to escape, and thus local search is most affected by plateaus of higher value. Therefore we follow the technique used by Frank et al. [4] and Smyth [8] employing a stochastic local search algorithm (WalkSat [13]) to sample the highest value plateaus in the search space.

Plateau measurement time depends on the number of vertices on the plateau. Thus large plateaus quickly become intractable to enumerate as they grow with depth and problem size. Some level sets can have a small number of extremely large plateaus which cannot be enumerated in a reasonable amount of time. Rather than omitting these data points (which would bias the results to make a lower bound appear tighter than it actually is) we only report the top three level sets for two benchmark sets.

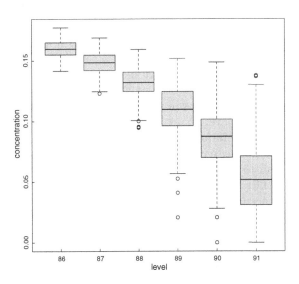

Fig. 4. Estimated concentration with respect to level set on uf20-91 problems

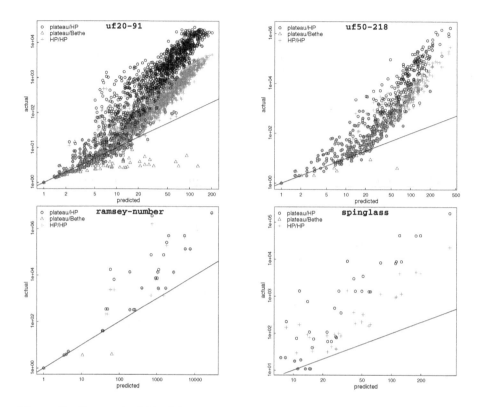

Fig. 5. Predictions for MAXSAT problems. Results on random uniform sets: 20 variables and 91 clauses uf20-91, and 50 variables and 218 clauses uf50-218 appear on the top; results on structured problem instances are plotted on the bottom.

We use two uniform random benchmark distributions from SATLIB: uf20-91, a 20 variable 91 clause set, and uf50-218, a 50 variable 218 clause set. We select 100 random instances from each set and perform WalkSat to generate 100 solutions each on the top six levels (for uf20-91) and the top three levels (for uf50-218). Note that all instances in these sets are satisfiable.

We estimate p for each level set by using the neutral walk method, taking 10 walks from each sampled solution. From each solution we exhaustively enumerate its plateau and its Hamming path set and compare the actual sizes to the bounds in Equations (5) and (6). The results from uf20-91 are plotted in the top left of Figure 5. The results from uf50-218 are plotted in the top right of Figure 5. Note the trends in accuracy when compared to each other and to the random landscape (see Figure 2).

We report the estimated p values found by the neutral walk method on the 20 variable uniform random SAT problem in Figure 4. The estimated concentration on each problem set of a particular size appears to decrease as a function of evaluation. This reflects the empirical decrease in plateau size with respect to level found originally by Hampson and Kibler [5] and later by Frank et al. [4]

and Smyth [8]. We also see a marked increase in variance as level increases which suggests plateau size becomes less uniform in better regions of the search space.

The random uniform problem instances show similar trends in accuracy. This could be an artifact of the inherent statistical regularity of random problems. To address this, we tested our predictions on structured problem instances. We performed the above experiments on the top three levels of a set of six Ramsey number problems from the MAXSAT 2007 problem competition. This problem set is comprised of several different instances with differing numbers of variables and clauses. The results are shown in Figure 5 on the bottom left. We also performed the above experiments on the top 10 levels of a 27 variable spin glass problem. This problem is unsatisfiable and the best solution by WalkSat was found on level set 145 (out of 162). These results are shown on the bottom right in Figure 5. The sparsity of the bottom plots is due to the smaller cardinality of the structured problem sets. The Ramsey numbers problems tended to have the largest concentration values: their nonzero concentration ranged from 0.09 to 0.68. The other instances had nonzero concentration values ranging from 0.01 to 0.2 or less. The concentrations were also higher relative to the critical value of $\frac{1}{n-1}$ on the structured instances, hence the paucity of data points from the Bethe model on the corresponding plots.

We see similar trends in accuracy with size across the random and structured problems. Furthermore, the trend is again similar to what we found on the hypercube graph model reported in Figure 2.

4   Impact on Algorithm Design

Accepting equal search moves can be beneficial or detrimental to a search algorithm depending on the immediate properties of a plateau region. Small, easy to escape plateaus offer little impediment to search while large, hard to escape plateaus are vast regions that lack "gradient" information and may result in search stagnation. A stochastic local search algorithm exhibits *plateau behavior* when a significant number of consecutive steps all have the same evaluation. This behavior signals that a plateau has been reached by the algorithm and certain measures may need to be taken to either exploit or react to the encountered plateau region.

Plateau moves can be *beneficial* to stochastic local search [1,3] because they provide neutral moves that may eventually lead to improving states. Plateau behavior is thus not always problematic. Frank et al. [4] point out that stochastic local search algorithms typically respond to plateau behavior by one or more of the following strategies 1) doing nothing, 2) detecting plateaus, 3) performing a short random walk, or 4) randomly restarting. The viability of each of these tactics depends on the size of the plateau in question, along with its exit density. Hence, knowledge of the expectation of plateau size can be beneficial in determining how an algorithm should react to plateau behavior.

For example, plateaus that are relatively small might easily be enumerated with breadth-first search whereas moderately sized plateaus (depending on exit density) might be escaped by taking a small "jump," e.g., flipping a number of variables at random [14]. On the other hand, a search that has reached a vast plateau region may obtain better results, depending on the evaluation level, by simply restarting. Even roughly identifying the size of moderate to large plateau regions can be difficult.

On large plateaus, several researchers [4,5] have discussed the inherent trade-off between continuing plateau search and changing the search strategy. In these studies, empirical measurements of plateau size are gathered off-line for a representative sample of a particular problem class and plateau characteristics are generalized to the entire class. The bound estimates presented in this paper allow rough plateau size approximations to be performed without much computational effort on-line. These estimates could be used in stochastic local search algorithms for strategic adaptation during execution: potentially providing information that allows search to quickly determine which of the above options (or other strategies) may be the best way to respond to plateau behavior.

We might also generalize their use to the prediction of *algorithm* performance. According to the well-known *no free lunch theorem* [15], no single algorithm performs consistently well across a set of problem instances. Indeed, specific algorithm performance often depends strongly on salient problem instance features. *Portfolio-based* approaches use different features to select among a set of algorithms to be applied [16]. For instance, Xu et al. [17] have recently introduced the SATzilla portfolio for satisfiability problems. The approach requires learning the relationship between a problem feature set and the likelihood of a particular algorithm's success in solving an instance with a given set of measurements. We conjecture that plateau size can provide additional problem space information. Hence the concentration and percolation estimates for MAXSAT presented in this paper may be beneficial as a computationally cheap, if rough estimate of a problem instance feature that may aid algorithm selection.

5 Conclusion

We have introduced methods for estimating bounds on plateau size for MAXSAT problems. These bounds may support portfolio approaches to MAXSAT by indicating problem difficulty for local search or principled adaptation for handling large plateaus.

We found that the accuracy in our estimates showed surprisingly similar trends across both random and structured problem instances. However, one inherent weakness with the approach is the large divergence in accuracy with plateau size. In the case of Bethe approximation, this is an artifact of the instability as the critical concentration is approached, thus the bound is not useful for larger values of p. For the Hamming path set, the bounds diverge as the cumulative effect from ignoring the internal path term increases.

We are continuing to refine the bounds on hypercube percolation, which would address divergence in accuracy. Furthermore, we would like to assess the influence of the phase transition on concentration.

The second important plateau characteristic is exit density, which we have not addressed in this paper. Future work also includes estimating plateau exit density and relating exit density and plateau size to problem difficulty and stochastic local search behavior.

References

1. Gent, I.P., Walsh, T.: An empirical analysis of search in GSAT. Journal of Artificial Intelligence Research 1, 47–59 (1993)
2. Selman, B., Levesque, H., Mitchell, D.: A new method for solving hard satisfiability problems. In: Proceedings of AAAI 1992, San Jose, CA (1992)
3. Mastrolilli, M., Gambardella, L.M.: How good are tabu search and plateau moves in the worst case? European Journal of Operations Research 166, 63–76 (2005)
4. Frank, J., Cheeseman, P., Stutz, J.: When gravity fails: Local search topology. Journal of Artificial Intelligence Research 7, 249–281 (1997)
5. Hampson, S., Kibler, D.: Plateaus and plateau search in boolean satisfiability problems: When to give up searching and start again. DIMACS Series in Discrete Math and Theoretical Computer Science 26, 437–453 (1993)
6. Yokoo, M.: Why adding more constraints makes a problem easier for hill-climbing algorithms: Analyzing landscapes of CSPs. In: Smolka, G. (ed.) CP 1997. LNCS, vol. 1330, pp. 356–370. Springer, Heidelberg (1997)
7. Hoos, H.H., Stützle, T.: Stochastic Local Search: Foundations and Applications. Morgan Kaufmann, San Francisco (2004)
8. Smyth, K.R.G.: Understanding stochastic local search algorithms: An empirical analysis of the relationship between search space structure and algorithm behaviour. Master's thesis, University of British Columbia (2004)
9. Reidys, C.M., Stadler, P.F.: Neutrality in fitness landscapes. Applied Mathematics and Computation 117, 321–350 (2001)
10. Reidys, C., Stadler, P., Schuster, P.: Generic properties of combinatory maps and neutral networks of RNA secondary structures. Bull. Math. Biol. 59, 339–397 (1997)
11. Stauffer, D., Aharony, A.: Introduction to Percolation Theory. Routledge, New York (1991)
12. Schuster, P., Fontana, W., Stadler, P.F., Hofacker, I.L.: From sequences to shapes and back: a case study in RNA secondary structures. In: Proceedings of the Royal Society London B, vol. 255, pp. 279–284 (1994)
13. Selman, B., Kautz, H., Cohen, B.: Local search strategies for satisfiability testing. In: Johnson, D.S., Trick, M.A. (eds.) DIMACS Series in Discrete Mathematics and Theoretical Computer Science, vol. 26. AMS, Providence (1996)
14. Gent, I., Walsh, T.: Unsatisfied variables in local search. In: Hallam, J. (ed.) Hybrid Problems, Hybrid Solutions, pp. 73–85. IOS Press, Amsterdam (1995)
15. Wolpert, D.H., Macready, W.G.: No free lunch theorems for optimization. IEEE Transactions on Evolutionary Computation 1(1), 67–82 (1997)
16. Leyton-Brown, K., Nudelman, E., Andrew, G., McFadden, J., Shoham, Y.: A portfolio approach to algorithm selection. In: Proceedings of the International Joint Conference on Artificial Intelligence, IJCAI 2003 (2003)
17. Xu, L., Hutter, F., Hoos, H., Leyton-Brown, K.: SATzilla: Portfolio-based algorithm selection for SAT. Journal of Artificial Intelligence Research 32, 565–606 (2008)

A Theoretical Analysis of the k-Satisfiability Search Space*

Andrew M. Sutton, Adele E. Howe, and L. Darrell Whitley

Department of Computer Science, Colorado State University,
Fort Collins CO, USA
{sutton,howe,whitley}@cs.colostate.edu

Abstract. Local search algorithms perform surprisingly well on the k-satisfiability (k-SAT) problem. However, few theoretical analyses of the k-SAT search space exist. In this paper we study the search space of the k-SAT problem and show that it can be analyzed by a decomposition. In particular, we prove that the objective function can be represented as a superposition of exactly k elementary landscapes. We show that this decomposition allows us to immediately compute the expectation of the objective function evaluated across neighboring points. We use this result to prove previously unknown bounds for local maxima and plateau width in the 3-SAT search space. We compute these bounds numerically for a number of instances and show that they are non-trivial across a large set of benchmarks.

1 Introduction

Local search methods for k-satisfiability (k-SAT) problems have received considerable attention in the AI search community. Though these methods are incomplete, they are usually able to quickly solve difficult problems that lie beyond the grasp of conventional complete solvers [1] and have been found to exhibit superior scaling behavior on soluble problems at the phase transition [2].

The behavior of local search algorithms closely depends on the underlying structure of the search space. A number of researchers have conducted empirical investigations on certain structural features of the k-SAT problem. Hoos and Stützle [3] introduced several metrics for measuring structure and presented an empirical examination of the characteristics of plateaus and their influence on the performance of local search. Clark et al. [4] studied the the relationship between problem hardness and the expected number of solutions on random problems. Frank et al. [5] analyzed the topology of the search space and experimentally probed the nature of local optima and plateaus. Yokoo [6] investigated the dependency of search cost on search space characteristics by studying how cost for local algorithms is related to the size of certain plateaus.

* This research was sponsored by the Air Force Office of Scientific Research, Air Force Materiel Command, USAF, under grant number FA9550-08-1-0422. The U.S. Government is authorized to reproduce and distribute reprints for Governmental purposes notwithstanding any copyright notation thereon.

T. Stützle, M. Birattari, and H.H. Hoos (Eds.): SLS 2009, LNCS 5752, pp. 46–60, 2009.
© Springer-Verlag Berlin Heidelberg 2009

In this paper, we take an analytical view of the k-SAT search space by formalizing it as a *landscape* [7] which captures the relationship between the *objective function* associated with the problem and a *neighborhood operator*. We use the landscape formalism to analyze the search space of the k-SAT problem. We show that the search landscape can be decomposed into k *elementary* components. We prove that this decomposition provides an equation that gives the expectation of a random variable that models the objective function value of states in a given neighborhood. This quantity is equal to the average objective function value of the neighbors of a given state.

Furthermore, we use the decomposition to prove bounds for two prominent search space features: local maxima and plateaus. We show local maxima do not exist below a certain objective function value. Plateaus are regions of the search space consisting of states that are interconnected by a neighborhood operator and share an objective function value. Hoos and Stützle [3] define the *width* of a plateau P: the minimal length path between any state in P and one not in P. For many SAT instances, empirical results suggest that plateaus of width greater than one do not exist, or are at least very rare [3]. We prove there are regions of the search space that *cannot* contain plateaus of width greater than 1 and show empirically that these regions encompass the majority of the range of the objective function value. To our knowledge, there are no analytical results on the existence (or non-existence) of plateaus of particular width. Our results apply to local search on k-SAT and MAX-k-SAT where the count of unsatisfied clauses is the state evaluation function.

1.1 The Landscape Formalism

Before we specialize the discussion to k-SAT problems, we begin by introducing the landscape formalism. A combinatorial search problem is characterized as a finite but very large set X of states (complete candidate solutions) and an objective function $f : X \to \mathbb{R}$ that assigns a measure of value $f(x)$ to each state x. The objective of a search algorithm is to quickly locate a state $x^* \in X$ that extremizes f. Since f is a function over a discrete domain, we can characterize it as a vector $f \in \mathbb{R}^{|X|}$.

Local search algorithms perform local perturbations on states to move through the search space toward more promising regions. The space explored by such local methods thus requires additional structure by imposing a connectivity on X that consists of pairs of states that are separated by a *move*. We can define a second function on X denoted $N : X \to 2^X$ where $N(x)$ represents the set of all possible states that can be derived from x by applying the move operator exactly once. We refer to this set as the *neighborhood* of x. The tuple (X, N, f) is called the *landscape* of the combinatorial search problem and encompasses both the objective function values and the connectivity of states via the neighborhood.

We define the $|X| \times |X|$ *Markov transition matrix* $\mathbf{T}$

$$\mathbf{T}_{xy} = \begin{cases} \frac{1}{|N(x)|} & \text{if } y \in N(x) \\ 0 & \text{otherwise} \end{cases}$$

This matrix quantifies the transition probabilities between states on a random walk of the graph of the state space induced by the neighborhood operator. We can also view $\mathbf{T}$ as a linear operator that acts on an arbitrary vector $g \in \mathbb{R}^{|X|}$:

$$(\mathbf{T}g) = \begin{bmatrix} \frac{1}{|N(x_1)|} \sum_{z \in N(x_1)} g(z) \\ \vdots \\ \frac{1}{|N(x_{|X|})|} \sum_{z \in N(x_{|X|})} g(z) \end{bmatrix} \tag{1}$$

where x_i is the ith element of X. Intuitively, $\mathbf{T}g$ is a discrete function where $\mathbf{T}g(x)$ gives the average value of g evaluated across the neighbors of the state x.

A landscape (X, N, f) is called *elementary* if the following equation is satisfied

$$\mathbf{T}f = \lambda f + \gamma \tag{2}$$

where both λ and γ are constants [8,7]. In other words, the objective function is an *eigenfunction* of the Markov transition matrix (up to an additive constant) corresponding to eigenvalue λ.

Several well-studied combinatorial problems along with natural neighborhood operators have been shown to satisfy the above equation (e.g., traveling salesman, graph coloring, not-all-equal satisfiability). Elementary landscapes possess a number of interesting properties. For example, Grover [8] has shown that no arbitrarily poor local optima can exist on an elementary landscape and that a solution with evaluation superior to the mean objective function value can be computed in polynomial time.

Landscapes that obey Equation (2) are called elementary because they behave as building blocks of more general combinatorial search landscapes. Provided that the neighborhood operator satisfies symmetry and regularity conditions, any arbitrary landscape can be represented as a linear combination of elementary landscapes [7]. We impose in this paper the following constraints.

1. $y \in N(x) \iff x \in N(y)$
2. $|N(x)| = |N(y)| = d; \quad \forall x, y \in X$

Most "natural" operators typically satisfy these constraints. The first constraint states all neighborhood relationships are symmetric, and the second asserts that all states have exactly d neighbors. Under these conditions $\mathbf{T}$ is a real symmetric $|X| \times |X|$ matrix and thus its $|X|$ eigenvectors $\{\phi_i\}$ with corresponding real eigenvalues λ_i form an orthonormal basis.

Thus we can represent an arbitrary function f in the eigenbasis $\{\phi_i\}$ as a linear combination.

$$f = \sum_{i=0}^{|X|-1} a_i \phi_i \tag{3}$$

Each ϕ_i is an eigenvector of $\mathbf{T}$. Note that each $a_i \phi_i$ can be considered again as a function $a_i \phi_i : X \to \mathbb{R}$. Each of these component functions satisfy Equation (2) and are thus elementary with respect to the neighborhood operator N.

In the general case, an arbitrary landscape f is represented by $|X|$ elementary constituents. Clearly, $|X|$ is exponential in the problem input size for landscapes of interest in this context. Thus this property is not obviously useful. However, in some interesting cases, it has been shown that the superposition is composed of a small number of elementary components. Examples are the asymmetric traveling salesman problem [9] and the quadratic assignment problem [10], both under traditional move operators.

1.2   The Neighborhood Expectation Value

We introduce a random variable that measures the objective function value of a neighbor selected uniformly at random. Later, we will use the expectation of this random variable in a simple probabilistic argument to prove the main results of the paper. Whitley et al. [11] studied elementary landscapes in the context of this random variable by connecting Equation (2) to the first moment of its distribution. In this section, we show this analysis can be easily extended to landscapes that are superpositions of elementary components.

Let $x \in X$ be an arbitrary state. Let $y \sim N(x)$ be an element drawn uniformly at random from the neighborhood of x, i.e., y is a random move using the operator defined by N. We define the random variable $Y = f(y)$ as the objective value of the neighboring state y.

Since y is selected uniformly at random, the expectation of Y is equivalent to the average of f evaluated over all of the neighbors of x.

$$\mathbb{E}[Y] = \frac{1}{d} \sum_{z \in N(x)} f(z)$$

If the objective function can be decomposed into a small number of components, the decomposition is useful in finding the expectation of Y. For example, suppose there are only $c+1$ nonzero coefficients $a_0, a_1, \ldots, a_c$ in the decomposition shown in Equation (3).

$$\begin{aligned}
\mathbb{E}[Y] &= \frac{1}{d} \sum_{z \in N(x)} f(z) \\
&= \mathbf{T}f(x) \qquad\qquad \text{by Eq. (1)} \\
&= \mathbf{T}\left(\sum_{i=0}^{c} a_i \phi_i(x) \right) \\
&= \sum_{i=0}^{c} \lambda_i a_i \phi_i(x) \qquad\qquad (4)
\end{aligned}$$

Therefore, given the $c + 1$ elementary components $a_i \phi_i$ and the corresponding eigenvalues λ_i we can immediately compute $\mathbb{E}[Y]$ without computing any elements of $N(x)$.

2   Decomposition of k-SAT

We now show that the k-SAT problem (and its optimization variant MAX-k-SAT) is decomposable into k elementary components. An instance of the k-SAT problem consists of a set of n Boolean variables $\{v_1, \ldots, v_n\}$ and a set of m clauses $\{c_1, \ldots, c_m\}$. Each clause is composed of exactly k *literals* in disjunction. The objective is to find a variable assignment that maximizes the number of satisfied clauses.

In this case, a state is a complete assignment to the n variables and can be characterized as a sequence of n bits $x = (x[1], x[2], \ldots x[n])$ where

$$x[b] = \begin{cases} 1 & \text{if and only if } v_b \text{ is true} \\ 0 & \text{if and only if } v_b \text{ is false} \end{cases}$$

The *state space* X is isomorphic to the set of all sequences $x \in \{0, 1\}^n$.

The objective function $f : X \to \{0, \ldots, m\}$ simply counts the number of clauses satisfied under the assignment given by x. The most natural neighborhood is the Hamming neighborhood N where $N(x)$ is the set of n states y that differ from x in exactly one bit.

Since f can be taken as a function over bit strings of length n, a natural decomposition is given by the Walsh transform. In the general case, an arbitrary pseudo-Boolean function $f : \{0, 1\}^n \to \mathbb{R}$ can be represented as a linear combination of 2^n *Walsh functions* which we will define shortly. Rana et al. [12] showed that the k-SAT objective function can be tractably decomposed into a polynomial number of such functions. We will use this result to obtain a decomposition of the k-SAT objective function into elementary components.

Given two bit strings x and y of length n, we denote the inner product $\langle x, y \rangle$ as $\sum_{b=1}^{n} x[b]y[b]$. We define the ith Walsh function $i \in \{0, \ldots, 2^n - 1\}$ as

$$\psi_i(x) = (-1)^{\langle i, x \rangle}$$

Here, the i that appears in the inner product of the exponent is taken to be the *bit string representation* of the index i, that is, the binary sequence of length n that corresponds to the integer i.

The objective function f can now be written as

$$f(x) = \sum_i w_i \psi_i(x) \tag{5}$$

where each Walsh coefficient w_i is the sum of contributions from each clause.

$$w_i = \sum_{j=1}^{m} w_{i,c_j}$$

where w_{i,c_j} is the contribution to w_i from clause c_j. This is defined as follows. Let $v(c_j)$ denote a bitstring of length n where

$$v(c_j)[b] = \begin{cases} 1 & \text{if variable } v_b \text{ appears in clause } c_j \\ 0 & \text{otherwise} \end{cases}$$

Similarly, let $u(c_j)$ be a bitstring of length n where

$$u(c_j)[b] = \begin{cases} 1 & \text{if variable } v_b \text{ appears } negated \text{ in clause } c_j \\ 0 & \text{otherwise} \end{cases}$$

If x and y are bitstrings of length n, we say

$$x \subseteq y \iff (x[b] = 1 \implies y[b] = 1)$$

for $b = \{1, \ldots, n\}$. The contribution of clause c_j to Walsh coefficient w_i is

$$w_{i,c_j} = \begin{cases} 0 & \text{if } i \not\subseteq v(c_j) \\ \frac{2^k - 1}{2^k} & \text{if } i = 0 \\ -\frac{1}{2^k}\psi_i(u(c_j)) & \text{otherwise} \end{cases} \tag{6}$$

The *order* of a Walsh coefficient w_i is the number of ones in the bitstring representation of i. This can be denoted following our notation as $\langle i, i \rangle$. Note that the order of any nonzero Walsh coefficient is bounded by k: the number of variables that appear together in a clause. Rana et al. showed it is enough to specify $f(x)$ by computing the $O(2^k m)$ non-zero Walsh coefficients and computing the superposition in Equation (5). Since k is typically taken to be $O(1)$, all nonzero Walsh coefficients can be found in polynomial time.

Lemma 1. *The Walsh function ψ_i of order $\langle i, i \rangle = p$ is an eigenvector of the Markov transition matrix $\mathbf{T}$ with eigenvalue $\left(1 - \frac{2p}{n}\right)$*

Proof. Let x be an arbitrary state.

$$\mathbf{T}\psi_i(x) = \frac{1}{n} \sum_{z \in N(x)} \psi_i(z) \qquad \text{by Eq. (1)}$$

A Hamming neighbor $z \in N(x)$ differs from x in exactly one bit position b. By definition, $\psi_i(z) = (-1)^{\langle i, z \rangle}$. Consider $i[b]$, that is, the bit located at position b in the bitstring representation of i. If $i[b] = 0$ then $\langle i, z \rangle = \langle i, x \rangle$ and $\psi_i(z) = \psi_i(x)$. On the other hand, if $i[b] = 1$ then $|\langle i, z \rangle - \langle i, x \rangle| = 1$ and $\psi_i(z) = -\psi_i(x)$.

Since each Hamming neighbor differs from x in each of the n possible bit positions, there are p elements z of $N(x)$ that satisfy the second condition and $n - p$ that satisfy the first. Thus we have

$$\frac{1}{n} \sum_{z \in N(x)} \psi_i(z) = \frac{1}{n}\left((n - p)\,\psi_i(x) - p\psi_i(x)\right)$$

$$= \left(1 - \frac{2p}{n}\right)\psi_i(x)$$

Since we chose x arbitrarily,

$$\mathbf{T}\psi_i = \left(1 - \frac{2p}{n}\right)\psi_i$$

and ψ_i is an eigenfunction of $\mathbf{T}$. $\square$

We define $\varphi^{(p)}$ as the *Walsh span* of order p.

$$\varphi^{(p)}(x) = \sum_{i:\langle i,i \rangle = p} w_i \psi_i(x)$$

Intuitively, $\varphi^{(p)}$ is an element of the linear space spanned by the Walsh functions of order p. Now we can write the objective function as a sum over Walsh spans of each order p (recall p is bounded by k).

$$f(x) = \sum_{p=0}^{k} \varphi^{(p)}(x) \tag{7}$$

We now show that this is a superposition of elementary components.

Proposition 1. *The pth Walsh span is an elementary landscape.*

Proof. We show that $\varphi^{(p)}$ is an eigenfunction of $\mathbf{T}$. Consider

$$\mathbf{T}\varphi^{(p)} = \mathbf{T}\left[\sum_{i:\langle i,i \rangle = p} w_i \psi_i \right]$$

$$= \sum_{i:\langle i,i \rangle = p} w_i \left(1 - \frac{2p}{n} \right) \psi_i \qquad \text{by Lemma 1}$$

$$= \left(1 - \frac{2p}{n} \right) \left[\sum_{i:\langle i,i \rangle = p} w_i \psi_i \right]$$

$$= \left(1 - \frac{2p}{n} \right) \varphi^{(p)}$$

thus $\varphi^{(p)}$ is an eigenfunction of $\mathbf{T}$ corresponding to eigenvalue $\left(1 - \frac{2p}{n} \right)$. □

We can use the decomposition from the previous section to compute the expectation of Y.

Corollary 1. *On any k-SAT instance, the expectation of the random variable Y is a linear combination of the $k + 1$ Walsh spans evaluated at x.*

$$\mathbb{E}[Y] = \sum_{p=0}^{k} \left(1 - \frac{2p}{n} \right) \varphi^{(p)}(x)$$

This follows directly from the proposition along with Equations (4) and (7).

The following two lemmas will be useful in the next section. First, we show that the Walsh span of order zero is always a constant that is equal to the mean objective function value over X.

Lemma 2. *Let $\bar{f}$ be the mean objective value over X,*

$$\bar{f} = \frac{1}{|X|} \sum_{x \in X} f(x)$$

For all $x \in X$, the zeroth Walsh span is the constant function

$$\varphi^{(0)}(x) = \bar{f}$$

Proof. Let $x \in X$. There is only one Walsh function of order zero: $\psi_0(x) = 1$. We have $\varphi^{(0)}(x) = w_0 \psi_0(x) = w_0$. Note that for $p \neq 0$ we have

$$\frac{1}{|X|} \sum_{x \in X} \varphi^{(p)}(x) = 0 \tag{8}$$

because of the parity of bitstrings of order p. By some algebraic manipulation,

$$w_0 = \left(\frac{1}{|X|} \sum_{x \in X} w_0 \right)$$

$$= \frac{1}{|X|} \sum_{x \in X} \varphi^{(0)}(x)$$

$$= \frac{1}{|X|} \sum_{x \in X} \varphi^{(0)} + \frac{1}{|X|} \sum_{x \in X} \sum_{p=1}^{k} \varphi^{(p)}(x) \qquad \text{by Eq. (8)}$$

$$= \frac{1}{|X|} \sum_{x \in X} \sum_{p=0}^{k} \varphi^{(p)}(x)$$

$$= \frac{1}{|X|} \sum_{x \in X} f(x) \qquad \text{by Eq. (7)}$$

$$\square$$

Corollary 2. *The objective function f for any k-SAT or MAX-k-SAT instance is a superposition of k elementary landscapes*

$$f(x) = \bar{f} + \sum_{p=1}^{k} \varphi^{(p)}(x)$$

In the next section, we will need to bound the value of $\varphi^{(p)}$ over all states $x \in X$. We use the absolute values of the Walsh coefficients w_i to do so.

Lemma 3. *For all $x \in X$,*

$$\sum_{\langle i,i \rangle = p} -|w_i| \leq \varphi^{(p)}(x) \leq \sum_{\langle i,i \rangle = p} |w_i|$$

Proof. Let x be an arbitrary state in X. By definition we have

$$\varphi^{(p)}(x) = \sum_{\langle i,i \rangle = p} w_i \psi_i(x) = \sum_{\langle i,i \rangle = p} \pm |w_i|$$

since $\psi_i(x) = \pm 1$ and $w_i = \pm |w_i|$. Clearly, the smallest that each term could be is $-|w_i|$ and the largest is $|w_i|$.   □

3   Some Bounds for 3-SAT

Two structural search space characteristics that directly affect the performance of local heuristic search algorithms are *local maxima* and *plateaus*. In this section we will use the results from the previous section to prove some bounds on the evaluation of states that are local maxima or belong to plateaus of width greater than 1.

Before we continue we prove the following lemma that provides an identity for a series expansion that will allow for some algebraic manipulation in the theorems below.

Lemma 4. *On 3-SAT we have the following identity.*

$$\sum_{p=0}^{3} p \varphi^{(p)}(x) = 2f(x) - 2\bar{f} - \varphi^{(1)}(x) + \varphi^{(3)}(x)$$

Proof. The series is equal to

$$\sum_{p=0}^{3} p \varphi^{(p)}(x) = \varphi^{(1)}(x) + 2\varphi^{(2)}(x) + 3\varphi^{(3)}(x)$$

We can group the terms on the right hand side as follows

$$\left[\varphi^{(1)}(x) + \varphi^{(2)}(x) + \varphi^{(3)}(x) \right] + \left[\varphi^{(2)}(x) + 2\varphi^{(3)}(x) \right]$$

By the decomposition in Equation (7),

$$\left[f(x) - \varphi^{(0)}(x) \right] + \left[f(x) - \varphi^{(0)}(x) - \varphi^{(1)}(x) + \varphi^{(3)}(x) \right]$$

By Lemma 2,

$$\left[f(x) - \bar{f} \right] + \left[f(x) - \bar{f} - \varphi^{(1)}(x) + \varphi^{(3)}(x) \right]$$

and simplifying gives the result.   □

A state x is said to be a *local maximum* if, for all $y \in N(x)$, $f(y) \leq f(x)$. We point out that this definition is distinct from studies that allow for multi-state local maxima (e.g., [5]). Our single-state definition coincides with Hoos and Stützle [3]. Furthermore, every *global maximum* is also a local maximum.

Grover [8] showed on *elementary* landscapes no local maxima (minima) lie below (above) the mean value of the objective function over X. This will not necessarily hold for arbitrary functions. However, we show here that the knowledge of the elementary components and their properties also allow us to bound the evaluation of local maxima on 3-SAT.

Theorem 1. *On any 3-SAT instance with n variables and m clauses, there exists a positive real number τ such that for any state x, if $f(x) < \bar{f} - \tau$, then x cannot be a local maximum.*

Proof. We begin by showing if $f(x) < \mathbb{E}[Y]$, it cannot be a local maximum. We will then use the previous results to bound the inequality. Let x be a state such that $f(x) < \mathbb{E}[Y]$. There exists some point y in the neighborhood of x that has an evaluation $f(y) > f(x)$. Thus x cannot be a local maximum. By Corollary 1 we thus have

$$f(x) < \mathbb{E}[Y]$$

$$f(x) < \sum_{p=0}^{3} \left(1 - \frac{2p}{n}\right) \varphi^{(p)}(x)$$

$$f(x) < \sum_{p=0}^{3} \varphi^{(p)}(x) - \frac{2}{n} \sum_{p=0}^{3} p\varphi^{(p)}(x)$$

The first term on the right hand side is simply the decomposition of $f(x)$ given by Equation (7). Thus we can make the following substitution.

$$f(x) < f(x) - \frac{2}{n} \sum_{p=0}^{3} p\varphi^{(p)}(x)$$

By Lemma 4,

$$f(x) < f(x) - \frac{2}{n} \left(2f(x) - 2\bar{f} - \varphi^{(1)}(x) + \varphi^{(3)}(x)\right)$$

Simplifying, we have

$$f(x) < \bar{f} + \frac{1}{2} \left(\varphi^{(1)}(x) - \varphi^{(3)}(x)\right) \tag{9}$$

Inequality (9) describes a threshold that depends on $\varphi^{(1)}(x)$ and $\varphi^{(3)}(x)$ such that if $f(x)$ is less than this threshold, x cannot be locally maximum. We now give a threshold that holds *over the entire search space*.

By Lemma 3, we have for *any* $x \in X$,

$$\left(\varphi^{(1)}(x) - \varphi^{(3)}(x)\right) \geq \left(\sum_{\langle i,i\rangle=1} -|w_i| - \sum_{\langle i,i\rangle=3} |w_i|\right)$$

and letting

$$\tau = \frac{1}{2} \left(\sum_{\langle i,i \rangle = 1} |w_i| + \sum_{\langle i,i \rangle = 3} |w_i| \right) \tag{10}$$

we now have the following bound on the r.h.s. of Inequality (9).

$$\bar{f} - \tau \leq \bar{f} + \frac{1}{2} \left(\varphi^{(1)}(x) - \varphi^{(3)}(x) \right)$$

and thus, for all $x \in X$, if $f(x) < \bar{f} - \tau$, then x cannot be a local maximum. The threshold $\bar{f} - \tau$ is simply computed (in polynomial time) by summing the absolute Walsh coefficients of order 1 and 3 and holds over the entire search space.   □

In a similar manner, we can bound the function value at which plateaus of width greater than one can appear. A plateau is a maximal set P of states such that for all $x, y \in P$ there is a path $(x = x_1, x_2, \ldots, x_t = y)$ of length $t \geq 1$ with $f(x) = f(x_i)$ for $i = 1, 2, \ldots, t$ and, if $t > 1$, $x_{i+1} \in N(x_i)$. The *level* of a plateau P is the evaluation $f(x_p), \forall x_p \in P$.

We say the neighborhood of a state x is *flat* if, for all $y \in N(x)$, $f(y) = f(x)$, that is, x has the same value as all the states in its neighborhood. We show that flat neighborhoods cannot exist at certain levels of the objective function.

Theorem 2. *On any 3-SAT instance with n variables and m clauses, there exists a positive real number τ such that for any state x, if $f(x) < \bar{f} - \tau$ or $f(x) > \bar{f} + \tau$, then x cannot have a flat neighborhood.*

Proof. We prove the equivalent contrapositive. Let x be a state with a flat neighborhood. We have

$$f(x) = \mathbb{E}[Y]$$

$$= \sum_{p=0}^{3} \left(1 - \frac{2p}{n} \right) \varphi^{(p)}(x)$$

$$= \sum_{p=0}^{3} \varphi^{(p)}(x) - \frac{2}{n} \sum_{p=0}^{3} p\varphi^{(p)}(x)$$

$$= f(x) - \frac{2}{n} \sum_{p=0}^{3} p\varphi^{(p)}(x) \qquad \text{by Eq. (7)}$$

Therefore, at such a point x we must have

$$\sum_{p=0}^{3} p\varphi^{(p)}(x) = 0$$

$$2f(x) - 2\bar{f} - \varphi^{(1)}(x) + \varphi^{(3)}(x) = 0 \qquad \text{by Lemma 4}$$

thus if x has a flat neighborhood, the following must hold.

$$f(x) = \bar{f} + \frac{1}{2}\left(\varphi^{(1)}(x) - \varphi^{(3)}(x)\right) \tag{11}$$

Using Lemma 3 we can bound the terms $\varphi^{(1)}(x)$ and $\varphi^{(3)}(x)$ giving the following

$$\bar{f} - \tau \le f(x) \le \bar{f} + \tau$$

where τ is given by Equation (10) in Theorem 1.   □

Recall the width of a plateau P is the minimal length path between any state in P and one not in P. We have the following corollary.

Corollary 3. *A plateau P with level less than $\bar{f} - \tau$ or greater than $\bar{f} + \tau$ cannot have width greater than 1.*

Proof. This follows directly from the fact that no flat neighborhoods exist outside of the range $\bar{f} - \tau$ to $\bar{f} + \tau$. Thus, for these points, every state on a plateau P must have at least one neighbor outside P and the width of P is at most 1. □

4   Derived Values in Practice

We have shown how the average value of the neighborhood can be obtained analytically for any particular state and that a region (τ from $\bar{f}$) can be defined outside of which plateaus of width greater than one cannot exist and certain local optima cannot be found. We illustrate the proved properties in Figure 1. In this section, we show empirically that the expectation value computation is informative and that the region is non-trivial in benchmark problem instances.

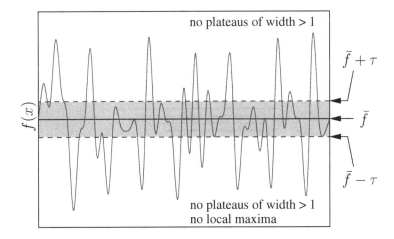

Fig. 1. An illustration of the proved properties. No plateaus of width strictly greater than one can lie outside the interval. No local maxima can lie below the interval.

4.1   Empirical Values of Neighborhood Expectation Value

The neighborhood expectation value computed in Equation (4) is useful because it can potentially provide algorithms with higher resolution information about states than the objective function. For example, given two states x and y with $f(x) = f(y)$, it is not necessarily the case that the neighborhood expectation values are equal for both x and y.

Stochastic local search algorithms applied to k-SAT problems often must select a neighboring state from a large set of moves with equal evaluation. This presents a problem for such algorithms due to the lack of gradient information in the neighborhood [3]. A collection of states at the same evaluation level are indistinguishable in terms of objective function value. However, we conjecture the expectation value can serve as a predictor of the number of *improving moves* that exit a particular state.

To illustrate this concept, we sampled 100 states at a particular objective function level ($f(x) = 390$) on each of 1000 instances that make up the uf100-430 benchmark set in SATLIB (100 vars, 430 clauses). For each point we calculated the correspondence between the expectation value given by Equation (4) and the actual number of improving moves in the neighborhood of the state. These data are plotted in Figure 2. A correlation test gives a strong positive correlation value of 0.51 with $p < 2.2 \times 10^{-16}$ indicating that better expectation leads to more potential for improvement. These data are preliminary indicators that the neighborhood expectation value can provide useful information about the neighborhoods of points even if they are equal in objective function value.

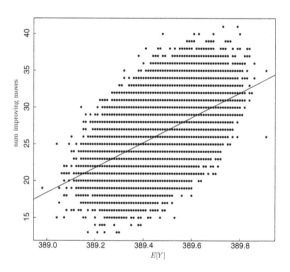

Fig. 2. Number of improving moves vs $\mathbb{E}[Y]$ at $f(x) = 390$ for 100 points each on 1000 instances of SATLIB benchmark set uf100-430. Line indicates linear best fit.

4.2 Empirical Values of τ

To demonstrate the region outside the interval is not trivial, we computed the values for τ as a percentage of the objective function range m across 18 benchmark distributions from SATLIB and the 2008 SAT competition. In Table 1 we report the mean (μ), standard deviation (σ), minimum, and maximum of the value τ/m over all N problems in each distribution.

The mean value of τ is consistently about 10% of the range m with a relatively low standard deviation. The maximum value of τ does not exceed 13% of the total objective function range over all the problem distributions we tested.

Table 1. Computed statistics for τ/m across several benchmark distributions from SATLIB and 2008 SAT competition

set	setsize	μ	σ	min	max
		SATLIB			
uf20-91	1000	0.10252	0.00707	0.08104	0.12775
uf50-218	1000	0.10467	0.00421	0.08945	0.11984
uf75-325	100	0.10487	0.00358	0.09538	0.11231
uf100-430	1000	0.10483	0.00307	0.0968	0.11483
uf125-538	100	0.10477	0.00241	0.09898	0.11245
uf150-645	100	0.10514	0.00221	0.10039	0.11027
uf175-753	100	0.10533	0.00239	0.0991	0.11155
uf200-860	100	0.10469	0.00203	0.09942	0.11047
uf225-960	100	0.10484	0.00194	0.0987	0.10898
uf250-1065	100	0.10478	0.00167	0.10082	0.10986
uuf50-218	1000	0.10131	0.00406	0.08888	0.1164
		2008 SAT competition			
v360	10	0.10382	0.00146	0.10046	0.10535
v400	10	0.1037	0.00198	0.10072	0.10651
v450	10	0.10369	0.00162	0.10016	0.10571
v500	10	0.10384	0.00177	0.09947	0.10616
v550	10	0.10366	0.00113	0.10137	0.10494
v600	10	0.10404	0.00107	0.1027	0.10603
v650	10	0.104	0.00108	0.10293	0.10627

5   Conclusion

Studying the structural characteristics of combinatorial search spaces is important to understanding the behavior of stochastic search algorithms. These characteristics, along with how algorithms respond to them, define how poorly or how well the algorithm performs, in some cases determining whether a problem or problem class is easily solved or not. We have presented analytical tools for analyzing the search space of k-SAT and MAX-k-SAT.

We have shown that the landscape formalism provides insight into certain structural relationships. We have shown that the decomposition of the objective function into elementary components supplies us with the expectation value of the objective function of neighboring states. We have also proved that the objective function of k-SAT can be decomposed into k computationally efficient elementary landscape functions. We have applied this result to obtain previously unknown bounds on the objective function levels for local maxima and plateau width in the 3-SAT search space.

We have shown empirically on a large number of cases that the region for which our results hold cover the majority of the objective function range. We also have demonstrated that neighborhood expectation varies across a set of states of equal evaluation and that this expectation correlates with improvement. Clearly the relationship between expectation and improvement needs to be carefully explored as does the implications of the theoretical results to algorithm design.

References

1. Gent, I.P., Walsh, T.: Towards an understanding of hill-climbing procedures for sat. In: Proc. of AAAI 1993, pp. 28–33. MIT Press, Cambridge (1993)
2. Parkes, A.J., Walser, J.P.: Tuning local search for satisfiability testing. In: Proc. of AAAI 1996, pp. 356–362. MIT Press, Cambridge (1996)
3. Hoos, H.H., Stützle, T.: Stochastic Local Search: Foundations and Applications. Morgan Kaufmann, San Francisco (2004)
4. Clark, D.A., Frank, J., Gent, I.P., MacIntyre, E., Tomov, N., Walsh, T.: Local search and the number of solutions. In: Freuder, E.C. (ed.) CP 1996. LNCS, vol. 1118, pp. 119–133. Springer, Heidelberg (1996)
5. Frank, J., Cheeseman, P., Stutz, J.: When gravity fails: Local search topology. J. of Artificial Intelligence Research 7, 249–281 (1997)
6. Yokoo, M.: Why adding more constraints makes a problem easier for hill-climbing algorithms: Analyzing landscapes of CSPs. In: Smolka, G. (ed.) CP 1997. LNCS, vol. 1330, pp. 356–370. Springer, Heidelberg (1997)
7. Stadler, P.F.: Toward a theory of landscapes. In: Lopéz-Peña, R., Capovilla, R., García-Pelayo, R., Waelbroeck, H., Zertruche, F. (eds.) Complex Systems and Binary Networks, pp. 77–163. Springer, Heidelberg (1995)
8. Grover, L.K.: Local search and the local structure of NP-complete problems. Operations Research Letters 12, 235–243 (1992)
9. Stadler, P.F.: Landscapes and their correlation functions. J. of Mathematical Chemistry 20, 1–45 (1996)
10. Rockmore, D., Kostelec, P., Hordijk, W., Stadler, P.F.: Fast Fourier transform for fitness landscapes. Applied and Computational Harmonic Analysis 12, 57–76 (2002)
11. Whitley, L.D., Sutton, A.M., Howe, A.E.: Understanding elementary landscapes. In: Proc. of GECCO, Atlanta, GA (July 2008)
12. Rana, S., Heckendorn, R.B., Whitley, L.D.: A tractable Walsh analysis of SAT and its implications for genetic algorithms. In: Proc. of AAAI 1998, pp. 392–397 (1998)

Loopy Substructural Local Search for the Bayesian Optimization Algorithm

Claudio F. Lima[1], Martin Pelikan[2],
Fernando G. Lobo[1], and David E. Goldberg[3]

[1] University of Algarve, Portugal
[2] University of Missouri at St. Louis, USA
[3] University of Illinois at Urbana-Champaign, USA
clima.research@gmail.com, pelikan@cs.umsl.edu,
fernando.lobo@gmail.com, deg@illinois.edu

Abstract. This paper presents a local search method for the Bayesian optimization algorithm (BOA) based on the concepts of substructural neighborhoods and loopy belief propagation. The probabilistic model of BOA, which automatically identifies important problem substructures, is used to define the topology of the neighborhoods explored in local search. On the other hand, belief propagation in graphical models is employed to find the most suitable configuration of conflicting substructures. The results show that performing loopy substructural local search (SLS) in BOA can dramatically reduce the number of generations necessary to converge to optimal solutions and thus provides substantial speedups.

1 Introduction

The Bayesian optimization algorithm (BOA) [1,2] replaces the standard crossover and mutation operators of evolutionary algorithms (EAs) by building a probabilistic model of promising solutions and sampling from the corresponding probability distribution. This feature allows BOA and other estimation of distribution algorithms (EDAs) [3,4] to automatically identify the problem decomposition and important problem substructures, leading to superior performance for many problems when compared to EAs with fixed, problem-independent variation operators.

Although EDAs are effective at exploring the search space to find promising regions, they inherit a common drawback from traditional EAs: slower convergence to optimal solutions when compared with appropriate local searchers that start the search within the basin of attraction of the optima. This observation has led to the combination of EAs with local search methods known as hybrid EAs or memetic algorithms [5,6]. In this context EDAs are no exception and many applications in real-world optimization have been accomplished with the help of some sort of local search. However, systematic methods for hybridizing and designing competent global and local-search methods that automatically identify the problem decomposition and important problem substructures are

T. Stützle, M. Birattari, and H.H. Hoos (Eds.): SLS 2009, LNCS 5752, pp. 61–75, 2009.
© Springer-Verlag Berlin Heidelberg 2009

still scarce. For instance, the probabilistic models of EDAs contain useful information about the underlying problem structure that can be exploited to speedup the convergence of EDAs to optimal solutions.

This paper makes use of the concept of substructural neighborhoods [7,8]—where the structure of the neighborhoods is defined by learned probabilistic models—to perform local search in BOA. The local search method proposed is inspired on loopy belief propagation, that is often used for obtaining the most probable state of a Bayesian network. To guide the propagation of beliefs, we use a surrogate fitness model that also relies on substructural information. Experiments are performed for a boundedly difficult problem with both non-overlapping and overlapping subproblems. The results show that incorporating loopy substructural local search (SLS) in BOA leads to a significant reduction in the number of generations, providing relevant speedups in terms of number of evaluations.

The next section briefly reviews the Bayesian optimization algorithm, while Section 3 details the notion of substructural local search in EDAs. Section 4 introduces belief propagation in graphical models and its potential for function optimization. A new substructural local search method based on loopy belief propagation is then presented in Section 5. Section 6 presents and discusses empirical results. The paper ends with a brief summary and conclusions.

2   Bayesian Optimization Algorithm

Estimation of distribution algorithms [3,2] replace traditional variation operators of EAs by building a probabilistic model of promising solutions and sampling the corresponding probability distribution to generate the offspring population. The Bayesian optimization algorithm [1,2] uses Bayesian networks as the probabilistic model to capture important problem regularities.

BOA starts with an initial population of candidate solutions that is usually randomly generated. In each iteration, selection is performed to obtain a population of promising solutions. This population is then used to build the probabilistic model for the current generation. After the model structure is learned and its parameters estimated, the offspring population is generated by sampling from the distribution of modeled individuals. The new solutions are then evaluated and incorporated into the original population by using any standard replacement method. The next iteration proceeds again from the selection phase until some stopping criterion is satisfied. Here, we use a simple replacement scheme where new solutions fully replace the original population.

2.1   Modeling Variable Interactions in BOA

Bayesian networks [9] are powerful graphical models that combine probability theory with graph theory to encode probabilistic relationships between variables of interest. A Bayesian network is defined by a structure and corresponding parameters. The structure is represented by a directed acyclic graph where the nodes correspond to the variables of the data to be modeled and the edges correspond to conditional dependencies. The parameters are represented by the conditional probabilities for each variable given any instance of the variables that this variable depends on. More formally, a Bayesian network encodes the following joint probability distribution,

$$p(X) = \prod_{i=1}^{\ell} p(X_i|\Pi_i), \tag{1}$$

where $X = (X_1, X_2, \ldots, X_\ell)$ is a vector of all the variables of the problem, Π_i is the set of *parents* of X_i (nodes from which there exists an edge to X_i), and $p(X_i|\Pi_i)$ is the conditional probability of X_i given its parents Π_i.

In BOA, both the structure and the parameters of the probabilistic model are searched and optimized to best fit the data (set of promising solutions). To learn the most adequate structure for the Bayesian network a greedy algorithm is usually used for a good compromise between search efficiency and model quality.

The parameters of a Bayesian network are represented by a set of conditional probability tables (CPTs) specifying the conditional probabilities for each variable given all possible instances of the parent variables Π_i. Alternatively, these conditional probabilities can be stored in the form of local structures such as decision trees or decision graphs, allowing a more efficient and flexible representation of local conditional distributions. In this work, decision trees are used to encode the parameters of the Bayesian network.

2.2 Modeling Fitness in BOA

Pelikan and Sastry [10] extended the Bayesian networks used in BOA to encode a surrogate fitness model that is used to estimate the fitness of a proportion of the population, thereby reducing the total number of function evaluations. For each possible value x_i of every variable X_i, an estimate of the marginal fitness contribution of a subsolution with $X_i = x_i$ is stored for each instance π_i of X_i's parents Π_i. Therefore, in the binary case, each row in the CPT is extended by two additional entries. The fitness of an individual can then be estimated as

$$f_{est}(X_1, X_2, \ldots, X_\ell) = \bar{f} + \sum_{i=1}^{\ell} \left(\bar{f}(X_i|\Pi_i) - \bar{f}(\Pi_i) \right), \tag{2}$$

where $\bar{f}$ is the average fitness of all solutions used to learn the surrogate, $\bar{f}(X_i|\Pi_i)$ is the average fitness of solutions with X_i and Π_i, and $\bar{f}(\Pi_i)$ is the average fitness of all solutions with Π_i.

Fitness information can also be incorporated in Bayesian networks with decision trees or graphs in a similar way. In this case, the average fitness of each instance for every variable must be stored in every leaf of the decision tree or graph. The fitness averages in each leaf are now restricted to solutions that satisfy the condition specified by the path from the root of the tree to the leaf.

3   Substructural Local Search

One of the key requirements for designing an efficient mutation operator is to ensure that it searches in the correct neighborhood. This is often accomplished by exploiting and incorporating domain- or problem-specific knowledge in the design of neighborhood operators. While these neighborhood operators are designed for a particular search problem, oftentimes on an ad-hoc basis, they do not generalize their efficiency beyond a small number of applications. On the other hand, simple bitwise hillclimbers are frequently used as local search methods with more general applicability, providing inferior but still competitive results, especially when combined with population-based search procedures. Clearly, there is a tradeoff between generalization and efficiency for neighborhood operators with fixed structure. Therefore, it is important to study systematic methods for designing neighborhood operators that can solve a broad class of search problems.

The exploration of neighborhoods defined by the probabilistic models of EDAs is an approach that exploits both the underlying problem structure while not loosing the generality of application. The resulting mutation operators explore a more *global*, problem-dependent neighborhood than traditional local, purely representation-dependent search procedures. Sastry and Goldberg [7] showed that a selectomutative algorithm that performs hillclimbing in the substructural space can successfully solve problems of bounded difficulty with subquadratic scalability.

Lima *et al.* [8] introduced the concept of substructural neighborhoods to the Bayesian optimization algorithm. The parental neighborhood, which considers all possible values for a given variable X_i and its corresponding parents Π_i, was adopted to perform local search in the subsolution space [8]. The substructural local search is performed for a proportion of the population in BOA to speedup convergence to good solutions, as in traditional hybrid EAs or memetic algorithms [5,6]. The SLS procedure essentially explores all substructural neighborhoods in a random order, choosing the best subsolution for each neighborhood according to $\bar{f}(X_i, \Pi_i)$.

Although this type of SLS succeeds in reducing the number of generations necessary to converge to optimal solutions for problems of bounded difficulty, the results do not carry over for problems with highly conflicting subsolutions [11]. This will become clear from the results presented in Section 6.

4   Loopy Belief Propagation

Belief propagation (BP) [9] is a method for performing exact and approximate inference in graphical models, which has enjoyed increasing popularity over the last years. Although BP has been reinvented several times in different fields [12,13], it is mainly applied to two tasks: (1) obtaining marginal probabilities for some of the variables, or (2) finding the most probable explanation or instance for the graphical model. These two versions are known as the sum-product and max-product algorithms.

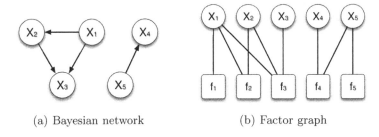

(a) Bayesian network   (b) Factor graph

Fig. 1. Example of a (a) Bayesian network and its equivalent representation as a (b) factor graph. Note that each factor corresponds to a conditional probability table, therefore the number of variable and factor nodes is the same.

BP algorithms are typically applied to factor graphs [12], which can be seen as a unifying representation for both Bayesian networks and Markov networks [14]. Factor graphs explicitly express the factorization structure of the corresponding probability distribution. Consider a function $g(X)$ whose joint probability distribution can be factorized in several local functions, such that

$$g(x_1, x_2, \ldots, x_\ell) = \frac{1}{Z} \prod_{I \in \mathcal{F}} f_I(x_{N_I}), \tag{3}$$

where $Z = \sum_x \prod_{I \in \mathcal{F}} f_I(x_{N_I})$ is a normalization constant, I is the factor index, N_I is the subset of variable indices associated with factor I, and factor f_I is a nonnegative function. Note that for a Bayesian network each factor corresponds to a conditional probability table.

A factor graph is a bipartite graph consisting of variable nodes $i \in \mathcal{V}$, factor nodes $I \in \mathcal{F}$, and an undirected edge $\{i, I\}$ between i and I if and only if $i \in N_I$, meaning that factor f_I depends on x_i. Factor nodes are typically represented as squares and variable nodes as circles.

An example of a Bayesian network, along with the corresponding representation as a factor graph, is presented in Figure 1. The factor graph represents the following factorization

$$g(x_1, x_2, x_3, x_4, x_5) = \frac{1}{Z} f_1(x_1) f_2(x_1, x_2) f_3(x_1, x_2, x_3) f_4(x_4, x_5) f_5(x_5). \tag{4}$$

If one substitutes the factor functions by the corresponding conditional probabilities, the joint probability distribution of a Bayesian network is obtained.

When BP is applied to cyclic graphs it is often referred as *loopy* belief propagation (LBP). In this situation, the convergence to exact beliefs can not be guaranteed as it is for acyclic graphs (without loops). However, empirical studies have shown that good approximate beliefs can be obtained for several domains (see [13] for an extensive list).

The inference performed by BP is done by message-passing between the nodes of the graphical model. Each node sends and receives messages from its neighbors until a stable state is reached. The outgoing messages are functions of incoming messages at each node. This iterative process is repeated according to some schedule that describes the sequence of message updates in time [13].

When performing BP in factor graphs, there are two types of messages: messages $m_{I \to i}$, sent from factors $I \in \mathcal{F}$ to neighboring variables $i \in N_I$, and messages $m_{i \to I}$, sent from variables $i \in \mathcal{V}$ to neighboring factors $I \in N_i$. The new messages m' are given in terms of the incoming messages by the following update rules:

$$m'_{i \to I}(x_i) = \prod_{J \in N_i \setminus I} m_{J \to i}(x_i) \qquad \forall i \in \mathcal{V}, \ \forall I \in N_i, \tag{5}$$

$$m'_{I \to i}(x_i) = \sum_{x_{N_I \setminus i}} f_I(x_{N_I}) \prod_{j \in N_I \setminus i} m_{j \to I}(x_j) \qquad \forall I \in \mathcal{F}, \ \forall i \in N_I, \tag{6}$$

$$m'_{I \to i}(x_i) = \max_{x_{N_I \setminus i}} \left(f_I(x_{N_I}) \prod_{j \in N_I \setminus i} m_{j \to I}(x_j) \right) \qquad \forall I \in \mathcal{F}, \ \forall i \in N_I, \tag{7}$$

where $N_i \setminus I$ represents the set of neighboring factor nodes of variable node i excluding node I, $N_I \setminus i$ represents the set of neighboring variable nodes of factor node I excluding node i, and $x_{N_I \setminus i}$ stands for a possible combination of values that all variables but X_i in X_{N_I} can take while variable X_i remains instantiated with value x_i.

For the sum-product algorithm, equations 5 and 6 are used, while for the max-product algorithm equations 5 and 7 should be used instead. When messages stop changing over time, the BP algorithm has converged and marginal functions (sum-product) or max-marginals (max-product) can be obtained as the normalized product of all messages received for X_i:

$$g_i(x_i) \propto \prod_{I \in N_i} m_{I \to i}(x_i). \tag{8}$$

For the max-product algorithm, the most probable configuration (MPC) for each variable X_i is obtained by assigning the value associated with the highest probability at each max-marginal.

When applying BP algorithms, three types of parameters need to be defined [15]: message scheduling, stopping criteria, and initial settings. For more details about parameter setting in BP algorithms the reader is referred elsewhere [15,13,9,12].

4.1   Message-Passing Techniques for Optimization

Several message-passing algorithms have been developed and applied to different optimization problems. The idea is to associate a probability distribution to the function to be optimized in such a way that the most probable value of the distribution is reached for the solution(s) that optimize the function [15]. Recent applications have been used to solve satisfiability problems [16,17] and for finding the maximum weight matching in a bipartite graph [18].

Recognizing the potential of BP for Bayesian EDAs, Mendiburu *et al.* [19] introduced belief propagation to the estimation of Bayesian networks algorithm (EBNA) [20], which is very similar to BOA. The idea is to combine probabilistic logic sampling (PLS) [21] with loopy belief propagation to sample the offspring population. Specifically, $n - 1$ individuals are sampled through PLS and the remaining individual is instantiated with the most probable configuration for the current Bayesian network. The Bayesian network is mapped into an equivalent factor graph so that the max-product algorithm can be applied to obtain the new individual. Although the authors concluded that this modification allowed an improvement in the optimization capabilities of EBNA, the results fail to demonstrate great improvements both in solution quality and number of function evaluations required [19].

While the calculation of the most probable configuration of the Bayesian network at each generation is expected to generate a good solution, its relative quality is strongly dependent upon the current stage of the search. It seems clear that high-quality solutions can only be generated by LBP when BOA starts focusing on more concrete regions of the search space. On the other hand, instead of performing loopy belief propagation based on the conditional probabilities, substructural fitness information can be used for the factor nodes. Although probabilities represent likely substructures, using the associated fitness provides more direct information when looking for solutions with high quality. That is what is proposed in the next section.

5   BOA with Loopy Substructural Local Search

This section describes a substructural local searcher based on loopy belief propagation that can be incorporated in BOA. The resulting method which is named as loopy substructural local search (loopy SLS) uses substructural fitness information $\bar{f}(X_i, \Pi_i)$ to guide the max-product algorithm in finding the MPC, which is the solution that is expected to maximize fitness based on the contribution of its substructures.

Regarding the parameterization of BP, the maximum number of iterations that the algorithm is allowed to run is set to 2ℓ, while the allowed difference when comparing two messages is of at least 10^{-6} (otherwise messages are considered to be similar). These are typical parameter values from the literature. The update schedule used is the maximum residual updating [22], which calculates all residuals (difference between updated and current messages) and updates only the message with the largest residual. Consequently, only the residuals that depend on the updated message need to be recalculated.

If the factor graph is acyclic, BP will converge towards a unique fixed point within a finite number of iterations, while the beliefs can be shown to be exact. However, if the factor graph contains loops, which is the typical situation when translating a Bayesian network from BOA, the result can be only interpreted as an approximate solution. Therefore, two different situations can arise when performing loopy SLS: (1) the max-product algorithm might not converge to a stable point and (2) even in case of convergence, the solution can present ties for certain positions.

If the LBP algorithm does not converge to a stable state, the configuration found after the maximum number of iterations (2ℓ) is still used as the result of loopy SLS. While this solution is not guaranteed to be the MPC, it is likely a local optimum and therefore should be inserted in the population. Another situation that can happen is the presence of ties for certain variables, where the MPC can not be decided between 0 and 1. Typically, for problems tested with BOA, this occasionally occurs but for very few variables. Therefore, when the MPC presents ties, the loopy SLS enumerates all possible configurations and insert them in the population as the result of local search. To account for the rare case where the number of ties n_t is beyond reasonable, the maximum number of possible configurations/individuals returned by local search is set to ℓ, in which case the configurations chosen are randomly selected from all possible 2^{n_t}.

The loopy SLS method presents several differences from the proposal by Mendirubu et al. [19]. The most significant difference is that the factor nodes use fitness information instead of the traditional approach in BP which is to use the conditional probabilities stored in CPTs. The motivation for doing so is discussed later with a detailed example. By using fitness information, the algorithm becomes a local search method based on loopy message-passing principles—therefore the name of loopy substructural local search. Another important innovation is the selection of relevant factor nodes to perform loopy SLS. Essentially, factor nodes (and corresponding edges) whose variable set is a subset of another factor are removed. Consider the previous example of a factor graph in Figure 1. The relevant factor nodes are f_3 and f_4 because the variable domain of the remaining factors is already included in these factors. Note that this simplification of the BN is possible because $\bar{f}(X_1, X_2, X_3)$ (stored in factor f_3) is more informative than both $\bar{f}(X_1, X_2)$ and $\bar{f}(X_1)$ (stored in factors f_2 and f_1). In the same way, $\bar{f}(X_4, X_5)$ already contains information from $\bar{f}(X_5)$. This straightforward procedure simplifies and improves the information exchange between nodes in the factor graph. In addition, the method for dealing with ties is also a novel contribution.

Figure 2 presents the pseudocode for the loopy substructural local searcher in BOA. The algorithm starts by mapping the current Bayesian network to a factor graph which stores fitness information in the factor nodes. The method proceeds by removing all factor nodes that are not relevant to local search, simplifying the search complexity for the MPC. The max-product algorithm is then applied to the resulting graph and the result is inserted in the population. Depending upon the number of possible ties for certain variable positions, up to ℓ different individuals can be inserted in the population. This is a reasonable number in terms of population-sizing which is known to scale as $\Theta(\ell \log \ell)$ [23]. Finally, it is important to mention that the loopy local search takes place after the offspring population is generated.

Loopy Substructural Local Search (Loopy SLS)

(1) Map the current Bayesian network B into a factor graph F, where factor nodes store substructural fitness information $\bar{f}(X_i, \Pi_i)$.

(2) Remove factor nodes (and corresponding edges) whose variable set is a subset of another factor in F.

(3) Perform loopy belief propagation in F. Return the most probable configuration MPC and possible number of tied positions n_t.

(4) **If** $n_t = 0$, instantiate an individual with the values from MPC;
    Else If $2^{n_t} \leq \ell$, enumerate all possible 2^{n_t} configurations and instantiate them in 2^{n_t} different individuals;
    Else enumerate ℓ randomly chosen configurations out of 2^{n_t} and instantiate them in ℓ different individuals.

(5) Evaluate the resulting individuals.

Fig. 2. Pseudocode of the loopy substructural local search in BOA

6   Results and Discussion

This section presents and discusses the results obtained for the standard BOA, BOA with loopy SLS, BOA with standard LBP (as proposed by Mendiburu *et al.* [19]), and BOA with the simpler SLS [8].

6.1   Experimental Setup

The test problem considered is the $m - k$ trap function, where m stands for the number of concatenated k-bit trap functions. Trap functions [24,25] are relevant to test problem design because they bound an important class of nearly decomposable problems [25]. The trap function used is defined as follows

$$f_{trap}(u) = \begin{cases} k, & \text{if } u = k \\ k - 1 - u, & \text{otherwise} \end{cases} \tag{9}$$

where u is the number of ones in the string, k is the size of the trap function. Note that for $k \geq 3$ the trap function is fully deceptive [24] which means that any lower than k-order statistics will mislead the search away from the optimum. In this problem the accurate identification and exchange of the building-blocks (BBs) is critical to achieve success, because processing substructures of lower order leads to exponential scalability [26]. Note that no information about the problem is given to the algorithm; therefore, it is equally difficult for BOA if the variables correlated are closely or randomly distributed along the chromosome string. A trap function with size $k = 5$ is used in our experiments.

Overlapping difficulty is an important problem feature because many problems can have different interactions that share common components. The difficulty of overlap is addressed by considering an overlapping version of m-k trap problem, where each variable index set corresponding to a subfunction shares o variables with two other neighboring subproblems. More precisely, a trap-k subfunction $f_j(x_i, x_{i+1}, \ldots, x_{i+k-1})$ will overlap with $f_{j-1}(x_{i-k+o}, x_{i-k+o+1}, \ldots, x_{i+o-1})$ and $f_{j+1}(x_{i+k-o}, x_{i+k-o+1}, \ldots, x_{i+2k-o-1})$.

For all experiments, we use the population size that minimizes the total number of function evaluations required to solve the problem in 10 out of 10 independent runs. The population size adjustment is performed for 10 independent runs using a modified bisection method [11,2]. Therefore, the total number of function evaluations is averaged over 100 (10×10) runs.

6.2   Loopy SLS *versus* Standard LBP

This section compares the proposed loopy SLS with the proposal by Mendiburu *et al.* [19]. It should be clear that the only difference between the two alternatives is that loopy SLS uses (1) substructural fitness information instead of conditional probabilities for the factor nodes and (2) removes non-relevant factors. Other aspects such as message-scheduling, ties management, and parameters are set similarly (as described for loopy SLS), to focus the experimental comparison on the capability for generating high-quality solutions, rather than comparing different configurations of the max-product algorithm. The results for BOA with both standard loopy BP (as proposed for EBNA) and loopy SLS are presented in Figure 3.

The two alternatives present a very different behavior. While the LBP algorithm behaves similarly to the original BOA, preferring smaller population sizes but taking more iterations and consequently evaluations, the loopy SLS seems to take advantage from using larger population sizes. Note that both alternatives use the same method to tune the population size. Nevertheless, increasing the population size for standard LBP does not reduce the number of generations necessary to solve the problem. Although minor gains are obtained with LBP for some problem instances, the corresponding speedup is very close to one.

Loopy SLS can effectively take advantage from larger populations to gather more accurate information to speedup the solution of the problem. More accurate fitness information allows the loopy local searcher to converge faster to optimal solutions. If conditional probabilities are used instead (as in standard LBP), the algorithm requires a certain number of generations for selecting and propagating the best substructures until their sampling probability becomes significant enough. For example, consider the trap-5 function with the local optimum at 00000 and the global optimum at 11111. Initially, the local optimum will dominate the population because it's much easier to climb. Later on, when both optima are the most frequent alternatives, the selection process starts propagating 11111 over 00000. Only at this stage, the max-product algorithm based of conditional probabilities is expected to return 11111 as the most probable configuration. On the other hand, when using substructural fitness information, once the fitness surrogate is accurate enough to identify 11111 as a better alternative than 00000, the MPC is expected to return the optimal solution. Consequently, BOA with loopy SLS takes advantage from using larger populations by building a more accurate fitness surrogate model.

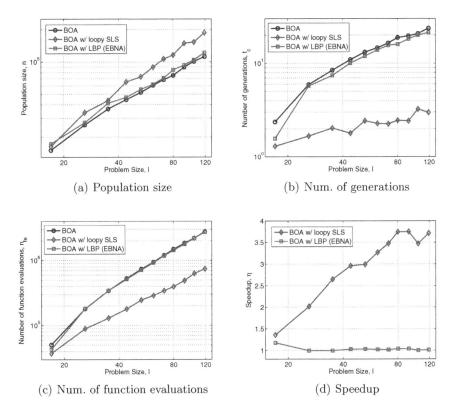

(a) Population size

(b) Num. of generations

(c) Num. of function evaluations

(d) Speedup

Fig. 3. Results for BOA with both standard LBP and loopy SLS when solving the trap-5 problem with two overlapping variables ($o = 2$)

Another important difference between the two approaches is the removal of factors which are not relevant to the MPC search. This is directly related to the dependency structure used by Bayesian networks to represent interactions among several variables. While this structure is required to be able to sample new instances with PLS, it is not necessary or even desirable when using BP methods. Given that $\prod_{i=1}^{k} p(X_i|X_{i+1}, X_{i+2}, \ldots, X_k) = p(X_1, X_2, \ldots, X_k)$, if a factor node relating k interacting variables stores the joint probability $p(X_1, X_2, \ldots, X_k)$, there is no need of having k factors, one for each conditional probability in the product above. In this case, the presence of k factors can be even prejudicial if the lower-order statistics are misleading, which is the case for deceptive problems. The factors corresponding to lower-order statistics will make judgments based on local/deceptive information, somehow discrediting the information sent by the factor nodes with $k-$order statistics. Only when lower-order statistics start guiding the search towards 11111 (as mentioned above), this configuration will get enough recommendations to set the MPC with the optimal substructure.

6.3   Loopy SLS *versus* Simple SLS for Increasing Overlap

Figure 4 details the performance of BOA with both substructural local searchers for the trap-5 problem without overlap. Clearly, both SLS versions succeed in reducing the number of generations required to solve the problem. Consequently, the total number of function evaluations required is significantly reduced, providing speedups superior to 10. This translates into an order of magnitude less evaluations to solve the same problem. More importantly, the speedup consistently increases with problem size approximately as $\Theta(\sqrt{\ell})$.

Figure 5 presents the results for the trap-5 problem with several degrees of overlapping ($o = \{1, 2, 3\}$). By using loopy substructural local search the savings in function evaluations are much greater than those obtained by the previous local searcher. For the simpler SLS, when the degree of overlapping between different subfunctions increases, the efficiency of performing local search reduces drastically. These results are not surprising given the nature of the local searcher. When searching for the best substructure at a given subproblem, the decision-making does not take into account the corresponding context. Because different subproblems are solved in a particular sequence, the best subsolution for a subproblem considered in isolation might not be the best choice when considering other subproblems that overlap with the first. While this is not the case for the overlapping trap-5 problem, because all subproblems have the same global optimum at 11111, the local searcher can still be deceived.

Consider the following example, where two different trap-5 subproblems overlap in two variables (X_4 and X_5), being the total problem size $\ell = 8$. When performing local search, the initial solution 00000000 has fitness $f = 4 + 4 = 8$, but when considering the best substructure for the first partition 11111000 the corresponding total fitness decreases to $f = 5 + 2 = 7$. While locally the best substructure is identified, the decrease in the overall fitness will not accept the

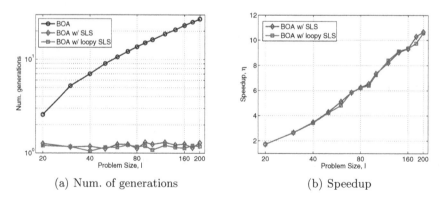

(a) Num. of generations   (b) Speedup

Fig. 4. Results for BOA with both simple SLS and loopy SLS when solving the non-overlapping trap-5 problem. The corresponding speedup scales approximately as $\Theta(\sqrt{\ell})$.

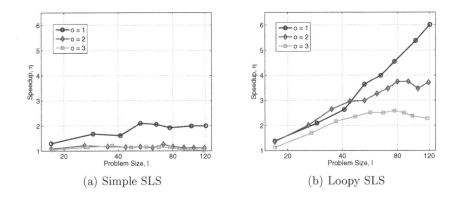

(a) Simple SLS   (b) Loopy SLS

Fig. 5. Speedup obtained for BOA with the simple SLS [8] and the loopy SLS when solving the trap-5 problem with overlap of $o = \{1, 2, 3\}$

move (see [8] for further details). Even if the order of visit for the neighborhoods is randomly shuffled each time local search is performed, there is no guarantee that all possibilities are covered for highly overlapping problems.

With loopy SLS the context for each variable is now taken into account. For 1-variable overlap ($o = 1$), the speedup grows up to 6, behaving very similarly to the non-overlapping case. For 2-variable overlap ($o = 2$), the speedup also increases with the problem size but with a more moderate slope. Finally, for 3-variable overlap, the speedup grows with even a more moderate slope, while for larger problem instances the speedup seems to stagnate. Notice that for a trap subfunction with $k = 5$ and $o = 3$, three out of five variables (60%) are shared with each of the two neighboring subfunctions, and each subfunction overlaps with another four on at least one variable. This translates into a considerable amount of noise at the decision-making for each subproblem, when looking for the best subsolution. Although the effect of overlapping variable interactions is similar to that of exogenous noise [25], which is known to be extremely hard for local search [7], the speedups obtained with loopy SLS for problems with overlap are still substantial for considerable proportions of overlap. Speedups of 6, 3.75, and 2.5 were obtained for proportions of overlap of 20%, 40%, and 60%, respectively.

7   Summary and Conclusions

This paper presents a substructural local searcher for the Bayesian optimization algorithm based on the principles of loopy belief propagation in graphical models. The concept of substructural neighborhoods is used to perform local search in BOA. The local search method proposed makes use of a message-passing algorithm to find the optimal assignment of variable values, adequate for solving problems with highly conflicting subsolutions. Experiments are performed for different instances of the trap problem.

For the non-overlapping trap problem, substructural local search is shown to substantially reduce the number of function evaluations, providing speedups superior to 10 for a problem size of $\ell = 200$. This translates into one order of magnitude less evaluations to solve the same problem. More importantly, the speedup consistently increases with problem size approximately as $\Theta(\sqrt{\ell})$.

For the overlapping trap problem, BOA with loopy SLS maintains the substantial speedups from the non-overlapping case, but as the dimension of overlapping increases (making the problem more noisy), its efficiency is reduced. Nevertheless, local search still succeeds in saving a significant number of function evaluations when compared to standard BOA. Speedups of 6, 3.75, and 2.5 were obtained for proportions of overlap of 20%, 40%, and 60%, respectively.

Acknowledgements. This work was sponsored by the Portuguese Foundation for Science and Technology under grants SFRH-BD-16980-2004 and PTDC-EIA-67776-2006, by the National Science Foundation under CAREER grant ECS-0547013, by the Air Force Office of Scientific Research, Air Force Materiel Command, USAF, under grant FA9550-06-1-0096, and by the University of Missouri in St. Louis through the High Performance Computing Collaboratory sponsored by Information Technology Services, and the Research Award and Research Board programs.

References

1. Pelikan, M., Goldberg, D.E., Cantú-Paz, E.: BOA: The Bayesian Optimization Algorithm. In: Banzhaf, W., et al. (eds.) Proceedings of the Genetic and Evolutionary Computation Conference GECCO 1999, pp. 525–532. Morgan Kaufmann, San Francisco (1999)
2. Pelikan, M.: Hierarchical Bayesian Optimization Algorithm: Toward a New Generation of Evolutionary Algorithms. Springer, Heidelberg (2005)
3. Larrañaga, P., Lozano, J.A. (eds.): Estimation of distribution algorithms: a new tool for Evolutionary Computation. Kluwer Academic Publishers, Boston (2002)
4. Pelikan, M., Goldberg, D.E., Lobo, F.: A survey of optimization by building and using probabilistic models. Computational Optimization and Applications 21(1), 5–20 (2002)
5. Moscato, P.: On evolution, search, optimization, genetic algorithms and martial arts: Towards memetic algorithms. Technical Report C3P 826, Caltech Concurrent Computation Program, California Institute of Technology, Pasadena, CA (1989)
6. Hart, W.E.: Adaptive global optimization with local search. PhD thesis, University of California, San Diego, CA (1994)
7. Sastry, K., Goldberg, D.E.: Let's get ready to rumble: Crossover versus mutation head to head. In: Deb, K., et al. (eds.) GECCO 2004. LNCS, vol. 3103, pp. 126–137. Springer, Heidelberg (2004)
8. Lima, C.F., Pelikan, M., Sastry, K., Butz, M., Goldberg, D.E., Lobo, F.G.: Substructural neighborhoods for local search in the bayesian optimization algorithm. In: Runarsson, T.P., Beyer, H.-G., Burke, E.K., Merelo-Guervós, J.J., Whitley, L.D., Yao, X. (eds.) PPSN 2006. LNCS, vol. 4193, pp. 232–241. Springer, Heidelberg (2006)

9. Pearl, J.: Probabilistic reasoning in intelligent systems: Networks of plausible inference. Morgan Kaufmann, San Mateo (1988)
10. Pelikan, M., Sastry, K.: Fitness inheritance in the bayesian optimization algorithm. In: Deb, K., et al. (eds.) GECCO 2004. LNCS, vol. 3103, pp. 48–59. Springer, Heidelberg (2004)
11. Lima, C.F.: Substructural Local Search in Discrete Estimation of Distribution Algorithms. PhD thesis, University of Algarve, Faro, Portugal (2009)
12. Kschischang, F., Frey, B., Loeliger, H.A.: Factor graphs and the sum-product algorithm. IEEE Transactions on Information Theory 47(2), 498–519 (2001)
13. Mooij, J.M.: Understanding and Improving Belief Propagation. PhD thesis, Radboud University Nijmegen, Nijmegen, Netherlands (2008)
14. Kindermann, R., Snell, J.L.: Markov Random Fields and Their Applications. American Mathematics Society, Providence (1980)
15. Mendiburu, A., Santana, R., Lozano, J.A., Bengoetxea, E.: A parallel framework for loopy belief propagation. In: GECCO 2007: Proceedings of the 2007 GECCO conference companion on Genetic and evolutionary computation, pp. 2843–2850. ACM, New York (2007)
16. Braunstein, A., Mezard, M., Zecchina, R.: Survey propagation: An algorithm for satisfiability. Random Structures and Algorithms 27(2), 201–226 (2005)
17. Feige, U., Mossel, E., Vilenchik, D.: Complete convergence of message passing algorithms for some satisfiability problems. In: Díaz, J., Jansen, K., Rolim, J.D.P., Zwick, U. (eds.) APPROX 2006 and RANDOM 2006. LNCS, vol. 4110, pp. 339–350. Springer, Heidelberg (2006)
18. Bayati, M., Shah, D., Sharma, M.: Max-product for maximum weight matching: Convergence, correctness, and LP duality. IEEE Transactions on Information Theory 54(3), 1241–1251 (2008)
19. Mendiburu, A., Santana, R., Lozano, J.A.: Introducing belief propagation in estimation of distribution algorithms: A parallel approach. Technical Report EHU-KAT-IK-11-07, Department of Computer Science and Artificial Intelligence, University of the Basque Country (2007)
20. Etxeberria, R., Larrañaga, P.: Global optimization using Bayesian networks. In: Rodriguez, A.A.O., et al. (eds.) Second Symposium on Artificial Intelligence (CIMAF 1999), Habana, Cuba, pp. 332–339 (1999)
21. Henrion, M.: Propagation of uncertainty in Bayesian networks by logic sampling. In: Lemmer, J.F., Kanal, L.N. (eds.) Uncertainty in Artificial Intelligence, pp. 149–163. Elsevier, Amsterdam (1988)
22. Elidan, G., Mcgraw, I., Koller, D.: Residual belief propagation: Informed scheduling for asynchronous message passing. In: Proceedings of the Twenty-second Conference on Uncertainty in AI, UAI (2006)
23. Yu, T.L., Sastry, K., Goldberg, D.E., Pelikan, M.: Population sizing for entropy-based model building in genetic algorithms. In: Thierens, D., et al. (eds.) Proceedings of the ACM SIGEVO Genetic and Evolutionary Computation Conference (GECCO 2007), pp. 601–608. ACM Press, New York (2007)
24. Deb, K., Goldberg, D.E.: Analyzing deception in trap functions. Foundations of Genetic Algorithms 2, 93–108 (1993)
25. Goldberg, D.E.: The Design of Innovation - Lessons from and for Competent Genetic Algorithms. Kluwer Academic Publishers, Norwell (2002)
26. Thierens, D., Goldberg, D.E.: Mixing in genetic algorithms. In: Forrest, S. (ed.) Proceedings of the Fifth International Conference on Genetic Algorithms, San Mateo, CA, pp. 38–45. Morgan Kaufmann, San Francisco (1993)

Running Time Analysis of ACO Systems
for Shortest Path Problems

Christian Horoba[1] and Dirk Sudholt[1,2,*]

[1] LS 2, Fakultät für Informatik, Technische Universität Dortmund,
Dortmund, Germany
[2] International Computer Science Institute, Berkeley, USA
{horoba,sudholt}@ls2.cs.tu-dortmund.de

Abstract. Ant Colony Optimization (ACO) is inspired by the ability of
ant colonies to find shortest paths between their nest and a food source.
We analyze the running time of different ACO systems for shortest path
problems. First, we improve running time bounds by Attiratanasunthron
and Fakcharoenphol [*Information Processing Letters*, 105(3):88–92, 2008]
for single-destination shortest paths and extend their results for acyclic
graphs to arbitrary graphs. Our upper bound is asymptotically tight
for large evaporation factors, holds with high probability, and transfers
to the all-pairs shortest paths problem. There, a simple mechanism for
exchanging information between ants with different destinations yields
a significant improvement. Our results indicate that ACO is the best
known metaheuristic for the all-pairs shortest paths problem.

1   Introduction

Ant Colony Optimization (ACO) is a rapidly growing field. It is inspired by the
foraging behavior of real ants, which enables an ant colony to find shortest paths
between its nest and a food source. Ants communicate by placing pheromone on
the ground while searching the environment for food. Other ants are attracted
by pheromone trails and therefore tend to follow previous ants. In case foraging
ants discover different paths between a nest and a food source, a short path
typically gets invested with pheromone more quickly than a longer path. The
more ants take the short path, the more pheromone is deposited, until almost
all ants follow the short path.

The communication mechanism of real ants has been transferred to many
optimization problems such as the TSP [1], routing problems [2,3], and many
other combinatorial problems, see the book by Dorigo and Stützle [4]. Despite a
plethora of applications, the theoretical knowledge on ACO is still very limited.
First theoretical investigations concerned convergence proofs [5] and simplified
models of ACO algorithms [6]. In 2006 the first rigorous investigations of the
running time of ACO algorithms were presented independently by Gutjahr [7]

* Dirk Sudholt acknowledges financial support by a postdoctoral fellowship from the
German Academic Exchange Service.

T. Stützle, M. Birattari, and H.H. Hoos (Eds.): SLS 2009, LNCS 5752, pp. 76–91, 2009.
© Springer-Verlag Berlin Heidelberg 2009

and Neumann and Witt [8] for the optimization of simple pseudo-Boolean functions. The latter authors presented an algorithm called 1-ANT. This algorithm memorizes the best solution found so far. In each iteration a new solution is constructed and the pheromones are updated in case another solution with at least the same quality is found. In other words, every new best-so-far solution is rewarded only once. Investigations of the 1-ANT [8,9] have shown that if the evaporation strength ρ is set too small the algorithm stagnates on even very simple problems and the expected time until an optimum is found is exponential. Other algorithms, variants of the MAX-MIN Ant System (MMAS) [10], reinforce the best-so-far solution in every iteration. This avoids the problem of stagnation and leads to efficient running times on various test problems [11,12].

Neumann, Sudholt, and Witt [13] investigated the effect of hybridizing ACO with local search. Regarding combinatorial problems, Neumann and Witt [14] presented an analysis for minimum spanning trees. Attiratanasunthron and Fakcharoenphol [15] presented a running time analysis of ACO algorithms on a shortest path problem, the single-destination shortest path problem (SDSP) on directed acyclic graphs (DAGs). Their algorithm n-ANT is inspired both by the 1-ANT [8] and the AntNet algorithm [3]. To our knowledge, this is the first and only rigorous running time analysis for ACO on a shortest path problem. This is surprising as shortest path problems crucially inspired the development of ACO.

The aim of this work is to bring forward the theory of ACO for shortest path problems. Shortest paths have already been investigated in the context of other metaheuristics. Scharnow, Tinnefeld, and Wegener [16] presented an analysis of a simple evolutionary algorithm, the (1+1) EA, for the single-source shortest path problem (SSSP). The problems SDSP and SSSP are in essence identical. Their results were later refined by Doerr, Happ, and Klein [17]. In [18] the latter authors investigated a genetic algorithm, simply called GA, for the all-pairs shortest path problem (APSP) and proved that the use of crossover leads to a speed-up compared to mutation-based evolutionary algorithms. Finally, Horoba [19] proved that an evolutionary multiobjective algorithm represents a fully polynomial-time approximation scheme for an NP-hard multiobjective shortest path problem. Table 1 gives an overview on the best known bounds in the single-objective case, including bounds that will be proven in this paper. We remark that problem-specific algorithms solve SDSP for graphs with n vertices and m edges in time $O(m + n \log n)$ and APSP in time $O(nm + n^2 \log n)$ [20].

In Section 2 we define an ACO algorithm $MMAS_{SDSP}$ for the SDSP that differs from the n-ANT [15] in two essential ways. Using our modified algorithm we are able to obtain significantly improved running time bounds (see Table 1 and Section 3) and to generalize previous results for DAGs to graphs with cycles. A corresponding lower bound shows that our upper bounds are asymptotically tight if the evaporation factor ρ is not too small. In Section 4 we transfer these results to a generalized ant system $MMAS_{APSP}$ for the APSP where ants with different destinations move independently. The main result concerns a modification of $MMAS_{APSP}$ where ants temporarily follow foreign pheromone traces. We prove that, surprisingly, this simple mechanism leads to a significant speed-up.

Table 1. Overview on the best known running time bounds on graphs with n vertices, m edges, maximum degree Δ, maximum number of edges ℓ on any shortest path, and $\ell^* := \max\{\ell, \ln n\}$. The rightmost column contains the number of path length evaluations in one iteration. The bound for MMAS$_{\mathrm{APSP}}$ with interaction holds for $\rho \leq 1/(23\Delta \log n)$; it simplifies to $O(n \log^3 n)$ for optimal ρ.

Algorithm	Problem	Iterations	Eval.
n-ANT [15]	SDSP on DAGs	$O\left(\frac{m\Delta\ell \log(\Delta\ell)}{\rho}\right)$	n
MMAS$_{\mathrm{SDSP}}$	SDSP	$O\left(\Delta\ell\ell^* + \frac{\ell \log(\Delta\ell)}{\rho}\right)$	n
MMAS$_{\mathrm{SDSP}}$	SDSP on G_{lb}	$\Omega\left(n^2 + \frac{n}{\rho \log(1/\rho)}\right)$	n
MMAS$_{\mathrm{SDSP}}$+adaptive $\tau_{\min}$	SDSP	$O\left(\ell m + \frac{n \log n}{\rho}\right)$	n
(1+1) EA [17]	SSSP	$\Theta\left(n^2 \ell^*\right)$	1
MMAS$_{\mathrm{APSP}}$	APSP	$O\left(\Delta\ell\ell^* + \frac{\ell \log(\Delta\ell)}{\rho}\right)$	n^2
MMAS$_{\mathrm{APSP}}$+interaction	APSP	$O\left(n \log n + \frac{\log(\ell) \log(\Delta\ell)}{\rho}\right)$	n^2
GA [18]	APSP	$O\left(n^{3.5}\sqrt{\log n}\right)$	1

2 Algorithms

We consider shortest path problems on weighted directed graphs $G = (V, E, w)$ where $w(e)$ denotes the weight of edge e. The number of vertices is always denoted by n. We define a *path* of length ℓ from u to v as a sequence of vertices $(v_0, \ldots, v_\ell)$ where $v_0 = u$, $v_\ell = v$, and $(v_{i-1}, v_i) \in E$ for all i with $1 \leq i \leq \ell$. For convenience, we also refer to the corresponding sequence of edges as path. Let $\deg(u)$ denote the out-degree of a vertex u and $\Delta(G)$ denote the maximum out-degree of any vertex $u \in V$. Let $\ell(G, v) := \max_u\{\text{\#edges on } p \mid p \text{ is a shortest path from } u \text{ to } v\}$ and $\ell(G) := \max_v \ell(G, v)$. For undirected non-weighted graphs $\ell(G, v)$ is called *eccentricity* of v and $\ell(G)$ *diameter* of G.

For the single-destination shortest path problem (SDSP) we are looking for shortest paths from every vertex to a specified destination vertex. The length $w(p)$ of a path p is defined as the sum of weights for all edges in p if the path ends with the destination vertex. If the path does not reach the destination, we define $w(p) := \infty$. In the following, we only consider positive weights as with negative-length cycles one can find arbitrarily short paths and the problem of computing a shortest *simple* path is NP-hard [15].

Attiratanasunthron and Fakcharoenphol [15] present the ACO algorithm n-ANT for the SDSP. Their algorithm is inspired by the 1-ANT [8] and the AntNet routing algorithm [3]. From every vertex $u \in V$ an ant a_u starts heading for the destination. The path is chosen by performing a random walk through the graph according to pheromones on the edges. Ant a_u memorizes the best path it has found from u to the destination so far. If it has found a path that

Algorithm 1. Path Construction from u to v for MMAS$_{\text{SDSP}}$

1: $i \leftarrow 0$
2: $p_i \leftarrow u$
3: $V_1 \leftarrow \{p \in V \setminus \{p_0\} \mid (p_0, p) \in E\}$
4: **while** $p_i \neq v$ and $V_{i+1} \neq \emptyset$ **do**
5:     $i \leftarrow i + 1$
6:     choose $p_i \in V_i$ with probability $\tau((p_{i-1}, p_i)) / \sum_{p \in V_i} \tau((p_{i-1}, p))$
7:     $V_{i+1} \leftarrow \{p \in V \setminus \{p_0, \ldots, p_i\} \mid (p_i, p) \in E\}$
8: **end while**
9: **return** $(p_0, \ldots, p_i)$

is at least as good as the previous best-so-far path, a pheromone update takes place and the new path is reinforced. The authors use a purely local update rule: each ant a_u is responsible for updating the edges leaving its start vertex u. If the new path is worse, the pheromones on the edges leaving u remain unchanged.

As the authors only consider acyclic graphs, the n-ANT is not supposed to deal with cycles. In particular, in [15] the authors state that in graphs with cycles their path construction procedure might take exponential time. Therefore, here we only allow ants to construct simple paths, i.e., an ant cannot visit a vertex more than once. The choice which edge to take next is made among all edges leading to unvisited vertices. This restriction bears the risk that the ant does not reach the destination. Recall that in this case the length of the path found is defined as $w(p) = \infty$. Due to the local pheromone update it is guaranteed that still one outgoing edge is rewarded for every vertex u with $\deg(u) \geq 1$ and $u \neq n$. The construction procedure is described in Algorithm 1.

We call our algorithm MMAS$_{\text{SDSP}}$ as we use the best-so-far update rule from the algorithm MMAS in [12] instead of the update rule used by the 1-ANT. The difference is that we always perform a pheromone update with the current best-so-far path, either with a new path or with the previous best-so-far path in case the new path is worse.

The update scheme is essentially taken over from [15]. We initialize the pheromones $\tau \colon E \to \mathbb{R}_0^+$ such that all edges leaving some vertex u receive the same amount of pheromone: if $e = (u, \cdot)$ then $\tau(e) = 1/\deg(u)$. If e is the only edge leaving u, we keep $\tau(e) = 1$ fixed. This means that vertices with a single outgoing edge are traversed in the only possible way; these vertices may therefore be disregarded when proving upper bounds on the running time. In case u has more than one outgoing edge, the pheromone for $e = (u, v)$ is computed as follows. Let p_u^* denote the best path from u found so far. Initially, we set p_u^* to an empty path, which has infinite length by definition of w. As in [10,15] we use pheromone borders to keep pheromones within an interval $[\tau_{\min}, \tau_{\max}]$. In a pheromone update then

$$\tau(e) \leftarrow \begin{cases} \min\left\{(1-\rho) \cdot \tau(e) + \rho, \ \tau_{\max}\right\} & \text{if } e = (u,v) \in p_u^*, \\ \max\left\{(1-\rho) \cdot \tau(e), \ \tau_{\min}\right\} & \text{if } e = (u,v) \notin p_u^*. \end{cases} \quad (1)$$

Algorithm 2. MMAS$_{\text{SDSP}}$

1: initialize pheromones τ and best-so-far paths $p_1^*, \ldots, p_n^*$
2: **loop**
3:     **for** $u = 1$ to n **do**
4:         construct a simple path $p_u = (p_{u,0}, \ldots, p_{u,\ell_u})$ from u to n w.r.t. τ
5:         **if** $w(p_u) \le w(p_u^*)$ **then** $p_u^* \leftarrow p_u$ **end if**
6:     **end for**
7:     update pheromones τ w.r.t. $p_1^*, \ldots, p_n^*$
8: **end loop**

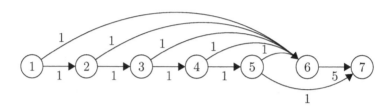

Fig. 1. Example graph for $n = 7$

The complete algorithm is shown in Algorithm 2. We are interested in the *optimization time* or *running time* of MMAS$_{\text{SDSP}}$, i.e., the number of iterations until shortest paths from $1, \ldots, n$ to n have been found. Another common performance measure for metaheuristics is the number of function evaluations. Note that in one iteration of MMAS$_{\text{SDSP}}$ we have n ants constructing n solutions and performing n function evaluations in parallel. Hence, the number of function evaluations is by a factor n larger than the number of iterations.

Before analyzing MMAS$_{\text{SDSP}}$ we motivate why it is essential to have ants starting from every vertex, even when we are only interested in the shortest path from a single source to a single destination and even when considering simple DAGs. Imagine a variant MMAS$_{\text{SPSP}}$ (SPSP for single-pair shortest paths) where one or multiple ants start from a single vertex, searching for the destination. Consider the following graph $G = (V, E, w)$ sketched in Figure 1. It contains a single heavy edge $(n - 1, n)$ with weight $n - 2$ and light edges $(u, n - 1)$ for $u \le n - 2$, $(u, u + 1)$ for $u \le n - 3$ and $(n - 2, n)$ of weight 1, each.

On each vertex $u \le n - 2$ an ant has to decide whether to move to $n - 1$ or to proceed on the shortest path. As all edges initially have equal pheromone, the probability that an ant follows the shortest path to vertex $n/2$ is $2^{-n/2+1}$. Assume the ant leaves the shortest path before reaching $n/2$. As the length of a path containing ℓ edges and traversing $n - 1$ is $\ell + n - 3$, no further path with a larger number of edges will be accepted in the following, except for the optimal path traversing $1, 2, \ldots, n - 2, n$. This implies that the pheromones for edges leaving the vertices $n/2, \ldots, n - 2$ will always remain equal, unless an ant finds the optimum. The probability of finding the optimum is $2^{-n/2+1}$, hence taking the union bound over 2^{cn} steps for some small constant $c > 0$, the optimization time is at least 2^{cn} with probability $1 - 2^{-\Omega(n)}$. Note that this also holds in case polynomially many ants search for the destination in parallel in one iteration.

Also using edge weights as heuristic information does not help. Many ACO algorithms use both pheromones and a heuristic function to guide the solution construction [4]. However, from a vertex $n/2 \leq u \leq n - 2$ both outgoing edges have the same weight and the same pheromone, with high probability, hence they look the same for every ant. This example also shows that heuristic information may be useless or even misleading for some problem instances.

3   Single-Destination Shortest Path Problem

When ants start from different vertices, ants starting close to the destination have a good chance of finding a shortest path. The pheromones deposited on the outgoing edges of a vertex v can then be used to guide different ants traversing v. This way, the shortest path for v can be extended towards a longer shortest path that contains v. This is the basic idea of the analysis by Attiratanasunthron and Fakcharoenphol [15], which is improved and generalized in this section. Their results are limited to directed acyclic graphs. We start with these graphs and extend the results to directed graphs with cycles.

Lemma 1. *If $\tau_{\min} + \tau_{\max} = 1$ then for every vertex u with $\deg(u) > 1$ always*

$$1 \leq \sum_{e=(u,\cdot)\in E} \tau(e) \leq 1 + \deg(u)\tau_{\min}.$$

Proof. The first inequality has already been proven in [15]. Initially the sum of pheromones equals 1. Assume for an induction that $\sum \tau(e) \geq 1$. If the phero- mones are not capped by pheromone borders, we have $(1 - \rho)\sum \tau(e) + \rho \geq 1$ as new sum. In case a pheromone drops below $\tau_{\min}$, setting the pheromone to $\tau_{\min}$ can only increase the sum. If at least one pheromone is capped at the upper bor- der $\tau_{\max}$ then the sum of pheromones is at least $\tau_{\min} + \tau_{\max} = 1$ as $\deg(u) > 1$.

For the second inequality observe that the sum of pheromones can only in- crease due to the lower pheromone border as $(1 - \rho)\sum \tau(e) + \rho \leq \sum \tau(e)$ follows from $\sum \tau(e) \geq 1$. Consider an edge e with $(1 - \rho)\tau(e) < \tau_{\min}$. Compared to this value, the pheromone increases by at most $\tau_{\min} \cdot \rho$ when setting the pheromone to $\tau_{\min}$. If currently $\sum \tau(e) \leq 1 + \deg(u)\tau_{\min}$ then the sum of the next pheromone values is at most $(1 - \rho)(1 + \deg(u)\tau_{\min}) + \rho + \deg(u)\tau_{\min} \cdot \rho = 1 + \deg(u)\tau_{\min}$. Hence, the second inequality follows by induction.   □

As an immediate consequence, we obtain the following direct relation between pheromones and probabilities for the ant a_u, i. e., the ant starting at u, of choos- ing an edge $(u, \cdot)$ in case $\tau_{\min} \leq 1/\deg(u)$. The last condition makes sense as $\tau_{\min}$ should be chosen below the initial pheromone value of $1/\deg(u)$.

Corollary 1. *If $\tau_{\min} \leq 1/\deg(u)$ and $\tau_{\min} + \tau_{\max} = 1$ for every edge $e = (u, \cdot)$*

$$\tau(e)/2 \leq \mathrm{Prob}(\text{ant } a_u \text{ chooses edge } e) \leq \tau(e).$$

The lower bound also holds for every other ant leaving vertex u and every edge
$e = (u, v)$ unless v has already been traversed by the ant. The upper bound also
holds for every other ant and every edge $e = (u, \cdot)$ if it has not traversed a
successor of u before arriving at u.

The penultimate statement holds as the probability of choosing an edge $e = (u, v)$
to an unvisited successor v increases if other successors of u have been visited
before. In particular, we always have $\tau_{\min}/2$ as lower bound on the probability of
choosing any specific outgoing edge. This is an improvement to Lemma 1 in [15].
We remark that using the improved lemma in [15], the running time bounds for
the algorithm n-ANT can be divided by m/n, where m is the number of edges.

    The following theorem gives upper bounds for $\text{MMAS}_{\text{SDSP}}$, each consisting
of two additive terms. Intuitively, the first terms cover waiting times until improvements of best-so-far paths are found. The second terms grow with $1/\rho$.
They reflect the time to adapt the pheromones after a change of the best-so-far
path. This time is called *freezing time* by Neumann, Sudholt, and Witt [12].

Theorem 1. *Consider a directed acyclic graph G with n vertices and positive*
weights. The expected optimization time of $MMAS_{SDSP}$ on G with $\tau_{\min} := 1/n^2$
and $\tau_{\max} = 1 - \tau_{\min}$ is $O(n^3 + (n \log n)/\rho)$. Let $\Delta := \Delta(G)$ and $\ell := \ell(G, n)$.
The expected optimization time of $MMAS_{SDSP}$ with $\tau_{\min} = 1/(\Delta\ell)$ and $\tau_{\max} =$
$1 - \tau_{\min}$ is $O(n\Delta\ell + n \log(\Delta\ell)/\rho)$.

Proof. We follow the analysis by Attiratanasunthron and Fakcharoenphol [15].
Call an edge (u, v) *incorrect* if it does not belong to any shortest path from u
to n. We say that a vertex u is *processed* if a shortest path from u to n has been
found and if all incorrect edges leaving u have pheromone $\tau_{\min}$.
    We estimate the expected time until a vertex u has been processed, given
that all vertices reachable from u on shortest paths from u to n have already
been processed. We first consider the expected time until a shortest path from u
to n has been found for the first time. We also say that then vertex u has been
optimized. By Corollary 1 the probability of choosing an edge that belongs to
a shortest path from u to n is at least $\tau_{\min}/2$. Such a shortest path is found
if the ant does not choose an incorrect edge until n is reached. As all vertices
on all shortest paths are processed, all incorrect edges at some vertex v have
pheromone $\tau_{\min}$ and the probability of choosing some incorrect edge is at most
$\deg(v)\tau_{\min}$. Hence, the probability of choosing an edge on a shortest path is
at least $1 - \deg(v)\tau_{\min} \geq 1 - 1/\ell$ if $\tau_{\min} \leq 1/(\deg(v)\ell)$. As all shortest paths
have at most ℓ edges, the probability that no incorrect edge is chosen is at
least $(1 - 1/\ell)^{\ell-1} \geq 1/e$ with $e = \exp(1)$. Together, the probability of finding a
shortest path from u to n is at least $\tau_{\min}/(2e)$.
    The expected time until u is optimized is thus at most $2e/\tau_{\min}$. Afterwards,
due to the best-so-far rule, a shortest path from u to n is reinforced automatically in each iteration. The precise path may change, but it is guaranteed that
only shortest paths are rewarded and hence the pheromone on incorrect edges
decreases in every step. Lemma 2 in [15] states that $\ln(\tau_{\max}/\tau_{\min})/\rho$ iterations

are enough for the vertex to become processed, hence the expected time until u is processed is bounded by $2e/\tau_{\min} + \ln(\tau_{\max}/\tau_{\min})/\rho$.

Let $v_1, \ldots, v_{n-1}$ be an enumeration of the vertices in $V \setminus \{n\}$ ordered with respect to increasing length of the shortest path to n. As all weights are positive, all shortest paths from v_{i+1} to n only use vertices from $\{n, v_1, \ldots, v_i\}$. If $v_1, \ldots, v_i$ have been processed then we can wait for v_{i+1} to become processed using the above argumentation. The expected time until all vertices $v_1, \ldots, v_{n-1}$ have been processed is bounded by $n2e/\tau_{\min} + n\ln(\tau_{\max}/\tau_{\min})/\rho$. Choosing $\tau_{\min} := 1/n^2$ and $\tau_{\max} = 1 - \tau_{\min}$, we obtain the bound $O(n^3 + (n \log n)/\rho)$. Choosing $\tau_{\min} := 1/(\Delta\ell)$ and $\tau_{\max} = 1 - \tau_{\min}$ yields the bound $O(n\Delta\ell + n\log(\Delta\ell)/\rho)$.   □

Observe that for $MMAS_{SDSP}$, once a shortest path from u has been found, the pheromones are continuously "frozen" towards shortest paths from u in the following $F = \ln(\tau_{\max}/\tau_{\min})/\rho$ iterations. The algorithm n-ANT from [15], however, only updates pheromones in case a new best-so-far path is found. This implies that a shortest path from u has to be found several times, in the worst case in F different iterations, in order to freeze the pheromones in the same way. Hence, using the best-so-far rule of MMAS algorithms leads to better performance results. This adds to the comparison of the 1-ANT and MMAS on pseudo-Boolean problems in [12].

We proceed by improving Theorem 1 in several respects. First, the bound on the expected optimization time is improved at least by a factor of ℓ^*/n. Second, the result not only holds for directed acyclic graphs but for all directed graphs with positive weights and unique shortest paths. Finally, we show that the running time bounds hold with high probability (i.e. with probability at least $1 - n^{-c}$ for some $c > 0$). In the proof we follow ideas from [17] showing that the random time until a short path of length $\ell = \Omega(\log n)$ is found is highly concentrated around the expectation[1].

Theorem 2. *Consider a directed graph G with n vertices and positive weights where all shortest paths are unique. Let $\Delta := \Delta(G)$, $\ell := \ell(G, n)$, and $\ell^* := \max\{\ell, \ln n\}$. The optimization time of $MMAS_{SDSP}$ on G with $\tau_{\min} = 1/(\Delta\ell)$ and $\tau_{\max} = 1 - \tau_{\min}$ is $O(\Delta\ell\ell^* + \ell\log(\Delta\ell)/\rho)$ with probability at least $1 - 1/n^2$. The optimization time bound also holds in expectation.*

Proof. When estimating the probability that an ant chooses an edge on a shortest path the lower bound from Corollary 1 always holds. In the proof of Theorem 1 we have shown that for ant a_u the probability of finding a shortest path from u to n, given that all successors of u on shortest paths have been processed, is bounded below by $\tau_{\min}/(2e)$ if $\tau_{\min} \leq 1/(\Delta\ell)$. This result also holds in the case of arbitrary directed graphs.

---

[1] There is a subtle difference to [17]: in their definition of ℓ the authors only consider shortest paths *with a minimum number of edges* (if there are several shortest paths between two vertices). Both definitions for ℓ are, however, equal if all shortest paths are unique or have the same number of edges.

Fix a vertex u and the unique shortest path $u = v_{\ell'}, v_{\ell'-1}, \ldots, v_0 = n$ with $\ell' \leq \ell$. We pessimistically estimate the expected time until u is processed. Let T_i be the random time until v_i is optimized. Consider random variables $X_1, \ldots, X_T$ that are independently set to 1 with probability $\tau_{\min}/(2e)$ and to 0 otherwise. The random first point of time T_1^* where $X_t = 1$ stochastically dominates the random time until v_1 is optimized. As v_1 becomes processed after an additional waiting time of $F := \ln(\tau_{\max}/\tau_{\min})/\rho$ steps, $T_1^* + F$ stochastically dominates T_1. Inductively, we have that $T_{\ell'}^* + \ell'F$ stochastically dominates $T_{\ell'}$ and hence the time until u is processed.

Let $T := 16e\ell^*/\tau_{\min}$ and $X := \sum_{i=1}^{T} X_i$. We have $\mathrm{E}(X) = T \cdot \tau_{\min}/(2e) = 8\ell^*$. By Chernoff bounds [21]

$$\mathrm{Prob}(X < \ell^*) \;\leq\; \mathrm{Prob}(X \leq (1 - 7/8) \cdot \mathrm{E}(X)) \;\leq\; e^{-8\ell^*(7/8)^2/2} < e^{-3\ell^*} \leq n^{-3}.$$

Hence, the probability that u is not processed after $T + \ell \ln(\tau_{\max}/\tau_{\min})/\rho$ steps is $1/n^3$. By the union bound, the probability that there is an unprocessed vertex remaining after this time is at most $1/n^2$. The result on the expectation follows from the first result, which holds for arbitrary initial pheromones. If the algorithm does not find all shortest paths within the first $T + \ell \ln(\tau_{\max}/\tau_{\min})/\rho$ steps, we repeat the argumentation with another phase of this length. The expected number of phases needed is clearly $O(1)$. $\qquad\square$

3.1   Lower Bounds for MMAS$_{\mathrm{SDSP}}$

We now turn to lower bounds on the expected optimization time of MMAS$_{\mathrm{SDSP}}$. We begin with a general lower bound, which holds for a wide range of graphs, including most acyclic graphs. The main idea is that the pheromones need some time to adapt, such that a shortest path with ℓ edges can be found with good probability. On the one hand, the bound grows with $1/\rho$ if ρ is not too small. On the other hand, it also applies to pure random search, i.e., $\rho = 0$.

Theorem 3. *Consider a directed acyclic graph G with n vertices and positive weights. Assume that G contains a unique shortest path $p_0, \ldots, p_\ell = n$ such that for $0 \leq i < \ell$ we have $\deg(p_i) \geq 2$ and no edges leading back from p_i to $\{p_0, \ldots, p_{i-1}\}$. Let $\Delta := \Delta(G)$ and $\ell := \ell(G, n)$. If $\rho \leq 1 - \Omega(1)$ then the expected optimization time of MMAS$_{\mathrm{SDSP}}$ on G with $\tau_{\min} \leq 1/(\Delta\ell)$ and $\tau_{\max} = 1 - \tau_{\min}$ is $\Omega(\min\{(\log \ell)/\rho, \; e^{\sqrt{\ell}/4}\})$.*

Proof. Initially all pheromones on edges $(u, \cdot)$ equal $1/\deg(u)$. During the first $t := \min\{(1/\rho - 1) \cdot \ln(\ell) \cdot 1/2, \; e^{\sqrt{\ell}/4}/2\} = \Omega(\min\{(\log \ell)/\rho, \; e^{\sqrt{\ell}/4}\})$ steps (using $1/\rho - 1 = \Omega(1)$ by assumption on ρ) the pheromone on every such edge is at least

$$\frac{1}{\deg(u)} \cdot (1 - \rho)^t \;\geq\; \frac{1}{\deg(u)} \cdot e^{-\ln(\ell) \cdot 1/2} = \frac{1}{\deg(u)} \cdot \frac{1}{\sqrt{\ell}}.$$

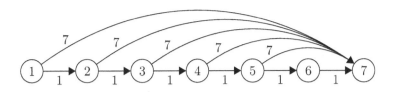

Fig. 2. Example graph G_{lb} from Definition 1 for $n = 7$

Note that this even holds in case the lower pheromone border is hit. Consider the ant starting at p_0 trying to create $p_0, \ldots, p_\ell$. As the probability of taking a specific incorrect edge is at least $p := 1/(2 \deg(u)\sqrt{\ell})$, the probability that the ant takes a correct edge on the path is at most $1 - (\deg(u) - 1) \cdot p = 1 - (\deg(u) - 1) \cdot 1/(2 \deg(u)\sqrt{\ell}) \leq 1 - 1/(4\sqrt{\ell})$. The probability that the path $p_0, \ldots, p_\ell$ is created in a specific iteration $t' \leq t$ is hence bounded by $(1 - 1/(4\sqrt{\ell}))^\ell \leq e^{-\sqrt{\ell}/4}$. The probability that this happens during the first t iterations is bounded by $t \cdot e^{-\sqrt{\ell}/4} \leq 1/2$ due to the definition of t. Hence with probability at least $1/2$ we have not found all shortest paths after t steps and the lower bound $t/2 = \Omega(\min\{(\log \ell)/\rho,\ e^{\sqrt{\ell}/4}\})$ follows. $\qquad\square$

In order to assess whether the upper bound from Theorem 2 is asymptotically tight, we consider the following input instance (see Figure 2). The basic idea is that the algorithm is forced to optimize the vertices one after another, from right to left.

Definition 1. Let $G_{\mathrm{lb}} = (V, E, w)$ with $V = \{1, \ldots, n\}$, $E = \{(i, i+1) \mid 1 \leq i \leq n-1\} \cup \{(i, n) \mid 1 \leq i \leq n-2\}$, and weights $w((u, v)) = 1$ if $v = u+1$ and $w((u, v)) = n$ if $v \neq u+1$.

Theorem 2 yields an upper bound $O(n^2 + (n \log n)/\rho)$ for G_{lb}. The following lower bound is tight with the upper bound if $\rho = \Omega((\log n)/n)$. For smaller ρ there is a gap of $O(\log^2 n)$.

Theorem 4. If $1/\mathrm{poly}(n) \leq \rho \leq 1/2$ then the expected optimization time of $MMAS_{\mathrm{SDSP}}$ on G_{lb} with $\tau_{\min} = 1/(2n)$ and $\tau_{\max} = 1 - \tau_{\min}$ is $\Omega\left(n^2 + \frac{n}{\rho \log(1/\rho)}\right)$.

Proof. Consider all paths from u to n with $u \leq n-2$. The path (u, n) has length n. All other paths start with the edge $(u, u+1)$. The length of the path only traversing edges with weight 1 is $n - u$. However, if the path ends with an edge (v, n) for $u < v \leq n-2$, the path has length $v - u + n > n$. Hence the path (u, n) is the unique second best path from u to n.

Call a vertex $u \leq n-2$ *wrong* if the best-so-far path found by ant a_u is (u, n). After initialization both edges have an equal probability of being chosen by the first ant. By Chernoff bounds at least $n/3$ ants a_u with $u \leq n-2$ choose incorrect edges with probability $1 - e^{-\Omega(n)}$ and then the edges remain incorrect until a shortest path has been found. We assume that we initially have $n/3$ wrong vertices. First, we show that with high probability after $F := \ln(\tau_{\max}/\tau_{\min})/\rho$ iterations we still have $n/3 - O(\log^2 n)$ wrong vertices. For these vertices u the pheromones then are frozen towards the incorrect edge.

As long as a vertex u remains wrong, the pheromone on its correct edge is at most $1/2$. (It even decreases continuously towards $\tau_{\min}$ unless a shortest path is found.) Fix the set of $r := 8\log(1/\rho)$ wrong vertices with largest index and let u be the vertex with the smallest index in this set. During a phase comprising the following $t := 1/\rho - 1$ steps the probability of choosing the correct outgoing edge is for each vertex bounded from above by $1 - \frac{1}{4}(1 - \rho)^t \leq 1 - \frac{1}{4e}$ using Corollary 1. The probability that a shortest path for u is found throughout the phase is at most $t(1 - \frac{1}{4e})^r \leq 2^{\log(1/\rho)}(1 - \frac{1}{4e})^{8\log(1/\rho)} \leq 1/2$.

We conclude that the time until all r vertices have found shortest paths is at least t with probability at least $1/2$ and the expectation is $\Omega(t)$. We may repeat these arguments with a new phase and another set of r vertices which are still wrong at that time and have maximal index. Consider $3F/t = \Theta(\log n)$ subsequent phases. Applying Chernoff bounds to random variables indicating whether a phase has found shortest paths for the considered r vertices within t iterations, with high probability F/t phases each need at least t iterations. Hence, with high probability after F steps at most $O(\log n) \cdot r = O(\log^2 n)$ wrong vertices have found shortest paths. It may happen that during a phase some vertices preceding the r considered vertices find shortest paths by chance. However, the probability that a vertex v finds a shortest path if the path still contains $3\log n + \log(1/\rho)$ wrong vertices is at most $2^{-3\log n - \log(1/\rho)} \leq \rho/n^3$. Taking the union bound for at most n vertices and F iterations, this does not happen within F iterations, with high probability. Hence, we correct at most $3\log n + \log(1/\rho) = O(\log n)$ wrong vertices per phase and $O(\log^2 n)$ wrong vertices in total this way.

With high probability we obtain a situation where for $n/3 - O(\log^2 n)$ wrong vertices pheromones are frozen towards the incorrect edge. We separately prove lower bounds $\Omega(n/(\rho\log(1/\rho)))$ and $\Omega(n^2)$ for the expected remaining optimization time.

The first bound follows from applying the above arguments on phases to the remaining $\Omega(n)$ wrong vertices, along with the fact that the probability of finding a shortest path containing i wrong vertices has decreased to $(\tau_{\min})^i \leq 1/n^i$. Hence, with high probability at most a constant number of wrong vertices is corrected unexpectedly per phase and the expected time to complete $\Omega(n/r) = \Omega(n/\log(1/\rho))$ phases yields the first bound.

For the second bound $\Omega(n^2)$ we observe that the expected time to find a shortest path for u if the path contains at least four wrong vertices is at most $(\tau_{\min})^4 \leq 1/n^4$. Hence, with high probability during $\Omega(n^2)$ iterations it does not happen that more than 4 wrong vertices are corrected in the same iteration. The expected time until the wrong vertex with largest index is corrected is $1/\tau_{\min} \geq n$. If the number of wrong vertices always decreases by at most 4, the expected time to correct $\Omega(n)$ wrong vertices is $\Omega(n^2)$. □

3.2   An Adaptive Choice of Pheromone Borders

The probability of constructing a shortest path from u, given that all successors of u on shortest paths have been processed, is bounded below by $\tau_{\min}/(2e)$ if $\tau_{\min} \leq 1/(\deg(u)\ell)$. This suggests to choose $\tau_{\min}$ as large as possible. However, if the same pheromone borders apply to all edges, the best feasible choice is $\tau_{\min} = 1/(\Delta\ell)$.

It thus makes sense to consider an ACO system where pheromone borders can be adapted to single vertices. The pheromone on an edge $e = (u, \cdot)$ is then bounded by the pheromone borders $\tau_{\min}(u)$ and $\tau_{\max}(u)$. If $\tau_{\min}(u) = 1/(\deg(u)\ell)$ and $\tau_{\max}(u) = 1 - \tau_{\min}(u)$ then the expected waiting time until u is optimized, given that all successors on shortest paths are processed, is bounded by $2e/\tau_{\min}(u) = 2e\deg(u)\ell$. The adaptation leads to the following bound.

Theorem 5. *Consider a directed graph G with n vertices, m edges, and positive weights. Let $\ell := \ell(G, n)$. The expected optimization time of $MMAS_{\mathrm{SDSP}}$ using adaptive pheromone borders with $\tau_{\min}(u) = 1/(\deg(u)\ell)$ and $\tau_{\max}(u) = 1 - \tau_{\min}(u)$ for all vertices u is $O(\ell m + (n \log n)/\rho)$.*

4   All-Pairs Shortest Path Problem

We now extend $MMAS_{\mathrm{SDSP}}$ towards an algorithm $MMAS_{\mathrm{APSP}}$ for the APSP. For each destination $v \in V$ we introduce a distinct pheromone function $\tau_v \colon E \to \mathbb{R}_0^+$. In each iteration, on each vertex u, and for each destination v we have an ant $a_{u,v}$ starting at u and heading for v. An ant heading for v uses the pheromone function τ_v for orientation and it updates τ_v as described in Section 2. $MMAS_{\mathrm{APSP}}$ remembers the best-so-far path $p^*_{u,v}$ from u to v for all $u, v \in V$.

The following result is an immediate implication from Theorem 2.

Theorem 6. *Consider a directed graph G with n vertices and positive weights where all shortest paths are unique. Let $\Delta := \Delta(G)$ and $\ell := \ell(G)$. The optimization time of $MMAS_{\mathrm{APSP}}$ on G with $\tau_{\min} = 1/(\Delta\ell)$ and $\tau_{\max} = 1 - \tau_{\min}$ is $O(\Delta\ell\ell^* + \ell\log(\Delta\ell)/\rho)$ with probability at least $1 - 1/n$. The optimization time bound also holds in expectation.*

We see that ants heading for different destinations do not collaborate in our ant system since ants heading for a destination v concern for the pheromone function τ_v exclusively. Therefore we could also run n instances of $MMAS_{\mathrm{SDSP}}$ in parallel to achieve the same result. An obvious question is whether the ants can interact in some clever way to achieve a better result.

Interestingly, the following very simple mechanism proves useful. Consider the ant $a_{u,v}$ heading for vertex v. Instead of always using the pheromone function τ_v to travel to v, with probability, say, $1/2$ the ant decides to follow foreign pheromones. It first chooses an intermediate destination w uniformly at random, then uses the pheromone function τ_w to travel to w, and afterwards uses the pheromone function τ_v to travel to the final destination v (see Algorithm 3). The pheromone update for ant $a_{u,v}$ always applies to the pheromones τ_v.

Algorithm 3. Path construction from u to v for MMAS$_{APSP}$ with interaction
1: **if** getRandomBit() = 0 **then**
2:    construct a simple path p from u to v w.r.t. τ_v
3: **else**
4:    choose $w \in V$ uniformly at random
5:    construct a simple path $p' = (p'_0, \ldots, p'_{\ell'})$ from u to w w.r.t. τ_w
6:    construct a simple path $p'' = (p''_0, \ldots, p''_{\ell''})$ from w to v w.r.t. τ_v
7:    **if** $p'_{\ell'} = w$ **then** $p \leftarrow (p'_0, \ldots, p'_{\ell'}, p''_1, \ldots, p''_{\ell''})$ **else** $p \leftarrow p'$ **end if**
8: **end if**
9: **return** p

With this mechanism the ant $a_{u,v}$ can profit from useful information laid down by other ants that headed towards w, in particular if w happens to be a vertex on a shortest path from u to v. The following theorem gives a significantly improved bound, without restriction to graphs with unique shortest paths.

Theorem 7. *Consider a directed graph G with n vertices and positive weights. Let $\Delta := \Delta(G)$, $\ell := \ell(G)$, and $\ell^* := \max\{\ell, \ln n\}$. If $\rho \le 1/(23\Delta \log n)$ then the optimization time of MMAS$_{APSP}$ using interaction on G with $\tau_{\min} = 1/(\Delta\ell)$ and $\tau_{\max} = 1 - \tau_{\min}$ is $O(n \log n + \log(\ell) \log(\Delta\ell)/\rho)$ with probability at least $1 - 1/n^2$. The optimization time bound also holds in expectation.*

Proof. We introduce similar notions as before. Consider a pair (u, v) of vertices. Let $\ell_{u,v}$ denote the maximum number of edges of a shortest path from u to v. We call an edge *incorrect* with respect to v if it does not belong to a shortest path to v. We call (u, v) *optimized* if a shortest path from u to v has been found. We call (u, v) *processed* if it has been optimized and if the pheromone $\tau_v(\cdot)$ on all incorrect edges $(u, \cdot)$ is $\tau_{\min}$.

Consider the first $t = (\ln 2)/\rho = O(1/\rho)$ iterations. Consider a pair (u, v) with $\ell_{u,v} = 1$. The probability of optimizing (u, v) in iteration i is at least $(1 - \rho)^{i-1}/(4\Delta)$ since the ant $a_{u,v}$ decides with probability $1/2$ to head for v and chooses (u, v) with probability at least $(1 - \rho)^{i-1}/(2\Delta)$ due to Corollary 1. Hence, the probability of *not* optimizing (u, v) within the considered phase is at most

$$\prod_{i=1}^{t}\left(1 - \frac{(1-\rho)^{i-1}}{4\Delta}\right) \le \exp\left(-\frac{1}{4\Delta}\sum_{i=0}^{t-1}(1-\rho)^i\right) = \exp\left(-\frac{1-(1-\rho)^t}{4\Delta\rho}\right).$$

Since $\rho \le 1/(23\Delta\log n) \le 1/(8\Delta\ln(2n^4))$, the above probability is at most $1/(2n^4)$. Because of the union bound, all pairs (u, v) with $\ell_{u,v} = 1$ are optimized within the considered phase with probability at least $1 - f_1$ where $f_1 := 1/(2n^2)$. We know that an optimized pair (u, v) is processed within $\ln(\tau_{\max}/\tau_{\min})/\rho$ iterations.

Consider a pair (u, v) and fix a shortest path $p_{u,v}$ from u to v with $\ell_{u,v}$ edges. Let i with $(3/2)^i < \ell_{u,v} \le (3/2)^{i+1}$. If all pairs (u', v') with $\ell_{u',v'} \le (3/2)^i$ are processed, the probability of optimizing (u,v) is at least $1/2 \cdot \ell_{u,v}/(3n) \cdot 1/e >$ $(3/2)^i/(6en)$ since the ant decides with probability $1/2 \cdot \ell_{u,v}/(3n)$ to choose an intermediate destination w on the middle third of p. Hence, the number of edges of all shortest paths $p_{u,w}$ $(p_{w,v})$ from u (w) to w (v) is at most $(3/2)^i$. Since (x,w) $((x,v))$ is processed for all vertices x on a shortest path from u (w) to w (v), the ant follows a shortest path from u to v with probability at least $(1-1/\ell)^{\ell-1} \geq 1/e$.

We divide a run of the ant system into phases. The ith phase finishes with all pairs (u,v) with $(3/2)^{i-1} < \ell_{u,v} \leq (3/2)^i$ being processed. Since $\ell_{u,v} \leq \ell$, we have to consider $\alpha := \lceil \log(\ell)/\log(3/2) \rceil$ phases.

Consider Phase i of length $t = 6en/(3/2)^i \ln(2\alpha n^4)$. The probability of not optimizing a pair (u,v) with $(3/2)^{i-1} < \ell_{u,v} \leq (3/2)^i$ within the phase is at most $(1-(3/2)^i/(6en))^t \leq 1/(2\alpha n^4)$. Due to the union bound, all such pairs (u,v) are optimized within t iterations with probability at least $1-1/(2\alpha n^2)$. We know that an optimized pair (u,v) is processed within $\ln(\tau_{\max}/\tau_{\min})/\rho$ iterations. Using the union bound, all phases are finished within

$$\sum_{i=1}^{\alpha} \left(\frac{6en\ln(2\alpha n^4)}{(3/2)^i} + \frac{\ln(\Delta\ell)}{\rho} \right) \leq 6en\ln(2\alpha n^4)\sum_{i=1}^{\alpha} \left(\frac{2}{3}\right)^i + \frac{\alpha\ln(\Delta\ell)}{\rho}$$

$$= O(n\log n + \log(\ell)\log(\Delta\ell)/\rho)$$

iterations with probability at least $1 - f_2$ where $f_2 := 1/(2n^2)$. The first part of the theorem follows since both failure probabilities f_1 and f_2 sum up to $1/n^2$. The second part can be derived using the bound $O(n^3 + (n\log n)/\rho)$ on the expected optimization time. This bound can be easily shown for all graphs (without restriction to unique shortest paths) using ideas from the proofs of Theorems 1 and 2. $\square$

We remark that the choice of the probability $1/2$ for choosing an intermediate vertex is not essential; using any other constant value $0 < p < 1$ would only affect the constants in Theorem 7. If $\Delta, \ell = \Omega(n)$ and $\rho = 1/(23\Delta\log n)$ the upper bounds given in Theorem 6 and Theorem 7 simplify to $O(n^3)$ and $O(n\log^3 n)$, respectively. Hence, the ant system clearly profits from our simple interaction mechanism and more collaboration between the ants.

5   Conclusions

ACO is motivated by the ability of real ant colonies to find shortest paths to a food source. Building on an initial study by Attiratanasunthron and Fakcharoenphol [15], we have conducted a rigorous analysis of the running time of ACO algorithms for shortest path problems. Our results (see Table 1) significantly improve and generalize the previous results for single-destination shortest paths. Taking the number of function evaluations as performance measure, the bound for MMAS$_{\text{SDSP}}$ is better than the bound for the (1+1) EA [17] if $\Delta\ell = o(n)$ and ρ is not too small.

For all-pairs shortest paths first results have been obtained using $\text{MMAS}_{\text{APSP}}$ as a direct generalization of $\text{MMAS}_{\text{SDSP}}$. We have proved that, surprisingly, letting ants temporarily follow foreign pheromone traces to random destinations yields drastically improved results. This is also the first result for combinatorial optimization where a slow adaptation for pheromones is crucial, i.e., low values for the evaporation factor ρ yield the best upper bounds. For an optimal choice of ρ the bound of $O(n^3 \log^3 n)$ function evaluations improves upon the best known bound $O(n^{3.5}\sqrt{\log n})$ for genetic algorithms [18]. This makes ACO the currently best known metaheuristic for the all-pairs shortest path problem from a theoretical perspective.

References

1. Dorigo, M., Gambardella, L.M.: Ant colony system: A cooperative learning approach to the traveling salesman problem. IEEE Transactions on Evolutionary Computation 1(1), 53–66 (1997)
2. Dorigo, M., Maniezzo, V., Colorni, A.: The ant system: An autocatalytic optimizing process. Technical Report 91-016 Revised, Politecnico di Milano (1991)
3. Di Caro, G., Dorigo, M.: AntNet: Distributed stigmergetic control for communications networks. Journal of Artificial Intelligence Research 9, 317–365 (1998)
4. Dorigo, M., Stützle, T.: Ant Colony Optimization. MIT Press, Cambridge (2004)
5. Gutjahr, W.J.: A generalized convergence result for the graph-based ant system metaheuristic. Probability in the Engineering and Informational Sciences 17, 545–569 (2003)
6. Merkle, D., Middendorf, M.: Modelling the dynamics of Ant Colony Optimization algorithms. Evolutionary Computation 10(3), 235–262 (2002)
7. Gutjahr, W.J.: First steps to the runtime complexity analysis of ant colony optimization. Computers and Operations Research 35(9), 2711–2727 (2008)
8. Neumann, F., Witt, C.: Runtime analysis of a simple ant colony optimization algorithm. In: Asano, T. (ed.) ISAAC 2006. LNCS, vol. 4288, pp. 618–627. Springer, Heidelberg (2006)
9. Doerr, B., Neumann, F., Sudholt, D., Witt, C.: On the runtime analysis of the 1-ANT ACO algorithm. In: Proc. of GECCO 2007, pp. 33–40. ACM Press, New York (2007)
10. Stützle, T., Hoos, H.H.: MAX-MIN ant system. Journal of Future Generation Computer Systems 16, 889–914 (2000)
11. Gutjahr, W.J., Sebastiani, G.: Runtime analysis of ant colony optimization with best-so-far reinforcement. Methodology and Computing in Applied Probability 10, 409–433 (2008)
12. Neumann, F., Sudholt, D., Witt, C.: Analysis of different MMAS ACO algorithms on unimodal functions and plateaus. Swarm Intelligence 3(1), 35–68 (2009)
13. Neumann, F., Sudholt, D., Witt, C.: Rigorous analyses for the combination of ant colony optimization and local search. In: Dorigo, M., Birattari, M., Blum, C., Clerc, M., Stützle, T., Winfield, A.F.T. (eds.) ANTS 2008. LNCS, vol. 5217, pp. 132–143. Springer, Heidelberg (2008)
14. Neumann, F., Witt, C.: Ant colony optimization and the minimum spanning tree problem. In: Maniezzo, V., Battiti, R., Watson, J.-P. (eds.) LION 2007 II. LNCS, vol. 5313, pp. 153–166. Springer, Heidelberg (2008)

15. Attiratanasunthron, N., Fakcharoenphol, J.: A running time analysis of an ant colony optimization algorithm for shortest paths in directed acyclic graphs. Information Processing Letters 105(3), 88–92 (2008)
16. Scharnow, J., Tinnefeld, K., Wegener, I.: The analysis of evolutionary algorithms on sorting and shortest paths problems. Journal of Mathematical Modelling and Algorithms 3(4), 349–366 (2004)
17. Doerr, B., Happ, E., Klein, C.: A tight analysis of the (1+1)-EA for the single source shortest path problem. In: Proc. of CEC 2007, pp. 1890–1895. IEEE Press, Los Alamitos (2007)
18. Doerr, B., Happ, E., Klein, C.: Crossover can provably be useful in evolutionary computation. In: Proc. of GECCO 2008, pp. 539–546. ACM Press, New York (2008)
19. Horoba, C.: Analysis of a simple evolutionary algorithm for the multiobjective shortest path problem. In: Proc. of FOGA 2009, pp. 113–120. ACM Press, New York (2009)
20. Cormen, T.H., Leiserson, C.E., Rivest, R.L., Stein, C.: Introduction to Algorithms, 2nd edn. The MIT Press, Cambridge (2001)
21. Mitzenmacher, M., Upfal, E.: Probability and Computing. Cambridge University Press, Cambridge (2005)

Techniques and Tools for Local Search Landscape Visualization and Analysis*

Franco Mascia and Mauro Brunato

DISI, Università di Trento, Trento, Italy
{mascia,brunato}@disi.unitn.it

Abstract. Because of their high dimensionality, combinatorial optimization problems are often difficult to analyze, and the researcher's intuition is insufficient to grasp the relevant features. In this paper we present and discuss a set of techniques for the visualization of search landscapes aimed at supporting the researcher's intuition on the behavior of a Stochastic Local Search algorithm applied to a combinatorial optimization problem.

We discuss scalability issues posed by the size of the problems and by the number of potential solutions, and propose approximate techniques to overcome them. Examples generated with an application (available for academic use) are presented to highlight the advantages of the proposed approach.

1 Introduction

Optimization problems arise from virtually all areas of science and engineering, and are often characterized by a large number of variables. The set of admissible values for such variables is called *search space*, and can usually be provided with a rich topological structure, which is determined both by the problem's intrinsic structure and by the solving algorithm's characteristics.

A search space complemented with the topological structure induced by the local search algorithm (evaluation function and neighborhood relation) is called a *search landscape*, and its structure determines, by definition, the behavior of the solving technique. *Search landscape analysis* is a research field aimed at providing tools for the prediction of the search algorithm's performance and its consequent improvement. Relevant features in this kind of analysis are, of course, the search space size and the number of degrees of freedom (i.e., the dimensionality).

In this work, we will focus on Stochastic Local Search (SLS) techniques [1], where a neighborhood operator is defined in order to map a configuration into a set of neighboring ones; the relevant topological structure is defined by the chosen neighborhood operator. An important feature influencing the behavior of SLS algorithms is the relative position and reachability of local optima with respect to the neighborhood topology, and some problem instances are known

---

* Work supported by project BIONETS (FP6-027748) funded by the FET program of the European Commission.

T. Stützle, M. Birattari, and H.H. Hoos (Eds.): SLS 2009, LNCS 5752, pp. 92–104, 2009.

to be hard with respect to SLS algorithms precisely because of "misleading" sets of good configurations. Researchers often resort to landscape metaphors such as peaks, valleys, plateaux and canyons to describe the possible pitfalls of the techniques, but the sheer dimensionality of the search space often defeats intuition.

We propose a tool for visual analysis of search landscapes for supporting the researcher's intuition via a careful selection of features to be maintained while the space dimensionality is reduced to a convenient size (2 or 3) for displaying. Visualization techniques for complex spaces usually suffer from a number of problems. In particular, the size of the search space requires the display technique to be highly scalable; moreover, the reduction method must be consistent in time, so that subsequent optimization steps correspond to small variations in the visualized landscape: such continuity is necessary to help the researcher consider the optimization process as a whole, rather than focus on single snapshots.

The Maximum Clique problem will be used as a paradigmatic example, together with two state of the art SLS algorithms for its optimization. By means of such examples, the scalability and continuity issues presented above will be discussed and tested, and the behavior of the solving techniques on hard instances will be analyzed.

The remainder of the paper is structured as follows. In Section 2 a brief overview of previous relevant work on visualization for optimization algorithms is presented. In Section 3 a representation of the search landscape in three dimension is proposed. In Section 4 an approximated representation is proposed, which scales better with the dimensions of the search landscapes, because it does not require the enumeration of the exponential number of sub-optimal solutions. In Section 5 a case study is presented, which shows how the behavior of a penalty based algorithm can be analyzed from the changes in the landscape after the penalization phases. Finally, in Section 6 conclusions are drawn and some ideas for further developing and leveraging this new type of analysis are presented.

2   Previous and Related Work

The area of stochastic local search algorithms has a long record of successes and improvements; applications are available on virtually all combinatorial problems. In this work, we will build upon two efficient techniques, namely Reactive Local Search (RLS) and Dynamic Local Search (DLS). The two techniques are paradigmatic examples of two approaches for ensuring diversification in combinatorial problem solving: RLS [2,3] is based on the temporary *prohibition* of selected moves in the neighborhood (and a history-dependent scheme is responsible of deciding the prohibition time), while DLS [4] is based on a diversification scheme that assigns *penalties* to solution components. Both algorithms have been applied to the *Maximum Clique* (MC) problem, the specialized version being known as RLS-MC and DLS-MC. The MC problem requires finding the largest *clique* (i.e., complete subgraph) in a given undirected graph, and is considered to be particularly hard among NP-complete problems due to classical non-approximability results.

The last years have witnessed a boost in the research on complex systems visualization, due to the general availability of inexpensive hardware for the fast computation of linear transformations involved in 3D polygon display. Graphics Processing Units (GPUs) are available in all display cards, and specialized expansions with hundreds to thousands of GPUs are available for common bus architectures for co-processing purposes. Therefore, the main scalability issues connected to large set visualization can be overcome by brute force. Work on dimensionality reduction via sampling with preservation of relevant graph properties has been presented in [5]. Online drawing of graphs is studied, for instance, in [6], where the effort is focused at preserving the presentation layout while the graph is changing.

Work that combines visualization and optimization dates back to [7], where multidimensional scaling and other techniques are applied to the visualization of evolutionary algorithms, while other contributions are aimed at human-guided search [8] where the computer finds local optima by hill-climbing while the user identifies promising regions of the search space. Visualization of Pareto-Sets in Evolutionary Multi-Objective Optimization is investigated in [9] by finding a mapping which maintains most of the dominance relationships. In [10] the authors propose a visualization suite for designing and tuning SLS algorithms. Starting from a selection of candidate solutions, the visualization tool uses a spring-based layout scheme to represent the solutions in two dimensions. The algorithm execution traces are then represented as trajectories around the laid out solutions, and the resulting analysis used by the researchers to tune the algorithm studied. While in [10] the authors focus on the behavior of the optimization algorithm and on the human interaction for the tuning of the algorithm parameters, we are interested in analyzing the intrinsic properties of the problem instance.

3   Complete Three-Dimensional Landscapes

The number of dimensions in the search space of a combinatorial optimization problem is equal to the number of variables in the instance. We propose a new way to represent it in a lower-dimensional space, describing the landscape as the variation of the solution quality (i.e., objective function) or the variation of a heuristic guidance function for the specific SLS algorithm (i.e., evaluation function).

For example, in order to reduce the problem landscape from the n dimensions to just 2, one could represent the feasible solutions as points plotted against their quality. In such two-dimensional plot, however, the ordering of the points representing the solutions is arbitrary, as it happens for example with plateau connection graphs and barrier-level basin graphs (see [1] for a thorough review of analysis methods).

A good layout for the solutions tries to preserve the distance (similarity) among the solutions in the original n-dimensional space. Our aim is to find a representation which can be easily visualized, therefore we will concentrate on reductions of the search space to a three-dimensional landscape, which also allows for some intuitive representation of the possible basic steps of a SLS algorithm.

In the following, we map the objective function value to the z axis, so that the z quota of a solution will always be fixed. The aim of the proposed techniques is to find convenient x and y coordinates of each solution. Since in our experience natural landscapes are in three dimensions, also the metaphor of *landscape* and of evaluation function can be easily represented and understood in three dimensions. It allows for a natural visualization of valleys, plateaus, and peaks, and fits perfectly with the basic operations of SLS algorithms.

3.1   The Technique

The first possible approach consists of computing a 3D layout of the search landscape of the problem instance. Figure 1 shows the landscape of an instance of the MC problem represented as a neighborhood graph in three dimensions, where nodes correspond to feasible solutions (cliques) and edges correspond to the neighborhood structure (i.e., cliques of Hamming distance 1 or 2). Node

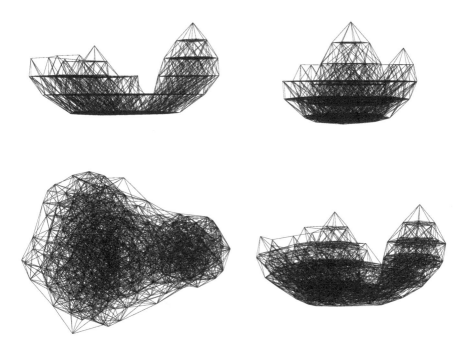

Fig. 1. Search Landscape corresponding to a Brockington-Culberson graph with 20 nodes, edge density 0.5, and maximum clique of size 7. The four subfigures are four different perspectives on the same 3D model. Brockington-Culberson graphs are designed with the aim of hiding the maximum clique [11].

heights represent the size of the corresponding clique, and the horizontal layout tries to retain the topology of the neighborhood graph.

The lowest vertices represent cliques with the smallest size (2). In all levels the number of vertices depends on the connectivity in the instance graph, and in the instance depicted in Figure 1 are bounded from above by $\binom{20}{k}$ where k is the size of the cliques in the level, and 20 the number of nodes in the specific instance.

The landscape depicted in Figure 1 is generated starting from 43 maximal cliques enumerated empirically with two state of the art heuristic algorithms for the MC problem: RLS-MC and DLS-MC. It has to be noted that a complete enumeration should always be used when possible, because using SLS algorithms for the empirical enumeration could lead to a bias in the representation. From every maximal clique, a tree containing all possible solutions within the maximal one is generated by means of a backtracking algorithm. Solution trees originated from different maximal cliques can overlap and share consistent parts of the search space. Therefore, during the enumeration all the solutions are added to a hash table, and when a solution is encountered twice the corresponding sub-tree is pruned. Once all the solution are enumerated, they are connected with arcs if a local search algorithm could move from one to the other by means of one of the neighborhood operations (*add*, *drop*, or *swap*). Once the graph is constructed a spring-based method is used to lay out the graph (with the further constraint that all vertices lay on the plane corresponding to their objective value). The nodes are treated as pointwise unit masses subject to pairwise forces of two types. The first is an attractive spring force based on a smoother version of Hooke's law [12]; it accounts for the node adjacency. The force acting on node a due to node b is

$$
F_{ab}^{H} = \begin{cases} k_{ab} \dfrac{b-a}{\|b-a\|_2} \log \dfrac{\|b-a\|_2}{r_{ab}} & \text{if } a \text{ and } b \text{ are adjacent} \\ 0 & \text{otherwise,} \end{cases} \tag{1}
$$

where a and b are the coordinate vectors of a and b in the low dimensional representation, r_{ab} is the ideal distance and k_{ab} is the spring stiffness, which depends on the desired layout. The second force is of Coulombian type and acts between every pair of nodes:

$$
F_{ab}^{C} = \frac{q_a q_b}{\|b-a\|_2^{D_{ab}}} \frac{a-b}{\|b-a\|_2}, \tag{2}
$$

where $q_a = q_b$ and the exponent D_{ab} depends on a threshold distance r_{th}:

$$
D_{ab} = \begin{cases} 2 & \text{if } \|b-a\|_2 \leq r_{th} \\ 4 & \text{otherwise.} \end{cases}
$$

The snapshots in Figure 1 show the landscape from the side, the front, the top, and in perspective. The almost flat area corresponding to a plateau bumped with several local optima is quite evident, as well as the clique of size 7 and the barrier between the points on the plateau and the maximum clique. This provides immediate information about the instance properties: because of the low number of nodes shared by the optimum and the flat area, algorithms with long plateau phases could be worse than algorithms with shorter plateau phases and more frequent restart policies. The layout can also embed extra information. For example, the vertices can be rendered with different colors depending on how frequently they are visited by the SLS algorithm, in order to analyze the attraction basins and how they are distributed with respect to the global optimum. Another example of information that could be easily embedded by means of a vertex coloring is the average degree distribution of the nodes in the solutions, which can give an immediate summary of the degree distribution and give some hints on the performance of greedy local search algorithms.

3.2   The Tool

The described technique works with all combinatorial optimization problems. Due to the way the application currently enumerates the possible solutions, the visualization is limited to the problems whose solutions can be encoded with binary strings and all sub-strings are also feasible solutions. Figure 1, as well as all the following figures are produced with *Graph Visualizer*, an application for Mac OS X that has been developed with the specific purpose of helping the researchers' intuition when studying the landscapes of combinatorial optimization problems[1]. Graph Visualizer is a general purpose tool for laying out graph structured data. Custom-designed tools for specific analysis purposes can be plugged into the main program; in particular, the Search Landscape Visualization (SLV) plugin produces three dimensional landscapes starting from a set of maximal solutions. The landscape generation is completely automated, the only input required is the list of local optima for the given instance, which we assume is automatically generated by the optimization program. Both the main multi-threaded application and the SLV plugin have been developed in Objective-C using the OpenGL libraries for the 3D visualization and Cocoa libraries for the native Mac OS X user interface. The whole application including the layout algorithm has been written from scratch by the authors.

3.3   NURBS Covers

For easier visualization, the search landscape can be covered with Non-uniform rational B-spline (NURBS) surfaces. These surfaces are superimposed over the three-dimensional landscapes by setting the height of the surface control points to the same heights of the corresponding vertices of the three dimensional neighborhood graph.

The NURBS surface has degree 3 and is controlled by a user-defined number of evenly spaced control points. The more the control points the more precise the

---

[1] The software is available for research purposes at http://graphvisualizer.org/

representation, but too many control points can lead to artificial local optima between the solutions where control point heights are not set by any solution.

The coloring of the NURBS surfaces as well as the clusters in the approximate landscapes varies from blue to red showing the quality of the solutions.[2]

4   Approximated Landscapes

While the search space analysis of small instances is interesting *per se*, every solution of size m contains $\binom{m}{k}$ solutions of size k, and the enumeration of all possible solutions at the lower levels (avoiding repetitions) does not scale with solution size. In order to handle larger instances, a number of approximated layouts can be introduced. The first solution considers clusters of subcliques as a unique object, the second operates by subsampling the solutions obtained by the SLS algorithm.

4.1   Clusters of Solutions

The following technique for generating an approximate landscape does not require the enumeration of all sub-optimal solutions, but just clusters of solutions having mutual Hamming distance 2.

Starting from local optimum solutions of size m, the cluster of solutions of size $m - k$ will contain $\binom{m}{m-k}$ solutions having mutual Hamming distance 2. The clusters can be scaled properly depending on the number of solutions they contain and the whole tree structure rooted in the local optimum is reduced to a stack of clusters with different sizes. Of course clusters belonging to stacks below different optimal solutions overlap for a volume which is proportional with the number of common solutions.

Let C_1 and C_2 be two maximal solutions; let $m = |C_1|$ be the size of the first, and $s = |C_1 \cap C_2|$ be the number of common components. The fraction of the cluster of solutions of size k below C_1 overlapping with the corresponding cluster of solutions of the same quality below C_2 is the following:

$$\binom{m}{k}\binom{s}{k}^{-1} = \frac{m!(s-k)!}{s!(m-k)!}. \tag{3}$$

With this technique, there is no need to enumerate the exponentially large number of sub-optimal solutions: knowing the size of the clusters and the fraction of their volume that overlaps is enough to render an approximated landscape like the one shown in Figure 2.

The multidimensional scaling is done with the spring based layout technique used in Section 3, but this time the vertices to be laid out are the clusters, their size is reflected in the charges q_a and q_b that determine their repulsive force in (2), and their overlapping volumes are encoded in the spring elastic constants K_{ab} and their zero-energy spring lengths r_{ab} of (1).

---

[2] Examples of colored surfaces are available at http://graphvisualizer.org/slv

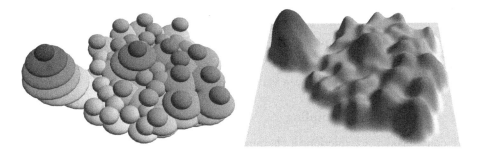

Fig. 2. On the left an approximated Search Landscape corresponding to a Brockington-Culberson graph with 20 nodes, edge density 0.5, and maximum clique of size 7. The approximated landscape retains the same shape as the complete landscape in Figure 1. On the right the approximated landscape is covered with a NURBS surface with 30×30 evenly spaced control points.

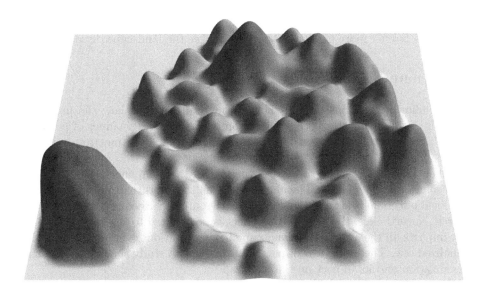

Fig. 3. Same Landscape of Figure 2 but subsampling the search space removing solutions with quality less than 3. This highlights the barrier between the plateau and the optimum.

The computation of large binomial coefficients is performed by the Stirling approximation of the factorials:

$$\ln n! \approx (n + 0.5)\ln n - n + \frac{\ln(2\pi)}{2}$$

therefore (3) can be approximated by

$$\binom{m}{k}\binom{s}{k}^{-1} \approx e^{(m+0.5)\ln m + (s-k+0.5)\ln(s-k) - (s+0.5)\ln s - (m-k+0.5)\ln(m-k)} \quad (4)$$

and it can be computed for large values of m and s.

4.2   Search Space Sampling

We can consider a reduction in the number of solutions around the global optimum, by filtering out the solutions which share fewer components with the global optimum. Another possible sampling strategy is to reduce the depth of the trees rooted in the local optima. The SLV plugin supports the combination of the two strategies. The sampled portion of the search landscape can improve the visualization by enhancing some of its features, but it can also drastically change the properties of the landscape. For example, Figure 3 shows the same landscape of Figure 2, obtained by applying the approximation technique in Section 4.1 and restricting the solutions to be considered to the ones having a quality (size) of at least 3. The restriction on the quality of the solutions to be considered makes the barrier more evident, but it also makes the landscape disconnected.

5   Dynamic Landscapes

In the following section, we will show through an example how the proposed analysis of the Search Landscape sheds some light on the dynamics of penalty-based SLS algorithms, and on the changes of the evaluation function g during the search.

When DLS-MC reaches a local optimum, all the components belonging to such solution are penalized. The aim of the penalization is to drop the quality of the local optimum and render it less attractive in the subsequent steps of local search. Nevertheless, the penalization effect is not limited to the local optimum, but impacts all the areas of the landscape having solutions overlapping with the penalized one. Therefore, it is of particular interest to study the behavior of the penalization and its impact on the landscape.

The adopted technique is composed of two steps. First, the three dimensional landscape corresponding to the objective function f is laid out by means of the force based multidimensional scaling technique described in Section 3. Then a landscape corresponding to the evaluation function g for each penalization step is produced. For the continuity reasons stated in Section 1, the horizontal layout of the objective function search landscape is retained throughout all penalization steps, the only thing that varies is the quality of the solutions whose components are penalized.

Figure 4 shows the penalization effect which transforms the landscape of the Brockington-Culberson instance of Figure 1. In Figure 4 the first NURBS surface is produced from the complete representation of the objective function. The second landscape in figure retains the same horizontal layout, and the plateau is

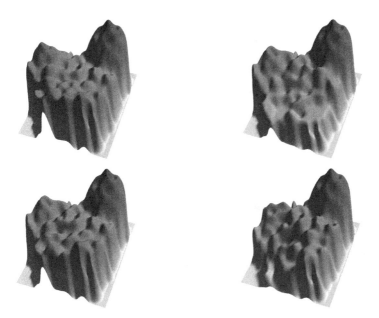

Fig. 4. Four penalization steps of DLS-MC on the Brockington-Culberson instance of Figure 1. The steps are shown chronologically from left to right and from top to bottom.

partly flattened by the penalization effect, which is then partially reverted after the penalties expiration in the third landscape. The fourth landscape shows the last penalization before DLS-MC is able to find the optimum solution. The effect is more clear in Figure 5, in which the plateau size reduction is quite evident. The increased number of levels in the graph after the penalization is due to the fact that the landscape corresponds to an evaluation function g and not an objective function. The algorithm whose steps are shown in figure associates integer penalties to the solution components belonging to local optima. The evaluation function g is computed as the cardinality of the solution minus the penalties associated to its components, therefore the landscape is on discrete levels, some of which have a negative quality.

The penalization strategy was effective in finding the well hidden global optimum, which does not share solution components with the penalized local optima.

On the contrary, in the instance of the MC problem depicted in Figure 6 the maximum clique has size 5, and the 30 smaller cliques of size 4 share a node with the maximum one. Therefore a penalization of a local maximum always impacts the global one.

Figure 7 represents the results of a DLS-MC run on the instance described above. The NURBS landscape on the top-left represents the unmodified objective function, and it shows in the middle the global optimum slightly above the other optima. The other three landscapes in figure show the evaluation function after

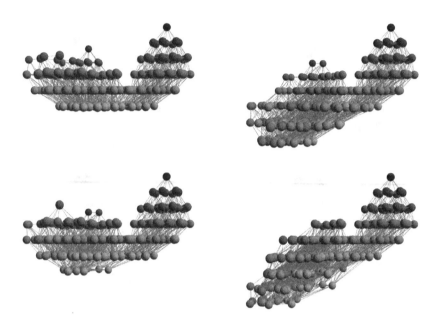

Fig. 5. Four penalization steps of DLS-MC on the Brockington-Culberson instance of Figure 1. The steps are shown chronologically from left to right and from top to bottom.

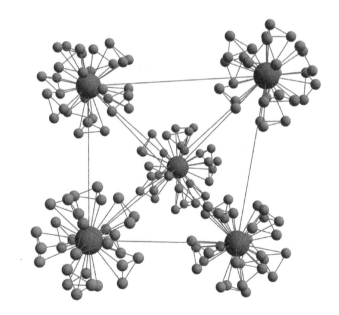

Fig. 6. A MC instance with 155 nodes. The maximum clique has size 5, and the 30 smaller cliques of size 4 share a node with the maximum one.

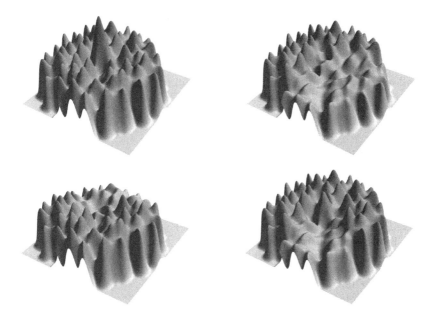

Fig. 7. Four penalization steps of DLS-MC on the instance depicted in Figure 6. The first landscape on the top-left shows the objective function with the global optimum in the middle.

subsequent penalization steps. The penalization always impacts on the global optimum.

In order to highlight the effect without using colors, the quality of the solutions in Figure 7 has been emphasized.

6   Conclusions and Future Work

We have presented a set of techniques for the visualization of search landscapes which can support the researcher's intuition on the behavior of a SLS algorithm applied to combinatorial optimization problems. The visualization also renders explicitly the geographic metaphors used by researchers to describe areas of interest of the landscape.

The examples presented in this paper are small instances useful to show how some features of the landscapes are rendered with the proposed techniques. The approximation techniques presented in Section 4 allow for the representation of instances otherwise intractable for the complete representation, while maintaining the features of the complete enumeration.

Current research is aimed towards more scalable layout algorithms with no exogenous parameters that can lay out landscapes with more than few thousand solutions and tens of thousands of relations among them. The convergence of a non-hierarchical spring-based layout algorithm depends strongly on the user provided parameters like the repulsion force, damping factor, zero energy spring lengths, spring elastic constants, which have to be appropriate for the graph structure.

The proposed techniques have been implemented in a Mac OS X application that allows for real-time manipulation and animation. The program is free for academic use and can be downloaded from

http://graphvisualizer.org/

Acknowledgments. We would like to thank the reviewers for their detailed feedback.

References

1. Hoos, H., Stützle, T.: Stochastic Local Search: Foundations and Applications. Morgan Kaufmann, San Francisco (2005)
2. Battiti, R., Protasi, M.: Reactive local search for the maximum clique problem. Technical Report TR-95-052, ICSI, 1947 Center St.- Suite 600 - Berkeley, California (September 1995)
3. Battiti, R., Mascia, F.: Reactive and Dynamic Local Search for the Max-Clique Problem: Engineering effective building blocks. Computers and Operations Research (2009) (in press)
4. Pullan, W., Hoos, H.H.: Dynamic Local Search for the Maximum Clique Problem. Journal of Artificial Intelligence Research 25, 159–185 (2006)
5. Rafiei, D., Curial, S.: Effectively visualizing large networks through sampling. In: WWW 2005 Proceedings (2005)
6. Frishman, Y., Tal, A.: Online dynamic graph drawing. IEEE Transactions on Visualization and Computer Graphics 14(4), 727–740 (2008)
7. Pohlheim, H.: Visualization of evolutionary algorithms-set of standard techniques and multidimensional visualization. In: Proceedings of the Genetic and Evolutionary Computation Conference, vol. 1, pp. 533–540. Morgan Kaufmann, San Francisco (1999)
8. Anderson, D., Anderson, E., Lesh, N., Marks, J., Perlin, K., Ratajczak, D., Ryall, K.: Human-guided simple search: combining information visualization and heuristic search. In: Proceedings of the 1999 workshop on new paradigms in information visualization and manipulation in conjunction with the eighth ACM international conference on information and knowledge management, pp. 21–25. ACM, New York (1999)
9. Koppen, M., Yoshida, K.: Visualization of Pareto-sets in evolutionary multi-objective optimization. In: 7th International Conference on Hybrid Intelligent Systems. HIS 2007, pp. 156–161 (September 2007)
10. Halim, S., Yap, R.: Designing and Tuning SLS Through Animation and Graphics: An Extended Walk-Through. In: Stützle, T., Birattari, M., Hoos, H.H. (eds.) SLS 2007. LNCS, vol. 4638, pp. 16–30. Springer, Heidelberg (2007)
11. Brockington, M., Culberson, J.C.: Camouflaging independent sets in quasi-random graphs. In: Johnson, D.S., Trick, M.A. (eds.) Cliques, Coloring, and Satisfiability: Second DIMACS Implementation Challenge, vol. 26, pp. 75–88. American Mathematical Society, Providence (1996)
12. Eades, P.: A heuristic for graph drawing. Congressus Numerantium 42, 149–160 (1984)

High-Performance Local Search for Solving Real-Life Inventory Routing Problems

Thierry Benoist[1], Bertrand Estellon[2], Frédéric Gardi[1], and Antoine Jeanjean[1]

[1] Bouygues e-lab, Paris, France
[2] Laboratoire d'Informatique Fondamentale–CNRS UMR 6166, Faculté des Sciences de Luminy, Université Aix-Marseille II, Marseille, France
{tbenoist,fgardi,ajeanjean}@bouygues.com,
bertrand.estellon@lif.univ-mrs.fr

Abstract. In this paper, a real-life routing and scheduling problem encountered is addressed. The problem, which consists in optimizing the delivery of fluids by tank trucks on a long-term horizon, is a generalization of the vehicle routing problem with vendor managed inventory replenishment. The particularity of this problem is that the vendor monitors the customers' inventories, deciding when and how much each inventory should be replenished by routing tank trucks. Thus, the objective of the vendor is to minimize the logistic cost of the inventory replenishment for all customers over the long run. Then, an original local-search heuristic is presented for solving the short-term planning problem. The engineering of this algorithm follows the three-layers methodology for "high-performance local search" recently introduced by some of the authors. A computational study demonstrates that our solution is both effective, efficient and robust, providing long-term savings exceeding 20 % on average, compared to solutions computed by expert planners or even a classical greedy algorithm. The resulting software is now exploited in North America by one of the French industry leaders.

1 Presentation of the Problem

The problem addressed in this paper is a real-life inventory routing problem (IRP) occurring in one of the world's leading companies in its field. For the sake of concision, the problem is not completely and formally described here, but its main characteristics are outlined.

Spread over a geographical area, some customers consume fluid products and plants produce it. Each customer is equipped with a storage; similarly, each plant has a storage from which product can be pumped. Reliable forecasts of production at plants are known over a short-term horizon. On the customer side, two kinds of resupply are managed by the vendor. The first one, called "forecasting-based resupply", corresponds to clients for which reliable forecasts of consumption are available over a short-term horizon. The inventory of each customer must be replenished by tank trucks so as to never fall under its safety level. The second one, called "order-based resupply", corresponds to customers

T. Stützle, M. Birattari, and H.H. Hoos (Eds.): SLS 2009, LNCS 5752, pp. 105–109, 2009.

which send orders to the vendor, specifying the desired quantity and the time window in which the delivery must be done. Some customers can ask for the both types of resupply management: their inventory is replenished by the vendor using monitoring and forecasting, but they keep the possibility of ordering (to deal with an unexpected increase of their consumption, for example). Constraints consisting in maintaining inventory levels above safety levels (no stock out) and in satisfying orders (no missed orders) are defined as soft, since the existence of an admissible solution is not ensured in real-life conditions.

The transportation is performed by vehicles composed of three kinds of heterogenous resources: drivers, tractors, trailers. Each resource is assigned to a base. A vehicle corresponds to the association of one driver, one tractor and one trailer. Some triplets of resources are not admissible (due to driving licences, for example). The availability of each resource is defined through a set of time windows. Each site (plant or customer) is accessible to a subset of resources (special skills or certifications are required to work on certain sites). Thus, scheduling a shift consists in defining: a base, a triplet of resources (driver, tractor, trailer), and a set of operations each one defined by a triplet (site, date, quantity) corresponding to the pickups or deliveries performed along the tour. A shift must start from the base to which are assigned the resources composing the vehicle and must end by returning to this base. The working and driving times of drivers are limited; as soon as a maximum duration is reached, the driver must take a rest with a minimum duration (Department of Transportation rules). In addition, the duration of a shift cannot exceed a maximal value depending on the driver. The sites visited along the tour must be accessible to the resources composing the vehicle. A resource can be used only during one of its availability time windows. The date of pickup/delivery must be contained in one of the opening time windows of the visited site. Finally, the inventory dynamics, which can be modeled by flow equations, must be respected at each time step, for each site inventory and each trailer. In particular, the sum of quantities delivered to a customer (resp. loaded at a plant) minus (resp. plus) the sum of quantities consumed by this customer (resp. produced by this plant) over a time step must be lower (resp. greater) than the capacity of its storage (resp. zero). Note that here the duration of an operation does not depend on the delivered or loaded quantity; this duration is fixed in function of the site where the operation is performed, the resulting approximation being covered by the uncertainties lying on the traveled times.

In our case, reliable forecasts (for both plants and customers) are known over a 15-days horizon. Thus, shifts are planned deterministically day after day with a rolling horizon of 15 days. It means that each day, a distribution plan is built for the next 15 days, but only shifts starting at the current day are fixed. The objective of the planning is to respect the soft constraints described above over the long run (satisfying orders, maintaining safety levels). In practice, the situations where these constraints cannot be met are extremely rare, because missed orders and stockouts are unacceptable for customers (on the other hand, safety levels must be finely tuned according to customer consumptions). Then, the second objective is to minimize over the long term a logistic ratio defined as the sum of the costs of shifts (which is composed of different terms related to the usage of resources) divided by the sum of the quantities delivered to customers. In other words, this logistic ratio corresponds to the cost per unit of delivered quantity.

Large-scale instances have to be tackled. A geographic area can contain up to 1500 customers, 50 sources, 50 bases, 100 drivers, 100 tractors, 100 trailers. All dates and durations are expressed in minutes (on the whole, the short-term planning horizon counts 21600 minutes); the inventory dynamics for plants and customers are computed with time steps of one hour (because forecasts are computed with this accuracy). The execution time for computing a short-term planning is limited to 5 minutes on standard computers.

2   Related Works

Since the seminal work of Bell et al. [1] on a real-life inventory routing problem encountered at AIR PRODUCTS (a producer and distributor of industrial gases), a vast literature has emerged on the subject. In particular, a long series of papers was published by Savelsbergh et al. [2,3,4,5,6], motivated by a real-life problematic encountered at PRAXAIR (another supplier of industrial gases). However, in many companies, inventory routing is still done by hand or supported by basic softwares, with rules like: serve "emergency" customers (that is, customers whose inventory is near to run out) using as many "full deliveries" as possible (that is, deliveries with quantity equal to the trailer capacity or, if not possible, to the customer tank capacity). For more references, the interested reader is referred to the recent papers by Savelsbergh and Song [5,6], which give a good survey of the research done on the IRP over the past 25 years.

To our knowledge, the sole papers describing practical solutions for problems similar to the one addressed here are the ones by Savelsbergh et al. [3,4,5,6]. The solution approaches described in these papers are the same in essence: the short-term planning problem is decomposed to be solved in two phases. In the first phase, it is decided which customers are visited in the next few days, and a target amount of product to be delivered to these customers is set. In the second phase, vehicle routes are determined taking into account vehicle capacities, customer delivery windows, drivers restrictions, etc. The first phase is solved heuristically by integer programming techniques, whereas the second phase is solved with specific insertion heuristics [7]. The experiments reported in the different works on the subject [1,3,4,5,6] show savings up to 10 % over the long run (with computation times of several minutes), compared to solutions obtained by a greedy algorithm based on the rules of thumb commonly used in practice (like the one cited above).

3   Contribution

To our acquaintance, no pure and direct local-search algorithm has been proposed for solving the IRP. A local-search approach is described by Lau et al. [8]

for solving an inventory routing problem with time windows, but their approach is based on a decomposition scheme (distribution and then routing). In this paper, an original local-search heuristic is described for solving the short-term planning problem. We insist on the fact that no decomposition is done in our approach: the short-term planning is optimized directly over the 15-days horizon. This algorithm has been designed and engineered following the methodology described by Estellon et al. [9] in a companion paper. A computational study demonstrates that our solution is both effective, efficient and robust, providing long-term savings exceeding 20 % on average, compared to solutions computed by expert planners or even a classical greedy algorithm.

Following the methodology exposed in [9], our local-search heuristic is designed according to three layers. The first layer corresponds to the search strategy; here a first-improvement descent heuristic with stochastic selection of transformations is employed (an initial solution is computed using an urgency-based insertion heuristic). The second layer corresponds to the pool of transformations which defines the neighborhood; here more than one hundred transformations are defined on the whole, which can be grouped into a dozen of types (for operations: insertion, deletion, ejection, move, swap; for shifts: insertion, deletion, rolling, move, swap). Finally, the third layer, corresponding to the "engine" of the local search, consists of three main procedures common to all transformations: evaluate (which evaluates the gain provided by the transformation applied to the current solution), commit (which validates the transformation by updating the current solution and the associated data structures), rollback (which clears all the data structures used to evaluate the transformation). Since the duration of an operation does not depend on the quantity loaded or delivered, the evaluation procedure is separated into two routines: first the scheduling of shifts and then the assignment of volumes. These routines, whose running time is critical for performance, relies on incremental algorithms supported by special data structures for exploiting invariants of transformations.

The whole algorithm was implemented in C# 2.0 programming language (for running on Microsoft .NET 2.0 framework). The resulting program includes nearly 30000 lines of code, whose 6000 lines (20 %) are dedicated to check the validity of all incremental data structures at each iteration (only active in debug mode). The whole project (specifications, research, implementation, tests), realized during the year 2008, required nearly 300 man-days. All statistics and results presented here have been obtained on a computer equipped with a Windows Vista operating system and a chipset Intel Xeon X5365 64 bits (CPU 3 GHz, L1 cache 64 Kio, L2 cache 4 Mio, RAM 8 Go). The local-search algorithm attempts more than 10000 transformations per second, even for large-scale instances (thousand sites and hundred resources). Then, our algorithm visits *nearly 10 million solutions in the search space during 5 minutes of running time* (which is the desired time limit in operational conditions). When planning over a 15-days horizon, the memory allocated by the program does not exceed 30 Mo for medium-size instances (hundred sites, ten resources), and 300 Mo for large-scale instances (thousand sites, hundred resources). Note that the running time of the urgency-based insertion heuristic is of few seconds for large-scale instances. The acceptance rate, which corresponds to the number of accepted transformations (that is, not strictly improving current solution) over the number of attempted ones, varies essentially between 1 and 10 % according to instances and optimization phases. Note that this rate is quasi constant all along the search (that is, during the 5 minutes of running time), allowing a large diversification of the search without the use of metaheuristics. On the other hand, the number of (strictly) improving transformations is of several hundreds.

The local-search algorithm has been extensively tested on several dozens of benchmarks with different characteristics: realistic (that is, matching the operational conditions), pathological (for example, with plants whose production is stopped several days), large-scale (for example, with 1500 sites and 300 resources). On 5 long-term real-life benchmarks (105 days), the gain obtained by the local-search algorithm with 5 minutes of running time per planning iteration reaches 21.8 % (resp. 25.3 %) on average compared to solutions obtained by the urgency-based insertion heuristic (resp. solutions built by the logistic experts of the company for which this R&D project was conducted).

References

1. Bell, W., Dalberto, L., Fisher, M., Greenfield, A., Jaikumar, R., Kedia, P., Mack, R., Prutzman, P.: Improving the distribution of industrial gases with an on-line computerized routing and scheduling optimizer. Interfaces 13(6), 4–23 (1983)
2. Campbell, A., Clarke, L., Kleywegt, A., Savelsbergh, M.: The inventory routing problem. In: Crainic, T., Laporte, G. (eds.) Fleet Management and Logistics, pp. 95–113. Kluwer Academic Publishers, Norwell (1998)
3. Campbell, A., Clarke, L., Savelsbergh, M.: Inventory routing in practice. In: Toth, P., Viego, D. (eds.) The Vehicle Routing Problem. SIAM Monographs on Discrete Mathematics and Applications, vol. 9, pp. 309–330. Kluwer Academic Publishers, Philadelphia (2002)
4. Campbell, A., Savelsbergh, M.: A decomposition approach for the inventory-routing problem. Transportation Science 38(4), 488–502 (2004)
5. Savelsbergh, M., Song, J.-H.: Inventory routing with continuous moves. Computers and Operations Research 34(6), 1744–1763 (2007)
6. Savelsbergh, M., Song, J.-H.: An optimization algorithm for the inventory routing with continuous moves. Computers and Operations Research 35(7), 2266–2282 (2008)
7. Campbell, A., Savelsbergh, M.: Efficient insertion heuristics for vehicle routing and scheduling problems. Transportation Science 38(3), 369–378 (2004)
8. Lau, H., Liu, Q., Ono, H.: Integrating local search and network flow to solve the inventory routing problem. In: Proceedings of AAAI 2002, the 18th National Conference on Artificial Intelligence, pp. 9–14. AAAI Press, Menlo Park (2002)
9. Estellon, B., Gardi, F., Nouioua, K.: High-performance local search for task scheduling with human resource allocation. In: Stützle, T., Birattari, M., Hoos, H.H. (eds.) SLS 2009. LNCS, vol. 5752, pp. 1–15. Springer, Heidelberg (2009)

A Detailed Analysis of Two Metaheuristics for the Team Orienteering Problem

Pieter Vansteenwegen[1,*], Wouter Souffriau[1,2], and Dirk Van Oudheusden[1]

[1] Centre for Industrial Management, Katholieke Universiteit, Leuven, Belgium
[2] Information Technology, KaHo St.-Lieven, Ghent, Belgium
{pieter.vansteenwegen,dirk.vanoudheusden}@cib.kuleuven.be
wouter.souffriau@kahosl.be

Abstract. This paper presents different techniques that can be used to improve the metaheuristic design and insight in the problem at hand. The presented techniques are applied to analyse the performance of two different metaheuristics for the team orienteering problem. Furthermore, the parameter setting problem is discussed and the parameter "sensitivity" is analysed.

1 Introduction

In the Orienteering Problem (OP) a set of n locations i is given, each with a score S_i and a service or visiting time T_i. The starting location (1) and the end location (n) are fixed. The time t_{ij} needed to travel from location i to j is known for all locations. Not all locations can be visited since the available time is limited to a given time budget T_{max}. The OP goal is to determine a single route, limited by T_{max}, that visits some of the locations and that maximises the total collected score. Each location can be visited at most once. The Team Orienteering Problem (TOP) is an OP where the goal is to determine m routes, each limited to T_{max}, that maximise the total collected score.

More details about the TOP and its applications can be found in the literature [1,2,3,4,5,6,7]. Many different algorithms have been designed for the TOP [1,3,4,5,6,7], but until now, they were only compared based on the quality of the results and the required computational effort. A thorough analysis of why certain algorithms perform well (or not) is missing. Little or no attention is given to gather real insight in the problem in order to "optimise" the design of (new) algorithms. This paper introduces techniques to analyse the performance of (certain components of) metaheuristics. The techniques are applied to the SVNS algorithm of Vansteenwegen et al. [5] and the PR algorithm of Souffriau et al. [7].

2 Importance of Local Search Moves

Souffriau et al. [7] compare the quality of the results and the required computational time of the PR algorithm with the best performing algorithms for the

T. Stützle, M. Birattari, and H.H. Hoos (Eds.): SLS 2009, LNCS 5752, pp. 110–114, 2009.

Table 1. Performance of SVNS moves

	Insert	Replace	TwoInsert	TwoReplace	Change	TwoOpt	Swap
CPA (%)	2.1	1.5	0.9	1.2	1.6	1.1	1.0
IC (%)	26.5	44.2	56.4	43.6	2.5	-	-
CPU (%)	6.2	4.9	8.8	9.4	242.2	-	-
AC (%)	0.6	0.5	0.0	0.3	0.8	0.4	0.2
CPU (%)	297.8	140.0	105.9	108.3	63.3	114.1	108.4

TOP [1,3,4,5,6]. We will only focus on the PR and SVNS algorithm described above and analyse their performance in detail. Seven local search moves are used by these algorithms. Five moves increase the total score of the solution: *Insert, TwoInsert, Replace, TwoReplace* and *Change*; and two moves reduce the travel time between the selected locations: *TwoOpt* and *Swap*. All moves are described in detail in [5] and [7]. 158 relevant instances, described in [7] are used for this analysis.

The importance of a move is illustrated by its "contribution per application", its "isolated contribution" and its "additional contribution". The "contribution per application" (CPA) is defined as the average score increase (or travel time decrease) over all the times the move is applied. CPA is given as a percentage of the total score (or travel time) of the final solution. The "isolated contribution" (IC) is defined as the decrease in score (in percentage) when only this move is implemented and no other moves. The "additional contribution" (AC) is defined as the decrease in score (in percentage) when this move is not implemented. The AC can be considered as the "added value" of adding this move to the implemented set of moves. All percentages mentioned in this section are average percentages over all 158 instances. An important move will have a high CPA and a low IC and AC. For each instance, the best result obtained by SVNS or PR will be used as a benchmark.

Skewed Variable Neighbourhood Search: Table 1 summarises the importance of all local search moves in the SVNS algorithm. The first row presents the contribution per application. The second and third row give the isolated contribution and the required computation time when only this move is implemented. The computation time is given as a percentage of the computation time of the original SVNS algorithm. Row four and five indicate the additional contribution of each move and the computation time (as a percentage) when only this move is left out.

The results for CPA should be interpreted with care, since the sequence wherein the moves are considered influences these results. Nevertheless, based on the CPA results, *Insert* appears to be the most contributing score increasing move and *TwoOpt* is the most contributing travel time decreasing move. When considering the IC, the result for *Change* stands out. If only *Change* is implemented, and no other local search moves, the average gap with the SVNS results is only 2.5%. However, the computational time would double at least. This implies that *Change* is very effective, but not really efficient. The fact that *Insert*

Table 2. Performance of PR moves

	Insert	Replace	TwoOpt	Swap
CPA (%)	2.2	1.2	1.5	1.1
IC (%)	1.9	0.3	1.1	1.6
CPU (%)	78.7	87.2	84.2	75.5
AC (%)	-	0.9	0.2	0.0
CPU (%)	-	82.6	120.7	93.6

is the next best move, based on IC, is not a surprise. *Insert* adds locations to all routes and the diversification procedures remove locations from the routes or move locations from one route to another. This combination allows an intensive exploration of the whole solution space. An important aspect that is still missing, resulting in a gap of 26.5%, is the lack of a travel time reduction move. No IC results are presented for *TwoOpt* or *Swap* since implementing these moves without any score increasing move, is irrelevant.

The percentages in the AC row are much smaller, but nevertheless very meaningful. These results confirm the previous results about the effectiveness of different moves. A rather surprising conclusion is that *Insert* and *Replace* are more important to reduce the computational effort than to increase the final quality of the results. This statement is only correct when enough alternative local search moves are implemented that increase the score and decrease the travel time.

Other interesting analysis results for SVNS (*not* in the table) are that without diversification procedures, the results are 7.3% worse on average.

GRASP with Path Relinking: Table 2 summarises the importance of each local search move in the PR algorithm, in the same way as Table 1. *Insert* is always applied during the initialisation and during the path relinking. This implies that the "Isolated Contribution" of the other moves is not really isolated, but always in combination with *Insert*.

Based on the CPA, the same conclusions as with SVNS can be made: *Insert* is the most important score increasing move and *TwoOpt* is the most contributing travel time decreasing move. The IC results for *Replace* (including *Insert*) illustrate that the travel time decreasing moves together increase the results with (only) 0.3%. The fact that PR considers many alternative initial solutions (diversification strategy), probably reduces the need for travel time decreasing moves, compared to the SVNS algorithm. The most significant result in this analysis, however, is that it would be better to leave out *Swap*. The quality would remain the same, and the computational effort would be reduced to 93.6%.

For both SVNS and PR *Insert* and *TwoOpt* are required to obtain high quality results with small computational times. Furthermore, *Replace* appears to be an efficient move and both algorithms require a good diversification strategy.

It would be interesting to know the contribution of the local search moves in the ant colony algorithm [4] and the tabu search and VNS algorithms [3], in order to draw more general conclusions about useful local search moves for the orienteering problem, independent from the metaheuristic framework that is implemented.

3 Parameter Settings

Next to selecting appropriate moves and the best sequence to apply them, another important design decision is the parameter setting. In almost all papers, not only about TOP algorithms, parameter settings are based on experimental results or preliminary testing. The parameters of the best performing TOP algorithms [1,3,4,5,6,7] are all determined in this way. Almost never, the "sensitivity" of the algorithm to a particular parameter setting is discussed. Sensitivity can be defined as to what extend small or larger changes in parameter settings will influence the quality and the computational effort of the algorithm.

SVNS: For SVNS, the only important parameters are the maximum number of iterations without improvement ($NoImproveMax = 40$) and the maximal number of locations to remove in each route ($KMax = 25$). In order to verify the influence of these parameters, the test instances are also solved with different combinations of higher and lower values: $NoImproveMax = 20$ and 80 and $KMax = 12$ and 50. Increasing $NoImproveMax$ increases the quality of the results, but the calculation time also increases significantly. This clearly illustrates the trade-off between the required calculation time and the quality of the results. Furthermore, the algorithm is not at all sensitive to changes in $KMax$; the influence on the result quality and the computational time is insignificant.

PR: The most important parameter in the PR algorithm is the maximum number of iterations. Based on this parameter slow and fast variants of the algorithm can be constructed (more details about this parameter can be found in [7]). In this paper only a slow variant is considered, with a maximum of 100 iterations without improvement. Other important PR parameters are the size of the elite pool ($EliteMax = 5$), the *Greediness* (0.5) of the initialisation method and the *SimilarityThreshold* (0.9) [7]. In order to verify the influence of these parameters, the test instances are also solved for other values of these parameters: $EliteMax = 3$ and 10, $Greediness = 0.3$ and 0.8 and $SimilarityThreshold = 0.5$.

Changing the number of elite solutions has a small influence on the quality of the results, but a significant influence on the computational efforts. The greediness value does not influence the result quality, however, a significant increase in computational effort is required when the greediness is increased or decreased. Further analysis should indicate if 0.5 can be considered as an optimal value and an "ideal" mix of greediness and randomness. Decreasing the similarity threshold decreases significantly the quality of the results on the one hand, but also the computational effort on the other hand. Again a trade-off should be made.

4 Conclusions

By analysing the "contribution" of individual local search moves and different variants of the solution algorithm, insight is gained in the implemented metaheuristics. These insights can help to optimise the design of the algorithm under study, other algorithms or future algorithms. Furthermore, in many papers, parameter setting are (only) based on experimental results or preliminary testing. Almost never, the "sensitivity" of the algorithm to a particular parameter setting is discussed. Nevertheless, this can give important information about the performance of an algorithm and the appropriateness of the trade-offs that were made during the implementation of the algorithm. In this paper, the parameter sensitivity and the importance of different moves are analysed for two different metaheuristics implemented to solve the team orienteering problem. In this way, important insights in these algorithms are gained.

In order to increase the statistical significance of the observed results, standard deviations should be taken into account and appropriate statistical tests should be used. "Multiple linear regression" analysis would allow a more thorough analysis of the test results in this paper. Multiple linear regression is a statistical technique to determine the contribution or significance of different parameters (local search moves or parameter settings) in obtaining certain results (high quality results or low computational times).

Acknowledgements. Pieter Vansteenwegen is a post doctoral research fellow of the Fonds Wetenschappelijk Onderzoek - Vlaanderen (FWO).

References

1. Tang, H., Miller-Hooks, E.: A tabu search heuristic for the team orienteering problem. Computer & Operations Research 32, 1379–1407 (2005)
2. Vansteenwegen, P., Van Oudheusden, D.: The mobile tourist guide: an OR opportunity. OR Insight 20(3), 21–27 (2007)
3. Archetti, C., Hertz, A., Speranza, M.: Metaheuristics for the team orienteering problem. Journal of Heuristics 13, 49–76 (2007)
4. Ke, L., Archetti, C., Feng, Z.: Ants can solve the team orienteering problem. Computers & Industrial Engineering 54, 648–665 (2008)
5. Vansteenwegen, P., Souffriau, W., Vanden Berghe, G., Van Oudheusden, D.: Metaheuristics for tourist trip planning. In: Geiger, M., Habenicht, W., Sevaux, M., Sörensen, K. (eds.) Metaheuristics in the Service Industry. Lecture Notes in Economics and Mathematical Systems, vol. 624, pp. 15–31. Springer, Berlin (2009)
6. Vansteenwegen, P., Souffriau, W., Vanden Berghe, G., Van Oudheusden, D.: A guided local search metaheuristic for the team orienteering problem. European Journal of Operational Research 196(1), 118–127 (2009)
7. Souffriau, W., Vansteenwegen, P., Vanden Berghe, G., Van Oudheusden, D.: A path relinking approach for the team orienteering problem. Computers & Operations Research (2009), doi:10.1016/j.cor.2009.05.002

On the Explorative Behavior of MAX–MIN Ant System

Daniela Favaretto[2], Elena Moretti[2], and Paola Pellegrini[1,2,*]

[1] Dipartimento di Elettrotecnica, Elettronica ed Informatica,
Università di Trieste, Trieste, Italy
[2] Dipartimento di Matematica Applicata,
Università Ca' Foscari di Venezia, Venezia, Italy
{paolap,favaret,emoretti}@unive.it

Abstract. Analyzing the behavior of stochastic procedures is generally recognized to be relevant. A possible way for doing so consists in observing the exploration performed. A formalization in this sense is proposed here: A method for studying this aspect regardless the type of approach used is defined and tested. The consequent measure of exploration is applied to MAX–MIN Ant System: The impact of the values of the parameters on the exploration is assessed. The conclusions drawn are put in relation with the indications provided by the average λ-branching factor.

1 Introduction

In combinatorial optimization, selecting the best algorithm for a given problem is a critical task. For doing it, it is crucial to understand what the characteristics of the various approaches are. In this sense, a fundamental element that must be investigated is the explorative behavior of the different procedures. Although the interest on this topic is quite intuitive, in the literature it has not been considered in general terms [1,7,2,8]. A widely applicable definition of exploration is proposed in Section 2, together with some details on how to measure exploration. Then, an application of this methodology is provided: the object of this study is MAX–MIN Ant System [3], an ant colony optimization (ACO) algorithm. In Section 3 the experimental analysis is reported and we conclude in Section 4.

2 Exploration: A Definition

Let a combinatorial optimization problem be mapped on a graph $G = (N, A)$, where N is the set of nodes and A the set of edges, and $|N| = n$ and $|A| = a$. A solution is a vector of a components. In particular, solution S is given by $S = (x_1, x_2, ..., x_a)$. $x_i = 0$ if the i-th edge is not included in it, and $x_i = P_i$ otherwise: Let P_i be the probability that the algorithm assigns to edge i when constructing

* The authors acknowledge the contribution of CINECA, Bologna, Italy, which provided computation resources for the experimental analysis presented in this paper.

T. Stützle, M. Birattari, and H.H. Hoos (Eds.): SLS 2009, LNCS 5752, pp. 115–119, 2009.

solution S. Since stochastic algorithms are considered, this probability is always computable, in a different way for each different approach. In this sense, solutions are observed from the point of view of the algorithm. Such a representation of solutions has been chosen for reflecting as much as possible the characteristics of stochastic algorithms.

Solutions represented in this way can be grouped in clusters [4,5]. To the aim of this analysis, all the solutions belonging to a cluster are close enough for being considered as a unique solution from the point of view of the algorithm. In this framework, it is possible to define the exploration: *The exploration performed by a stochastic algorithm is given by the number of clusters of solutions visited.* In order to compute this value, one only needs to know how the stochastic algorithm associates probabilities to edges. As an application of this concept, from here on, an ACO algorithm is studied.

For using such definition, a clustering procedure needs to be defined. In particular, an agglomerative hierarchical procedure [6] appears suitable. For what the stopping criterion is concerned, the aggregative procedure is concluded when the distance between the two closest clusters is greater than a predefined threshold. Let the threshold ϵ_x be such that solutions that differ for more than $x\%$ of their edges must not be included in the same cluster.

3   Experimental Analysis

In this section the impact of the values of the parameters on the exploration performed by MAX–MIN Ant System is analyzed. The stopping criterion considered in this analysis consists in the fulfillment of 20000 objective function evaluations. At this early stage, no local search procedure is applied. One hundred TSP instances with 50 nodes are used. The set of experiments described below have been performed also on one instance with 100 and 200 nodes. The results can be downloaded from the web page http://www.paola.pellegrini.it and they appear qualitatively equivalent. On the same web site the code used for computing the exploration and the instances used are available. The distance measure considered is the Euclidean distance. A very short experimental analysis with two different distances. The results appear substantially analogous to the ones reported in this Section. Following the computation described above and setting $x = 10$, the value of the parameter ϵ_{10} is 3.16.

MAX–MIN Ant System is run varying the values of the parameters. According to the literature [9] these values have an impact on the exploration. The following analysis aims at observing this difference of exploration during the evolution of a run. The solutions are considered iteration by iteration, i.e. in groups of 50 elements. In the literature, the problem of measuring the exploration performed by ACO algorithms has been shortly tackled [3]. The measure that is generally accepted as a measure of stagnation is the average λ-branching factor. The conclusions drawn with the cluster analysis are considered in the light of the results obtained by studying the trend of the average λ-branching factor computed in the same horizon.

The parameters analyzed are α, β, ρ. The values $\alpha = 1, \beta = 1, \rho = 0.02$ are considered as reference. A colony of 50 ants is used. Then, one parameter at a time is varied. The values used for parameters are the following: $\alpha \in \{1, 2, 3, 4\}, \beta \in \{1, 2, 3, 4\}, \rho \in \{0.02, 0.05, 0.2, 0.7\}$.

In figure 1 (left column), the exploration is reported for the different values of the parameters. It can be observed that an increase of the value of α has three main effects: First of all a significant level of exploration is achieved earlier in the run, as well as its peak. Moreover, the higher the value of α, the higher this maximum level. It has to be remarked that an exploration equal to 1 characterizes the beginning of the run whatever value is set for α. In this phase the algorithm is moving in the search space in a quite random fashion. Any exploration performed in this moment is then neither intentional not controlled. It is reasonable, then, to interpret it as non-exploration. This phase will be referred to as *random–like*. Until the probability of some edges passes a certain threshold the behavior remains substantially the same and the exploration is equal to 1.

For what β is concerned a very similar trend can be noted. The main difference consists in the fact that the *random–like* phase is completely absent when $\beta = 3$ and $\beta = 4$. In general, moreover, the peaks of exploration are much less pronounced, and they are reached after a smoother ascent.

Finally, ρ implies the same trend: When it increases, the duration of the *random–like* phase is shorter. Peaks are much less stressed than in the case of α. An actual decrease of exploration after the maximum is reached is not even evident. An explanation of this effect can be found in the pheromone update rule. In MAX–MIN Ant System pheromone evaporates on all the edges, and is deposited only on those belonging to the best so far (or iteration best) solution. It implies that if the evaporation rate is large, even after few updates the differences in the pheromone trails may be very strong.

In figure 1 (right column) the average λ-branching factor is reported. For all the values of the parameters, it increases for a while and then starts descending, more or less steeply. This reflects the observations made on the exploration: The period in which the average λ-branching factor is high, and the pheromone is almost uniformly distributed on the edges, corresponds to the *random–like* phase: The algorithm has not yet defined any real difference among the solutions.

A point that deserves a deeper analysis is the fact that when the average λ-branching factor reaches a very low value, the corresponding exploration appears to be quite high. In this framework the nature of the two measures needs to be taken into account: The former concerns only the pheromone distribution. The latter considers both the probability distribution (which is indeed connected to the pheromone trails) and the solutions actually visited. Figure 2 aims at underlying this difference. The last 50 solutions generated in the run with $\alpha = 1$, $\beta = 1$ and $\rho = 0.7$ are considered. In figure 2(a) the probability associated to each node to node edge is presented. It is evident that the distribution is coherent with a very low average λ-branching factor: not more that a couple of edges incident on each node have high probability. On the other hand, figure 2(b) investigates the difference among the solutions found. In particular, they

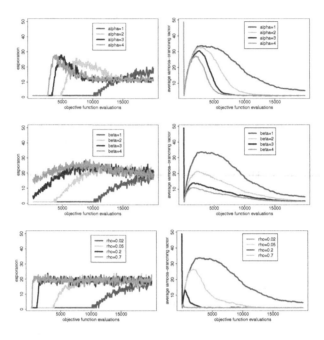

Fig. 1. Number of clusters (left) and average λ-branching factor (right)

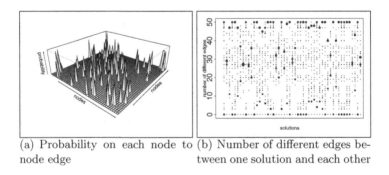

(a) Probability on each node to node edge

(b) Number of different edges between one solution and each other

Fig. 2. Observations on the last 50 solutions visited ($\alpha = 1, \beta = 1, \rho = 0.7$)

are considered here in a TSP-wise sense: only the permutations matter, while probabilities are completely neglected. The number of different edges between one solution and each other is reported. For each pair $(\hat{x}, \hat{y})$, the size of the bullet used is proportional to the number of solutions differing from solution $\hat{x}$ for $\hat{y}$ edges. It is evident that, despite the very concentrated pheromone trails, the solutions visited are far from being always the same. In this sense, despite that the average λ-branching factor is a fundamental measure for the effectiveness of MAX–MIN Ant System, the assessment of the number of clusters represents much more accurately the actual behavior of the procedure.

If the objective function value is considered for the different configurations, it is interesting that the ACO algorithm behaves significantly differently from random search only when exploration passes the *random–like* phase. This is true for any value of the parameters. The results obtained for all the 100 instances allow to draw the same conclusions.

4 Conclusions

This paper deals with the observation of the behavior of stochastic procedures, intended in terms of explorative attitude of the algorithms. A definition of exploration independent on the algorithm is presented, and a consequent measurement method is provided. It is applied to MAX–MIN Ant System: The impact of the values of the parameters on the exploration is assessed. The conclusions drawn in this sense are put in relations with the indications provided by the average λ-branching factor. In these first experiments, only one parameter at a time is varied, and no local search is applied. Both these points will be overcome in future research. In particular, it is expectable that the interaction between parameters has an impact on the exploration performed.

References

1. Bhattacharya, M.: A synergistic approach for evolutionary optimization. In: GECCO 2008: Proceedings of the 2008 GECCO conference companion on Genetic and evolutionary computation, pp. 2105–2110. ACM, New York (2008)
2. Devarenne, I., Mabed, H., Caminada, A.: Intelligent neighborhood exploration in local search heuristics. In: ICTAI 2006: Proceedings of the 18th IEEE International Conference on Tools with Artificial Intelligence, pp. 144–150. IEEE Computer Society, Los Alamitos (2006)
3. Dorigo, M., Stützle, T.: Ant Colony Optimization. MIT Press, Cambridge (2004)
4. Everitt, B., Landau, S., Leese, M.: Cluster Analysis. Arnold, London (2001)
5. Kaufman, L., Rousseeuw, P.J.: Finding groups in data. An introduction to cluster analysis. Wiley Series in Probability and Mathematical Statistics. Applied Probability and Statistics. Wiley, New York (1990)
6. Jardine, N., Sibson, R.: The construction of hierarchic and non-hierarchic classifications. The Computer Journal 11(2), 177–184 (1968)
7. Orosz, J.E., Jacobson, S.H.: Finite-time performance analysis of static simulated annealing algorithms. Computational Optimization and Applications 21(1), 21–53 (2002)
8. Pellegrini, P., Ellero, A.: The small world of pheromone trails. In: Dorigo, M., Birattari, M., Blum, C., Clerc, M., Stützle, T., Winfield, A.F.T. (eds.) ANTS 2008. LNCS, vol. 5217, pp. 387–394. Springer, Heidelberg (2008)
9. Pellegrini, P., Favaretto, D., Moretti, E.: On MAX–MIN ant system's parameters. In: Dorigo, M., Gambardella, L.M., Birattari, M., Martinoli, A., Poli, R., Stützle, T. (eds.) ANTS 2006. LNCS, vol. 4150, pp. 203–214. Springer, Heidelberg (2006)

A Study on Dominance-Based Local Search Approaches for Multiobjective Combinatorial Optimization

Arnaud Liefooghe, Salma Mesmoudi, Jérémie Humeau,
Laetitia Jourdan, and El-Ghazali Talbi

Laboratoire d'Informatique Fondamentale de Lille, UMR CNRS 8022,
INRIA Lille-Nord Europe, Université Lille 1, Villeneuve d'Ascq, France
{Arnaud.Liefooghe,Laetitia.Jourdan,talbi}@lifl.fr,
{Salma.Mesmoudi,Jeremie.Humeau}@inria.fr

Abstract. The purpose of the current paper is twofold. First, a unified view of dominance-based multiobjective local search algorithms is proposed. We focus on methods based on the iterative improvement of the nondominated set by means of a neighborhood operator. Next, the effect of current solutions selection and of neighborhood exploration techniques for such purpose is studied. Experiments are conducted on a permutation flowshop scheduling problem in a two- and a three-objective variant.

1 Introduction

The aim of this study is to provide a unified view of dominance-based local search for multiobjective optimization. Contrary to the single-objective case, a Multiobjective Combinatorial Optimization Problem (MCOP) does not yield a unique optimal solution. Instead, a set of compromise solutions, known as efficient solutions must generally be identified. Since they are naturally well-suited to find multiple efficient solutions in a single simulation run, a tremendous number of multiobjective evolutionary algorithms have been proposed over the last two decades [1]. However, local search methods are known to be efficient metaheuristics for single-objective optimization. Local search, also referred to as hill-climbing, descent, iterative improvement, etc., is likely the oldest and simplest metaheuristic [2]. But multiobjective local search principles based on a dominance relation appeared quite recently [1,3]. Hence, some dominance-based multiobjective local search methods have been proposed in the literature, including the Pareto Archived Evolution Strategy (PAES) [4], the Pareto Local Search (PLS) [5] or the Bicriteria Local Search (BLS) [6]. Such methods generally combine the definition of a neighborhood structure with the use of a population of solutions. They maintain a set of potentially efficient solutions, and iteratively improves this set by exploring part of its neighborhood. Our first purpose is to give a unified view of dominance-based multiobjective local search. We describe the basic components shared by all these algorithms and we introduce a general-purpose model for their design. Afterwards, we concentrate on a subpart of

T. Stützle, M. Birattari, and H.H. Hoos (Eds.): SLS 2009, LNCS 5752, pp. 120–124, 2009.

components involved into the unified model in order to study their respective behavior on a multiobjective permutation flowshop scheduling problem.

2 Dominance-Based Multiobjective Local Search

Until now, each DMLS algorithm was designed independently of the others, and was implemented as a self-contained method with its own specific components. In the following, we identify the common components shared by all DMLS algorithms and propose a unifying model that takes them into account. Hence, whatever the MCOP to be solved, the common concepts for the design of a DMLS algorithm can be stated as follows: (1) design a representation, (2) design a initialization strategy, (3) design a way of evaluating a solution, (4) design a suitable neighborhood structure, (5) design a way of evaluating a neighboring solution incrementally (if possible), (6) decide a current set selection strategy, (7) decide a neighborhood exploration strategy, (8) decide an archive management strategy, (9) decide a stopping condition. When dealing with any kind of metaheuristics, one may distinguish problem-related and problem-independent components. Hence, the first five issues presented above strongly depend of the MCOP under consideration, whereas the last four ones can be seen as generic components. In addition, three data structures are used to store (i) the archive contents, (ii) the *current set* of solutions whose neighborhood is to be explored, and (iii) the *candidate set* of neighbor solutions that will potentially enter the archive. Problem-related components are assumed to be designed for the MCOP at hand, so that they are not discussed in the paper due to space limitation.

2.1 Problem-Independent Issues

Current set selection. The first phase of a local search step deals with the selection of a set of solutions from which the neighborhood will be explored. Generally speaking, in the frame of the DMLS model presented in the paper, two strategies can be applied. Firstly, an *exhaustive selection*, where all solutions from the archive are selected. Second, a *partial selection*, where only a subset of solutions is selected. Such a set may be selected at random, or also with respect to a diversity measure. Of course, if some archive members are marked as visited, they must be discarded of the current set selection for obvious efficiency reasons.

Neighborhood exploration. From the current set, a number of candidate solutions must be generated by means of a neighborhood structure. Such a set is obtained by a repeated local transformation of every solution contained in the current set. For a given current solution, two classes can be clearly distinguished. Firstly, an *exhaustive neighborhood exploration*, where the neighborhood is evaluated in a full and deterministic way. Every possible move of the current solution is applied and the neighboring solutions are all added to the candidate set. The solutions of the current set can then all be marked as visited. Second, a *partial neighborhood exploration*, where only a subset of moves are applied. The number of moves to be applied is generally defined by a user-given parameter.

Archiving. The archive allows to store either all or a subset of nondominated solutions found during the search process. Its main aim is to prevent the loss of interesting solutions. But archive members are also integrated into the search process by providing solutions to exploit in the DMLS model presented in this paper. Different archiving techniques can be distinguished depending on the problem properties, the designed algorithm and the number of desired solutions: (*i*) an *unbounded archive* or (*ii*) a *bounded archive*. Firstly, when an archive is maintained, it usually comprises the current nondominated set approximation, as dominated solutions are discarded. Then, an unbounded archive can be used in order to save the whole set of nondominated solutions. However, as some MCOPs may contain an exponential number of nondominated solutions, additional operations must be used to bound the archive size.

Stopping condition. Since an iterative method computes successive approximations, a practical test is generally required to determine when the process must stop. Popular examples are a given number of iterations or a given runtime. However, when it is possible to mark archive members as visited, a natural stopping criterion arises when all archive solutions are marked as visited.

3   Computational Experiments

The goal of this section is to experiment the efficiency of some state-of-the-art strategies for both current set selection and neighborhood exploration. For each component, a set of 2 different schemes are investigated. This gives rise to a combination of 4 DMLS algorithms. Hence, with regards to the current set selection, either (*i*) each or (*ii*) a random single unvisited solution is selected from the archive. Next, with regards to the neighborhood exploration, either (*i*) all or (*ii*) a single random neighbor per solution is proposed as a candidate for integrating the archive. The corresponding algorithms are denoted by $DMLS^{(1\cdot1)}$, $DMLS^{(1\cdot\star)}$, $DMLS^{(\star\cdot1)}$ and $DMLS^{(\star\cdot\star)}$. Note that the algorithm denoted by and $DMLS^{(1\cdot1)}$ is closely related to PAES [4], $DMLS^{(1\cdot\star)}$ to PLS [5], and $DMLS^{(\star\cdot\star)}$ to BLS [6]. For each problem instance to be solved, different maximum runtime values, from 2 to 20 minutes, have been investigated in order to study the evolution of the search efficiency over time. However, as some algorithms stop in a natural way, a simple random restart has been performed to continue the search process until the maximum runtime is reached. For all the experiments, the initial population size is set to 1, and an unbounded archive is maintained.

3.1   A Permutation Flowshop Scheduling Problem

The Flowshop Scheduling Problem (FSP) consists of scheduling N jobs on M machines. We here focus on a permutation FSP, where the operating sequences of the jobs are identical and unidirectional on every machine. We will consider a two-objective FSP (denoted by FSP-2), where both the makespan and the total tardiness are to be minimized. Additionally, we will also consider a three-objective variant (denoted by FSP-3), where the maximum tardiness is the additional objective to be minimized. The reader is referred to [7] for more information on multiobjective scheduling.

The problem-related components used for the specific case of the FSP presented above are the following ones. Firstly, the representation is based on a permutation of size N. Next, the initialization strategy consists of generating solutions randomly. At last, the neighborhood is based on the *insertion* operator, *i.e.* a job at position i is inserted at position $j \neq i$, and the jobs located between positions i and j are shifted.

3.2   Results and Discussion

To evaluate the performance of the algorithms experimented in this paper, we consider various benchmark test instances[1]. Six problem instances involving from 20 jobs and 5 machines to 50 jobs and 20 machines are experimented. A set of 10 runs per instance has been performed for each search method. For a given instance, let Z^{all} denote the union of the outputs we obtained during all our experiments. We first compute a reference set $Z_N^\star$ containing all the nondominated points of Z^{all}. Now, to measure the quality of an output set A in comparison to $Z_N^\star$, we compute the difference between these two sets by using the unary hypervolume metric and the additive ϵ-indicator [8].

DMLS$^{(1\cdot1)}$ and DMLS$^{(\star\cdot1)}$ can generally not compete with other algorithms on small size problem instances. This can be explained by the fact that they do not handle any kind of natural stopping condition, so that they are never able to restart. On the contrary, DMLS$^{(1\cdot\star)}$ and DMLS$^{(\star\cdot\star)}$ quickly reach a state where each archive member is marked as visited, and can then restart with a different initial solution. However, DMLS$^{(1\cdot1)}$ and DMLS$^{(\star\cdot1)}$ perform better on bigger instances. In particular, these two algorithms appear very efficient in comparison to the others on the 50_10_01 and 50_20_01 instances when a short amount of runtime is available. Moreover, on the 50_20_01 instance of FSP-3, they perform better than all the other algorithms, even when a large runtime is allowed. Now, with regards to DMLS$^{(\star\cdot\star)}$, this approach performs very well on 20-job instances. For larger ones, the convergence is really slow in the biobjective case, but finally reaches competitive results after a long runtime. However, in the three-objective case, this method appears inefficient for problem instances of 50 jobs. Finally, the DMLS$^{(1\cdot\star)}$ algorithm, that embeds similar techniques than PLS [5], seems to reach the best overall performances. Indeed, it appears to be as good as DMLS$^{(\star\cdot\star)}$ on 20-job instances for both FSP-2 and FSP-3. For the 50_05_01 instance, it clearly outperforms the other algorithms all time long. For bigger instances, even if it is slightly dominated at the beginning of the search, it finally reaches the better results in the two-objective case. For FSP-3, same conclusions can be drawn on the 50_10_01 instance. But the last instance is the single one where DMLS$^{(1\cdot\star)}$ is always dominated by DMLS$^{(1\cdot1)}$ and DMLS$^{(\star\cdot1)}$.

---

[1] These instances are available at http://www.lifl.fr/~liefooga/benchmarks/

4   Conclusion

In this paper, a unification of dominance-based local search approaches for multiobjective combinatorial optimization has been attempted. Such methods can be seen as a generalization of the classical single-objective hill climbing, combined with the use of a population of solutions. They are based on the iterative improvement of the set of nondominated solutions by means of a neighborhood operator. A unified model has been proposed and its main issues have been identified. The problem-independent components of current set selection, neighborhood exploration as well as archiving strategies have been especially discussed. This model has been used as a starting point for the design and the implementation of an open-source software framework for dominance-based multiobjective local search. This contribution has been conceived as a plug-in to be integrated into the ParadisEO-MOEO software framework[2]. At last, the issues of current set selection and neighborhood exploration have been experimentally compared on a multiobjective flowshop scheduling problem. We showed the benefit of performing a full neighborhood exploration in order to avoid the revaluation of some neighboring solutions and to reach a natural stopping criterion. Furthermore, we concluded that selecting a single solution from the current population to explore its neighborhood in an exhaustive manner was especially efficient for the problem under consideration. As a next step, we will investigate larger instances for the flowshop scheduling problem as well as other kinds of multiobjective problems.

References

1. Ehrgott, M., Gandibleux, X.: Approximative solution methods for multiobjective combinatorial optimization. TOP 12(1), 1–89 (2004)
2. Talbi, E.G.: Metaheuristics: from design to implementation. Wiley, Chichester (2009)
3. Paquete, L., Stützle, T.: Stochastic local search algorithms for multiobjective combinatorial optimization: A review. In: Handbook of Approximation Algorithms and Metaheuristics. Chapman & Hall / CRC (2007)
4. Knowles, J.D., Corne, D.: Approximating the nondominated front using the Pareto archived evolution strategy. Evolutionary Computation 8(2), 149–172 (2000)
5. Paquete, L., Chiarandini, M., Stützle, T.: Pareto local optimum sets in the biobjective traveling salesman problem: An experimental study. In: [9], pp. 177–199
6. Angel, E., Bampis, E., Gourvés., L.: A dynasearch neighbohood for the bicriteria traveling salesman problem. In: [9], pp. 153–176
7. T'Kindt, V., Billaut, J.C.: Multicriteria Scheduling: Theory, Models and Algorithms. Springer, Berlin (2002)
8. Zitzler, E., Thiele, L., Laumanns, M., Foneseca, C.M., Grunert da Fonseca, V.: Performance assessment of multiobjective optimizers: An analysis and review. IEEE Transactions on Evolutionary Computation 7(2), 117–132 (2003)
9. Gandibleux, X., Sevaux, M., Sörensen, K., T'Kindt, V. (eds.): Metaheuristics for Multiobjective Optimisation. Lecture Notes in Economics and Mathematical Systems, vol. 535. Springer, Berlin (2004)

---

[2] The plug-in is available at `http://paradiseo.gforge.inria.fr/DMLS/`

A Memetic Algorithm for the Multidimensional Assignment Problem

Gregory Gutin and Daniel Karapetyan

Royal Holloway, University of London, London, UK
gutin@cs.rhul.ac.uk, daniel.karapetyan@gmail.com

Abstract. The Multidimensional Assignment Problem (MAP or s-AP in the case of s dimensions) is an extension of the well-known assignment problem. The most studied case of MAP is 3-AP, though the problems with larger values of s have also a number of applications. In this paper we propose a memetic algorithm for MAP that is a combination of a genetic algorithm with a local search procedure. The main contribution of the paper is an idea of dynamically adjusted generation size, that yields an outstanding flexibility of the algorithm to perform well for both small and large fixed running times.

1 Introduction

The Multidimensional Assignment Problem (MAP or s-AP in the case of s dimensions) is an extension of the well-known Assignment Problem (AP, linear AP) which is exactly two dimensional case of MAP. MAP has a host of applications, for details see [1].

For a fixed $s \geq 2$, s-AP is stated as follows. Let $X_1 = X_2 = \ldots = X_s = \{1, 2, \ldots, n\}$ and let $X = X_1 \times X_2 \times \ldots \times X_s$. For a vector $e \in X$, the component e_j denotes its jth coordinate, i.e., $e_j \in X_j$. Each vector $e \in X$ is assigned a non-negative weight $w(e)$. A collection A of $t \leq n$ vectors $e^1, e^2, \ldots, e^t$ is a *(feasible) partial assignment* if $e_j^i \neq e_j^k$ holds for each $i \neq k$ and $j \in \{1, 2, \ldots, s\}$. The *weight* of a partial assignment A is $w(A) = \sum_{i=1}^{t} w(e^i)$. An *assignment* (or *full assignment*) is a partial assignment with n vectors. The objective of s-AP is to find an assignment of minimum weight.

While AP can be solved in a polynomial time [2], s-AP for every $s \geq 3$ is NP-hard [3]. MAP is a very hard problem in the following sense. The weight matrix of MAP contains n^s values, there exist $n!^{s-1}$ possible assignments and the fastest known algorithm to find the optimal assignment takes $O(n!^{s-2}n^3)$ time. Indeed, without loss of generality set $e_1^i = i$ for $i = 1, 2, \ldots, n$ and for each feasible combination of e_j^i ($i = 1, 2, \ldots, n$ and $j = 2, 3, \ldots, s - 1$) find the optimal values for the last dimension e_s^i by solving corresponding linear AP in $O(n^3)$.

Compare it with, e.g., the Travelling Salesman Problem which has only n^2 weights, $(n-1)!$ possible tours and that can be solved in $O(n^2 2^n)$ time.

T. Stützle, M. Birattari, and H.H. Hoos (Eds.): SLS 2009, LNCS 5752, pp. 125–129, 2009.
© Springer-Verlag Berlin Heidelberg 2009

2   The Algorithm

A memetic algorithm is a combination of genetic algorithm with local search. A typical scheme of a memetic algorithm is as follows.

1. Produce the first generation, i.e., a set of solutions.
2. Apply the local search procedure to every solution in the first generation.
3. Repeat the following while a termination criterion is not met:
   (a) Produce a set of new solutions by applying so-called genetic operators to solutions from the previous generation.
   (b) Improve every solution in this set with the local search procedure.
   (c) Select several best solutions from this set to the next generation.

While the general scheme of the algorithm is quite common for all memetic algorithms, the set of genetic operators and the way they are applied can vary significantly. In our algorithm, we use the following procedure to obtain the next generation:

$$g^{i+1} = selection(\{g_1^i\} \cup mutation(g^i \setminus \{g_1^i\}, p_m, \mu_m) \cup C) \ ,$$

where g^k is the kth generation and g_j^k is the jth assignment of the kth generation; g_1^k is the best assignment in the kth generation. Constants $p_m = 0.5$ and $\mu_m = 0.1$ define the probability and the strength of mutation operator respectively. The function $selection$ simply returns m_{i+1} best distinct assignments among the given ones, where m_k is the size of the kth generation (if the number of distinct assignments in the given set is less than m_{i+1}, $selection$ returns all the distinct assignments and updates the value of m_{i+1} accordingly). To obtain the set of assignments C (crossover part) we repeat $LocalSearch(crossover(g_u^i, g_v^i))$ operation $(p \cdot m_{i+1} - m_i)/2$ times, where $u, v \in \{1, 2, \ldots, m_i\}$ are chosen randomly for every $crossover$ run and $p = 3$ defines how many times more assignments should be produced for the selection operator. The mutation function for a set of solutions is defined as follows:

$$mutation(G, p, \mu) = \bigcup_{g \in G} \begin{cases} LocalSearch(perturb(g, \mu)) \text{ if } r < p \\ g \hspace{3.5cm} \text{otherwise} \end{cases}$$

where $r \in [0, 1]$ is chosen randomly every time. The functions $crossover(x, y)$, $perturb(x, \mu)$ and $LocalSearch(x)$ are discussed later.

Coding. In genetic algorithms, coding is a way to represent a solution as a sequence of atom values such as boolean values or numbers; genetic operators are applied to such sequences.

Huang and Lim [4] use a local search procedure that, having first two dimensions of an assignment, determines the third dimension (note that the algorithm from [4] is designed only for 3-AP). Since the first dimension can always be fixed with no loss of generality, one needs to store only the second dimension of an assignment. Unfortunately, this coding requires a specific local search and is robust for 3-AP only. We use a different coding: a vector of an assignment is considered as an atom in our algorithm and, thus, a coded assignment is just a list of its vectors. The vectors are always stored in the first coordinate ascending order, e.g., an assignment $\{(2, 4, 1), (4, 3, 4), (3, 1, 3), (1, 2, 2)\}$ would be represented as $(1, 2, 2), (2, 4, 1), (3, 1, 3), (4, 3, 4)$. Two assignments are considered equal is they have equal codings.

Termination Condition. Usually, a termination condition in a memetic algorithm tries to predict the point after which any further effort is useless or, at least, not efficient. A typical approach is to count the number of subsequent generations which did not improve the best result and to stop the algorithm when this number reaches some predefined value.

We use a different approach. To be able to compare different algorithms correctly and to satisfy real world requirements, we bound our algorithm within some fixed running time. Apart from the mentioned advantages of this termination condition, it is worth to note that it gives flexibility to produce either fast or high quality solutions depending on one's needs.

Generation Size. The most natural way to fit the running time of a memetic algorithm into the given bound is to produce generations of some fixed size until the time is elapsed. However, it is clear that one memetic algorithm cannot work efficiently in both cases if there are just a few generations and if there are hundreds of generations. Thus, instead, we fix the number of generations and vary the generation size.

Our computational experiments show that, with a fixed running time, the most appropriate number I of generations for our algorithm is always around 50; this number does not depend on the local search procedure or the given time. Since the running time of the local search procedure can vary significantly (e.g., last generations usually contain better solutions than the first ones and, thus, are processed faster) and also to make our algorithm easily portable, we decided to adjust the generation size dynamically according to the remained time such that the total number of generations would always be close to I.

In particular, the size of the next generation is calculated as follows:

$$m'_{i+1} = \begin{cases} m'_i \cdot \max\left\{\min\left\{\frac{T-t}{\Delta \cdot (I-i)}, k\right\}, \frac{1}{k}\right\} & \text{if } i < I \\ m'_i \cdot k & \text{otherwise} \end{cases},$$

where T is the given time, t is the elapsed time, Δ is the time spent to produce the previous generation, I is the prescribed number of generations and $k = 1.25$ is a constant that limits the generation size change. Note that the values m'_i are real numbers, and the actual size m_i of the ith generation is defined as follows:

$$m_i = \max\left\{4, \begin{cases} \lfloor m'_i \rfloor & \text{if } (p \cdot \lfloor m'_i \rfloor - m_{i-1}) \text{ is even} \\ \lfloor m'_i \rfloor + 1 & \text{otherwise} \end{cases}\right\},$$

which guarantees that the value $p \cdot m_{i+1} - m_i$, i.e., the number of assignments produced by crossover, is even and that the generation size is never too small.

The size of the first generation is obtained in a different way (see below).

First Generation. As it was shown in [5] (and we also confirmed it by experimentation with our memetic algorithm and the construction heuristics from [6]), it is good to start any MAP local search or metaheuristic from a Greedy construction heuristic. Thus, we start from running the Greedy algorithm [5] and then perturb it using our *perturb* procedure to obtain every item of the first generation as follows:

$$g_j^1 = LocalSearch(perturb(greedy, \mu_f)) ,$$

where *greedy* is an assignment obtained by the Greedy heuristic and $\mu_f = 0.2$ is the perturbation strength coefficient. Since *perturb* performs a random modification, it guarantees some diversity in the first generation.

The algorithm produces assignments for the first generation until T/I time elapses but at least 4 assignments (recall that T is the time given for the whole memetic algorithm and I is the prescribed number of generations).

Crossover. A typical crossover operator combines two solutions, parents, to produce two new solutions, children. Crossover is the main genetic operator, i.e., it is the source of a genetic algorithm power. Due to the selection operator, it is assumed that good fragments of solutions are spread wider than others and that is why, if both parents have some similar fragments, these fragments are probably good and should be copied without any change to the children solutions. Other parts of the solution may be randomly mixed and modified though they should not be totally destroyed.

Most standard crossovers, like one-point and some others, do not preserve feasibility of MAP assignments since not every sequence of vectors can be decoded into a feasible assignment. We propose a special crossover operator. Let x and y be the parent assignments and x' and y' be the child assignments. First, we retrieve equal vectors in the parent assignments and initialize both children with this set of vectors: $x' = y' = x \cap y$. Let $k = |x \cap y|$, i.e., the number of equal vectors in the parent assignments, $p = x \setminus x'$ and $q = y \setminus y'$, where p and q are ordered sets. Let π and ω be random permutations of size $n - k$. For every $j = 1, 2, \ldots, n - k$ the crossover sets either $x' = x' \cup p_{\pi(j)}$ and $y' = y' \cup q_{\omega(j)}$ (with probability 80%), or $x' = x' \cup q_{\omega(j)}$ and $y' = y' \cup p_{\pi(j)}$ (with probability 20%).

Since this procedure can yield infeasible assignments, it requires additional correction of the child solutions. For this purpose, the following is performed for every dimension $d = 1, 2, \ldots, s$ for every child assignment c. For every i such that $\exists j < i : c_d^j = c_d^i$ set $c_d^i = r$ where $r \in \{1, 2, \ldots, n\} \setminus \{c_d^1, c_d^2, \ldots, c_d^n\}$ is chosen randomly. Finally, the vectors in the assignment are sorted in the ascending order of the first coordinate as it is required by the coding.

In other words, our crossover copies all equal vectors from the parent assignments to the child ones, then copies the rest of the vectors randomly choosing every time a pair of vectors, one from the first parent and one from the second one, and then adding them either to the first and to the second child respectively (with probability 80%) or to the second and to the first child respectively (with probability 20%). Since the obtained child assignments can be infeasible, the crossover corrects each of them; for every dimension of every child it replaces all duplicate coordinates with randomly chosen correct ones, i.e., with the coordinates which are not currently used for that dimension.

Perturbation Algorithm. The perturbation procedure $perturb(x, \mu)$ is intended to modify randomly the assignment x with the given strength μ. In our memetic algorithm, perturbation is used to produce the first generation and to mutate existing assignments when producing the next generation.

Our perturbation procedure $perturb(x, \mu)$ performs $\lceil n\mu/2 \rceil$ random swaps. Each swap randomly selects two vectors and some dimension and then swaps the corresponding coordinates: swap x_u^d and x_v^d, where $u, v \in \{1, 2, \ldots, n\}$ and $d \in \{1, 2, \ldots, s\}$ are chosen randomly; repeat the procedure $\lceil n\mu/2 \rceil$ times. For example, $perturb(x, 1)$ modifies up to n vectors in the assignment x.

Computational Experience. An extensive computation experiments were conducted for a number of instance families [1] and for several local search procedures described in [5]. As a result MDV2, which is a combination of MDV with 2-opt [5], was selected as the best local search procedure for our memetic algorithm. It was shown [1] that, given the same running time, the proposed algorithm clearly outperforms all high quality MAP algorithms known from the literature.

It is worth to note that we experimented with different values of the GK algorithm parameters such as I, μ_f, μ_m etc. and concluded that small variations of these values do not significantly influence the algorithm performance.

References

1. Gutin, G., Karapetyan, D.: A memetic algorithm for the multidimensional assignment problem. Preprint in arXiv (2009), `http://arxiv.org/abs/0906.0862`
2. Kuhn, H.W.: The hungarian method for the assignment problem. Naval Research Logistic Quarterly 2, 83–97 (1955)
3. Garey, M.R., Johnson, D.S.: Computers and Intractability: A Guide to the Theory of NP-Completeness. W.H. Freeman, New York (1979)
4. Huang, G., Lim, A.: A hybrid genetic algorithm for the three-index assignment problem. European Journal of Operational Research 172(1), 249–257 (2006)
5. Gutin, G., Karapetyan, D.: Local search heuristics for the multidimensional assignment problem. In: Proc. Golumbic Festschrift. LNCS, vol. 5420, pp. 100–115. Springer, Heidelberg (2009)
6. Karapetyan, D., Gutin, G., Goldengorin, B.: Empirical evaluation of construction heuristics for the multidimensional assignment problem. In: Chan, J., Daykin, J.W., Rahman, M.S. (eds.) London Algorithmics 2008: Theory and Practice. Texts in Algorithmics, pp. 107–122. College Publications (2009)

Autonomous Control Approach for Local Search

Julien Robet, Frédéric Lardeux, and Frédéric Saubion

LERIA, University of Angers, France
{robet,frederic.lardeux,frederic.saubion}@info.univ-angers.fr

Abstract. We propose here an approach for the autonomous control of a local search algorithm, which has several moves operators, whose efficiency can be diverse and whose application is adjusted according to the observation of the current status of search, in order to adapt to the balance between exploitation and exploration of search space.

1 Introduction

Local search algorithms are metaheuristics which have been widely used for solving complex combinatorial problems. Their efficiency relies on their ability to suitably explore various areas of the search space but also on its propensity to converge to a local optimum (the locality is defined here with respect to the notion of neighborhood). The concept of balance between intensification and diversification, especially well-known in evolutionary computation, is a crucial point when designing and using a local search algorithm. Indeed, one of the classic pitfalls encountered by these algorithms is the excessive attraction of local optima, which may trap the search process when all the potential neighbors are not as good as the current configuration and when the move strategy is mainly based on improvement. To cope with this excessive exploitation of the search space (i.e., intensification), alternative mechanisms must be used to insure enough diversification.

Inspired by the recent book of R. Battiti et al.[1] and our previous work on the autonomous management of multiple operators in genetic algorithms [2], we propose an original approach in order to design a local search algorithm that will include several move operators, corresponding to different neighborhoods and different strategies for choosing the neighbors. The control of these operators will then be achieved automatically. We have tested our algorithm on the famous quadratic assignment problem (QAP), which has been widely studied and for which an extensive library of instances and results is available [3].

2 Toward a More Integrated View of Neighborhood

In this paper, our idea is to combine parameters and components in the notion of move operators and to automatically control their application along the search process. We therefore introduce, within the local search algorithm, an adaptive operator selection method, as we have already proposed for genetic algorithms

T. Stützle, M. Birattari, and H.H. Hoos (Eds.): SLS 2009, LNCS 5752, pp. 130–134, 2009.

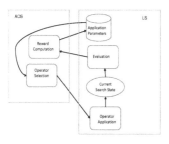

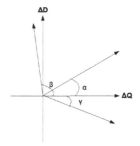

Fig. 1. Autonomous control in local search

Fig. 2. Balance between intensification and diversification

[2]. This selection mainly consists in evaluating the effect of the operator on the current state of the search in order to reward them and to be able to choose the most suitable one for the next computation step. Therefore, our objective is to evaluate the impact of the operators and to adjust their use according to the current the search. This approach is summarized in Figure 1.

This figure allows us to highlight the main issues that we have to address in an autonomous local search algorithm: How to evaluate the current search state ? How to reward operators with regards to this evaluation ? How to use these rewards to select the operator for the next move ?

If the notion of quality helps to guide and evaluate the ongoing search process, the concept of diversity should also deserves more attention. It has appeared indeed in previous works [2] that this notion can be used jointly with the quality in order to efficiently manage the balance between diversification and intensification. In the next section, we will therefore propose a definition of a diversity measure according to local search specificities.

3   A Diversity Measure for Local Search

To quantify the diversity of a local search path, our measure consists in analyzing, for each variable of the problem , the distribution of its successive assigned values with regards to its domain. Our approach relies indeed on a simple observation: if a search path is very diversified, successive assigned values to variables will tend to "cover" their domains. Otherwise, a non diversified path will be characterized by assigning a small number of different values to each variable (with regards to the cardinal of its domain), especially for the variable whose value remains unchanged along the considered path. The evaluation consists in observing, for each decision variable, the standard deviation of the number of occurrences of each possible value for this variable (i.e., for each element of its domain). The average of these deviations assesses the intrinsic similarity of the path. Indeed, the calculated standard deviations will be even lower as the path will be diverse. In order to normalize the measure, this average value is then divided by the theoretically maximum possible similarity. We obtain then a value between 0 and 1 that we subtract from 1 to reflect the diversity of the path.

4   The ALS Algorithm

The aim of our algorithm, called ALS (Autonomous Local Search), is to manage a set of local search operators. The challenge is thus to make three main modules work together: current solving state evaluation, internal components rewarding, and selection of the next operator using these rewards.

4.1   Operator Evaluation

The process used to analyze internal components is inspired by our previous works on evolutionary algorithms [2]. Its principle is to maintain along the search a history of recent performances for each operator. The originality of the method relies in the fact that the evaluation is not limited to one criterion (quality variations), but also takes into account diversity gaps. Quality and diversity variations between two iterations are thus computed as:

$$\Delta Q = \frac{eval(op(c)) - eval(c)}{eval(c) + 1} \text{ and } \Delta D = div(P_{i,j}) - div(P_{i-1,j-1})$$

where $op(c)$ is the configuration produced by the application of op on the current configuration c and $P_{i,j}$ the path from iteration i to iteration j. Given an operator op we then define $\Delta Q_{op,t}$ (resp. $\Delta D_{op,t}$) the mean quality (resp. diversity) variation over the t last applications of op where t corresponds to the size of the sliding window that stores information about each operator.

4.2   Control Issues

Applying the same memorization principles to the variations of the search state, we may collect important information about how the search process evolves among the search space. Indeed, a diversity loss reflects a focus on a particular search space areas, whereas a diversity gain appears when moving away from the current area. During the solving process, the choice of next operator to apply is achieved according to probabilities defined in the following section, 4.3. These probabilities are widely influenced by a parameter α, which models the desired balance between intensification and diversification. We thus introduce three values (see figure 2):

- α: desired balance between intensification and diversification ($0 \leq \alpha \leq \pi/2$)
- β: the angle formed by the current search trajectory (actual current angle)
- γ: the resulting commanded angle for next search step, in order to counteract the search in the right direction

The application strategy can thus been seen as the way to compute γ's value according to collected information. For example, if one gets trapped into a local optima, it will be beneficial to increase γ in order to promote search diversification. Furthermore, the closest to α the search trajectory is, the more efficient the solving process is. We designed then a formula to compute γ according to α and β, reducing the gaps between them as much as possible:

$$\gamma = \begin{cases} \alpha - gap(\alpha, \beta)/2 & \text{if } gap(\alpha, \beta) \leq \pi/2 \\ \alpha - gap(\alpha, \beta + \pi)/2 & \text{otherwise} \end{cases}$$

where gap corresponds to the difference between two angles values.

4.3   Operator Rewarding

Relying on operator evaluation (cf. section 4.1) and current execution state (cf. section 4.2), we defined the following rewarding system: first of all, measures introduced in section 4.1 have to be normalized. We thus divide them by the highest absolute values found among all operators.

Then, for each operator op, we have to compute its corresponding $angle(op)$ (between 0 and 2π) and its norm $||op||$ (between 0 and $\sqrt{2}$, as measures are normalized) in (Δ_Q, Δ_D). Operator rewards are then defined as follows:

$$score(op) = \begin{cases} (||op||.(1 - \frac{4.gap(\gamma, angle(op))}{\pi}))^2 & \text{if } gap(\gamma, angle(op)) \leq \pi/4 \\ (||op||.\frac{\pi - 4.gap(\gamma, angle(op))}{3\pi})^2 & \text{otherwise} \end{cases}$$

Those rewards are finally used to define operators' application probabilities:

$$p(op_k) = \begin{cases} max(0, \frac{score(op_k)}{\Sigma_{o \in Op} score(o)}) & \text{if } \exists o \in Op, score(o) > 0 \\ \frac{[\Sigma_{o \in Op} score(o)] - score(op_k)}{\Sigma_{o \in Op} score(o)} & \text{otherwise} \end{cases}$$

where Op is the set of all possible operators.

In order to insure fairness for less used operators, a simulation step is achieved every 20 iterations. It consists in applying every operator on the current configuration, only keeping the best resulting combination. This method, although computationally expensive, allows relatively up-to-date evaluations.

5   Application to the Quadratic Assignment Problem

We have experimented ALS on instances from QAPLIB [3]. We consider ALS with 10 operators, and tried several values for α. As a baseline, we have implemented an uniform choice version. ALS is also compared against the optimized robust taboo search [4] with the same experimental conditions. Table 1 summarizes the results. For each instance, we compute the average percentage deviations of the tested algorithms over 20 runs, each executed for 40 000 iterations. The best value is indicated in bold-face.

Table 1. Mean deviation of ALS, uniform choice, and robust taboo search from BKV

Instance	BKV	UC	ALS				RTS
			$\alpha = 0.25\pi$	$\alpha = 0.15\pi$	$\alpha = 0.1\pi$	$\alpha = 0$	
bur26a	5426670	0,1177	0,0196	0,0020	**0,0000**	0,0020	**0,0000**
bur26c	5426795	0,0359	0,0029	**0,0000**	**0,0000**	0,0217	**0,0000**
bur26f	3782044	0,0153	0,0019	**0,0000**	**0,0000**	0,0679	**0,0000**
chr25a	3796	42,4341	10,2160	**6,6228**	8,3298	8,6828	7,6765
els19	1,7E+07	4,8532	0,0003	**0,0000**	**0,0000**	**0,0000**	**0,0000**
kra30a	88900	3,8774	0,8931	0,7627	0,4027	1,1755	**0,0000**
kra30b	91420	2,4251	0,3227	**0,0131**	0,0459	0,1181	0,0230
tai30b	6,4E+08	1,5794	0,1882	0,2319	0,0372	0,8525	**0,0326**
tai50b	4,6E+08	1,4307	0,2330	0,3693	0,2566	0,5376	**0,1078**
nug20	2570	1,9767	0,0156	**0,0000**	**0,0000**	**0,0000**	**0,0000**
nug30	6124	2,0901	0,2449	**0,0000**	**0,0000**	0,0131	0,0065
sko42	15812	2,0529	0,5237	0,0443	**0,0202**	0,0620	0,0342
sko49	23386	2,0174	0,6431	0,2279	0,2407	0,2382	**0,1403**
sko56	34458	2,1139	0,5305	0,1843	0,1660	0,2783	**0,1051**
tai30a	1818146	3,6971	1,7781	0,4163	0,6008	0,3973	**0,3933**
tai35a	2422092	3,9348	2,1099	0,8157	**0,6868**	0,9082	0,7705
tai50a	4941410	4,4437	2,4926	1,1522	**1,1269**	1,3648	1,3733
wil50	48816	1,0005	0,2176	0,0520	0,0385	0,0713	**0,0361**
Average		4,4498	1,1352	0,6053	0,6640	0,8217	**0,5944**

Basically, results from table 1 clearly highlights the controller's advantages, since among 18 tested instances, ALS is systematically better than UC. When compared to RTS, we may remark that with α set to 0.15π or 0.1π, we obtain very similar results since about half of the instances are better solved with ALS. Nevertheless, we should insist here on the fact that the 10 operators are not really optimized and could be seen as general purpose operator for permutation based coded problems. The average values, mentioned at the bottom of the table and which are not so different for α between 0 and 0.15π, highlights that the tuning of α, although having a noticeable impact, seems to bear a greater tolerance than the tuning of all the operators' parameters. Let us also mention that according to other tests, not reported here, enlarging the set of handled operators improves solving efficiency. Indeed, ALS-10 (10 operators set) was better than ALS-2 (2 operators set) for all the instances. Therefore, using our controller, the user may expect benefits from a multi-operators algorithm whose parameters would be actually difficult to tune with regards to their combinatorial interactions.

References

1. Battiti, R., Brunato, M., Mascia, F.: Reactive Search and Intelligent Optimization. Operations Research/Computer Science Interfaces, vol. 45. Springer, Heidelberg (2008)
2. Maturana, J., Fialho, A., Saubion, F., Schoenauer, M., Sebag, M.: Compass and dynamic multi-armed bandits for adaptive operator selection. In: Proceedings of IEEE Congress on Evolutionary Computation (2009)
3. Burkard, R.E., Karisch, S., Rendl, F.: QAPLIB-a quadratic assignment problem library. European Journal of Operational Research 55(1), 115–119 (1991)
4. Taillard, É.: Robust taboo search for the quadratic assignment problem. Parallel Computing 17(4-5), 443–455 (1991)

EasyGenetic: A Template Metaprogramming Framework for Genetic Master-Slave Algorithms

Stefano Benedettini[1], Andrea Roli[1], and Luca Di Gaspero[2]

[1] DEIS, Alma Mater Studiorum Università di Bologna, Cesena, Italy
[2] DIEGM, Università di Udine, Udine, Italy
{s.benedettini,andrea.roli}@unibo.it, l.digaspero@uniud.it

Abstract. We present `EasyGenetic`, a genetic solver based on *template metaprogramming*, that enables the user to configure the solver by instantiating template parameters. The framework allows to combine flexibility with efficiency. The framework is mainly designed to be applied to problems for which a master-slave solution strategy can be defined.

1   Introduction

Genetic algorithms (GAs) are applied since several decades to problem solving and a plethora of successful cases demonstrates the effectiveness of this paradigm as a tool for building "automatic problem solvers".

Among other domains, GAs are particularly suitable for design problems, in which the construction of an artifact depends on a set of design choices and parameter values. From an abstract point of view, these problem can be seen as a composite master-slave task: a low-level (slave) task consists of building the artifact on the basis of a parametrized constructive procedure that is instructed by the parameter setting determined by a high-level (master) task.

In this work we adopt this very perspective and present `EasyGenetic`, a tool that enables the algorithms designer to implement a genetic solver by combining basic components and to tackle combinatorial optimization problems for which a parametric constructive procedure is available. `EasyGenetic` is a framework for implementing genetic solvers based on the master-slave decomposition of the problem which is developed employing *template metaprogramming*, a technique that allows to combine flexibility with efficiency.

The remainder of this paper is structured as follows. In Section 2 we provide the bird's-eye view of the genetic master-slave solver, whose architecture and implementation is detailed in Section 3. A more detailed description of `EasyGenetic` is provided in [1].

2   The Prototypical Genetic Master-Slave Algorithm

The general idea of the genetic master-slave algorithm we propose is based on the hypothesis that it is possible to split solution construction in two phases: in

T. Stützle, M. Birattari, and H.H. Hoos (Eds.): SLS 2009, LNCS 5752, pp. 135–139, 2009.

the first phase, the parameters of a constructive procedure are set by a *master* solver whereas in the second phase the solution is actually built by a *slave* solver (see Algorithm 1). For instance, the constructive procedure can be based on a sequence of decisions whose order is defined by the master solver. Many problems allows such a decomposition, for example planning or assignment problems.

Algorithm 1. Master-slave high-level framework

Procedure master
1: $\mathcal{P} \leftarrow$ buildInitialPopulation(n)
2: evaluate($\mathcal{P}$)
3: **while** terminating conditions not met **do**
4:     $\mathcal{P}' \leftarrow$ applyGeneticOperators($\mathcal{P}$)
5:     evaluate($\mathcal{P}'$, slave)
6:     $\mathcal{P} \leftarrow$ bestOf(n, $\mathcal{P}$, $\mathcal{P}'$)
7: **end while**
8: **return** min($\mathcal{P}$)

Procedure slave
1: **Input:** population $\mathcal{P}$
2: **Output:** evaluation of individuals of $\mathcal{P}$
3: **for all** $p \in \mathcal{P}$ **do**
4:     $s \leftarrow$ buildSolution(p)
5:     fitness[p] $\leftarrow$ eval(s)
6: **end for**

In `EasyGenetic`, the master is a GA, while the slave algorithm can be, in general, any deterministic constructive procedure that accepts an initial set of parameters that completely define solution construction. For example, for combinatorial problems there exist constructive procedures based on the following parameters: the sequence of objects to be included in the solution and/or the decisions to be taken, the set of preassigned variables or the set of hard constraints to be satisfied. In a sense, the master explores the search space of "parameter settings", employing the solution returned by the slave as the evaluation of those search space points.

3   The `EasyGenetic` Framework

As already mentioned, `EasyGenetic` is based on template metaprogramming and generic programming techniques. *Template metaprogramming* is a programming technique used to generate source code at compile time. The main applications of this technique include compile time generation of classes, compile time optimizations (such as implementation selection and loop unrolling), and generic programming. In this sense, templates can be regarded as a Turing-complete purely functional sub-language embedded in the C++ language, which allows compile time computation on the space of types. Prominent examples of applications of these techniques are the C++ Standard Template Library [2] and the Boost Libraries [3].

Generic programming is a programming style that focuses on building algorithms applicable to the widest possible variety of types. To do so, the programmer has to identify the minimal set of requirements on the types involved in an algorithm and to ensure that any type conforming to those constraints could be used with the algorithm. Moreover, *Concepts* play a central role in generic

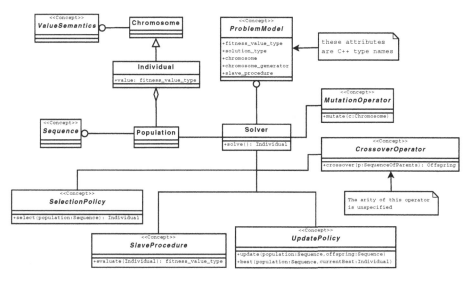

Fig. 1. Architecture of `EasyGenetic`

programming because they enable a programmer to express the required operations on a type in a concise and effective way. Specifically, in C++ a *concept* embodies a set of requirements on a template type parameter coded in terms of valid expressions that involve that type. More precisely, a concept is a structural interface in the sense that any type that syntactically matches the required expressions is a model of that concept.

An overview of the architecture of `EasyGenetic` is depicted in Figure 1 in form of a UML class diagram. Each component in the diagram represents either a concrete class or a concept.

The main component in the architecture is the `Solver` class that contains the actual skeleton of the generic master-slave genetic algorithm (Figure 2). The `Solver` is a class template whose type parameters are actual types conforming to the relative concepts. One of the advantages of this approach is that we obtain a solver that is configurable in every aspect at compile time by providing the desired type parameters.

Other significant components are the following ones:

- An `Individual` is an actual class that models a population individual and encapsulates its genetic material, i.e. the representation of a chromosome, and its fitness function value, which is computed by the slave procedure.
- The *SlaveProcedure* concept defines the interface to which the slave component must comply. A model of this concept must provide a static function which accepts an *Individual* as its argument and returns the related fitness function value.
- The *ChromosomeGenerator* concept specifies how to generate a new chromosome. The chromosomes generated by means of the procedure related to this concept are used in the initialization step of the algorithm.

```
class Solver {
  Individual solve() {
    std::vector<Individual> pop(pop_size);
    for (uint i = 0; i < pop_size; ++i) {
        Chromosome c = ChromosomeGenerator::generate(model);
        fitness_value_type v = SlaveProcedure::evaluate(model, c);
        pop[i] = Individual(c, v); // Individual is-a Chromosome
    }
    std::sort(pop.begin(), pop.end());
    Individual best = pop.back();
    for (/* termination conditions not met */) {
        std::vector<Individual> offspring(offspring_size);
        while(/* offspring is not full */){
        //select chromosome with SelectionPolicy::select(pop)
        //apply crossover and mutation operators
        for (uint i = 0; i < offspring_size; ++i)
            offspring[i].value = SlaveProcedure::evaluate(model, offspring
                [i]);
        UpdatePolicy::update(pop, offspring);
        UpdatePolicy::best(pop, offspring, best);
    }
    return best;
  }
}
```

Fig. 2. `Solver` simplified main method

- The *UpdatePolicy* concept specifies the interface for updating the population for the next generation of the genetic algorithm.
- The *SelectionPolicy* concept provides the interface for components that implement a selection procedure.
- *CrossoverOperator* and *MutationOperator* specify the interfaces required by those components that implement genetic operators. `EasyGenetic` seamlessly supports crossover operators with arbitrary number of parents and offspring (up to a reasonable amount).

ProblemModel. The central entity of the architecture is the *ProblemModel* concept, whose specification is given below.

```
T::fitness_value_type
T::solution_type
T::chromosome
T::chromosome_generator
T::slave_procedure
```

The purpose of *ProblemModel* is to provide the `Solver` with the actual problem-specific type information about various key entities of the system. Each member of the *ProblemModel* concept represents an actual type (such as a scalar C++ type like `int` or `double`, or user-defined classes), and some of them must conform to specific concepts.

Starting from the top, we have the following requirements: *fitness_ value_ type* is a scalar C++ type of the fitness value, while *solution_type* is the actual type of a solution to the problem. *chromosome* is the type of the *Chromosome* that brings the genetic information of a single *Individual. Chromosome* type is obviously problem-specific, therefore it has to be defined by the user. It represents the actual input to the slave procedure and must be model of the *ValueSemantics* concept. *chromosome_ generator* and *slave_ procedure* are the actual types that model the *ChromosomeGenerator* and *SlaveProcedure* concepts.

4   Applications

`EasyGenetic` can be used in a variety of problems, thanks to the generality of the master-slave approach and the flexibility offered by generic programming. As an example, a master-slave solver implemented with `EasyGenetic` has been developed to tackle two hard combinatorial problems, namely the Haplotype Inference Problem and the Capacitated Vehicle Routing Problem. For both problems, an effective constructive procedure was already available and it was employed as s slave solver. Details and results on these applications can be found in [1].

References

1. Benedettini, S., Roli, A., Di Gaspero, L.: Easygenetic: A template metaprogramming framework for genetic master-slave algorithms. Technical Report DEIS-LIA-09-005, University of Bologna (Italy), LIA Series no. 95 (May 2009)
2. Standard Template Library, http://www.sgi.com/tech/stl/ (viewed: April 2009)
3. Boost C++ libraries, http://www.boost.org/ (viewed: April 2009)

Adaptive Operator Selection
for Iterated Local Search

Dirk Thierens

Institute of Information and Computing Sciences,
Universiteit Utrecht, Utrecht, The Netherlands
dirk.thierens@cs.uu.nl

Abstract. Iterated local search is a simple yet powerful metaheuristic. It is only drawback is that it is quite sensitive to its only parameter: the perturbation step size. Adaptive operator selection methods are on-line adaptive algorithms that adjust the probability of applying the search operators to the current solutions. In this short note, we show the use of the adaptive pursuit algorithm to automatically select the perturbation step size for ILS when optimizing a blind, single-constraint knapsack problem. The resulting adaptive ILS achieves almost the same performance as the ILS with the best perturbation step size but without the need to determine the optimal parameter setting.

1   Introduction

Metaheuristics are search methods that aim to enhance the performance of multi-start local search by applying a problem independent strategy. For many combinatorial optimization problems, metaheuristic search algorithms are among the best performing techniques. Iterated local search (ILS) is a simple yet powerful metaheuristic. The search strategy of ILS consists of applying small perturbations on local optima and restarting local search from the perturbed solution. Ideally, the ILS perturbation step should move the search just outside the basin of attraction of the current local optimum [1]. If the new local optimum is better than the old one, ILS will continue searching from the new solution, otherwise it will return to the previous local optimum. ILS actually performs a stochastic greedy search in the space of local optima. It will be most successful in search space structures where the neighboring local optima have highly correlated fitness values. The only drawback of ILS is that it is rather sensitive to the size of the perturbation step.

Adaptive operator selection (AOS) methods are on-line adaptive algorithms that adjust the probability of applying the search operators to the current solutions. In the literature, AOS algorithms have been tested on artificial or trivial problems [2] [3]. Here, we show that the adaptive pursuit algorithm [3] can be successfully applied to design an adaptive ILS algorithm for a knapsack problem.

T. Stützle, M. Birattari, and H.H. Hoos (Eds.): SLS 2009, LNCS 5752, pp. 140–144, 2009.

2   Iterated Local Search

2.1   Knapsack Problem

The knapsack problem consists of m knapsacks K_i with fixed capacity c_i, and n items that have a weight and profit for each knapsack. The weights w_{ij} are specified in a $i \times j$ matrix W, the profits p_{ij} are stored in a $i \times j$ matrix P. The binary vector $X^s \in \{0, 1\}^n$ indicates whether item x_k is present or absent in solution s. Items are either present or absent in all m knapsacks. The goal is to maximize the profits in all knapsacks K_i under the constraint that the sum of the weights of the selected items does not exceed the capacity of any knapsack:

$$\texttt{maximize} \quad \forall i : F_i(X) = \sum_{j=1}^{n} p_{ij} \quad \texttt{with} \quad \forall i : \sum_{j=1}^{n} w_{ij} \leq c_i.$$

Most algorithms for solving the multi-constraint knapsack problem first reduce the multiple constraints to a single surrogate constraint. Here, we are only interested to see the effect of adaptive operator selection on iterated local search for a non-trivial problem. Therefore, we only consider the blind version of the single-constraint knapsack problem, meaning that the search algorithm has no knowledge of the specific profit and weight of the individual items. The benchmark problem used here has $\ell = 500$ profits and weights that are uniformly distributed random integers from the interval $[10 \ldots 50]$. The capacity of the knapsack is half the sum of all the weights.

2.2   Local Search

Our local search algorithm runs in $O(\ell^2)$ and consists of 3 steps:

1. Solutions of the problem are represented by a binary vector, where a 1 denotes the presence of the corresponding item in the knapsack, and a 0 its absence. Random solutions start from a uniformly random binary string. When the capacity constraint is violated, items are randomly selected and removed from the solution until the knapsack is filled below its capacity.
2. All items are considered in a random order. The feasible solution from step 1 is enlarged by adding items that do not make the solution become unfeasible.
3. The feasible solution is further improved by considering all possible swaps between items that are in the current solution and those that are not. Whenever an item can be replaced by another item such that the fitness increases but the capacity constraint does not become violated the swap is performed. The last 2 steps are repeated until a local optimum is reached.

Recall that the local search as outline above is optimizing the blind knapsack problem. The non-blind knapsack has a well-known fast and efficient heuristic. This heuristic first sorts all items in descending order of their profit/weight ratio's. Subsequently, items are added to the solution in this order when their addition does not make the solution unfeasible. Table 1 shows the fitness values

Table 1. Profit values for the knapsack problem found with the greedy heuristic and the greedy heuristic + local search, and the median profit of 30 runs for the blind version of the same knapsack problem with multi-start local search

Knapsack problem [10:50]	Greedy solution 10544	Greedy + local search 10545	Multi-start local search 10170

found by this greedy heuristic on our test problem. We also show the results of applying the local search operator to the greedy solution. This way we obtain a solution of very high quality which serves as a benchmark to the ILS and adaptive ILS that are solving the blind version of the problem.

Table 1 also shows the median profit values for multi-start local search with 1000 independent restarts of the local search algorithm. Clearly, the solutions obtained by multi-start local search are substantially inferior to the solutions obtained by the greedy heuristic (+ local search). Of course the former solves the blind knapsack problem while the latter uses the knowledge of the profits and weights of each individual item. The results indicate however that there is a lot of room for improvement left for the ILS and adaptive ILS metaheuristics.

2.3   Iterated Local Search

Iterated local search has only one parameter that needs to be chosen, unfortunately it is a very sensitive and important one. The size of the perturbation determines the success or failure of ILS. Too large perturbations reduce ILS to MLS, too small perturbations make ILS inefficient as most of the time the search will return to the local optimum it started from. Choosing a good value is basically guess work since one usually has no idea about the size of the basins of attractions of the local optima.

Our local search algorithm ensures that solutions to the knapsack problem are as close as possible to the capacity boundary. Therefore, it only makes sense to perturb the solutions by randomly removing some of the selected items with probability P_{mut}. The perturbation probabilities applied here are $P_{mut} = 0.01, 0.02, 0.03, 0.04$ and 0.05. As in the previous experiments with MLS the ILS calls the local search algorithm 1000 times. Figure 1 and Table 2 show the experimental results averaged over 30 independent runs. Clearly, the smallest perturbation probability $P_{mut} = 0.01$ has the best performance. It is interesting to note that the highly fit solutions of our 500 items knapsack have about 300 items selected. Perturbing only 1% of them means that the perturbed solution has - in expectation - only 3 items less than the local optimum. This is surprising as with such a small perturbation step one would expect that most of the time the local search would not leave the basin of attraction of the current local optimum. Apparently the basins of attractions for the 2-step local search operator are very small, highly correlated in fitness, and extremely connected: it is possible to move to the final best solution with small incremental perturbations by following a greedy path of increasingly better local optima.

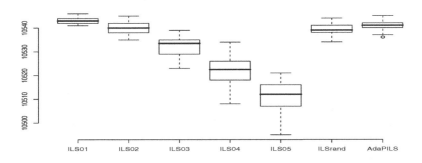

Fig. 1. The box and whisker plots show the median, 25th and 75th percentile, minimum and maximum values. Small circles represent outliers.

Table 2. Data summary over 30 runs

	ILS0.01	ILS0.02	ILS0.03	ILS0.04	ILS0.05	ILSrand	AdaPILS	MLS
Min.	10541	10535	10523	10508	10495	10534	10536	10120
1st Q.	10542	10538	10530	10518	10507	10538	10540	10160
Median	10543	10540	10534	10522	10512	10539	10541	10170
Mean	10543	10540	10532	10522	10511	10539	10541	10170
3rd Q.	10544	10542	10535	10526	10516	10541	10542	10180
Max.	10546	10545	10539	10534	10521	10544	10545	10220

The result of ILS with $P_{mut} = 0.01$ exceed or match the results of the greedy heuristic followed by local search on the non-blind knapsack version. For larger values of P_{mut} the performance of ILS deteriorates but it is still a lot better than the performance of MLS.

3   Adaptive Iterated Local Search

As shown above, ILS is very sensitive to the choice of the perturbation step size, and in general it is impossible to know the optimal value beforehand. Here, we investigate whether the adaptive pursuit allocation strategy can be used to design an adaptive ILS algorithm which is not dependent on knowing the optimal perturbation step size. Adaptive pursuit is an adaptive operator selection algorithm [3]. The allocation strategy applies each of the K operators with a minimum probability P_{min}. After an operator has been applied the environment returns a reward R - possibly zero. An exponential weighted recency vector Q estimates the current rewards for each operator. The probability vector P keeps track of the probability with which each operator will be selected. When a reward is received the adaptive pursuit allocation strategy increases the selection probability of the operator with the current highest Q-value and decreases the selection probabilities of the other operators.

In the experiment here we have $K = 5$ ILS operators with perturbation sizes $P_{mut} = 0.01, 0.02, 0.03, 0.04$, and 0.05. The reward equals 1 whenever the off-spring local optimum has a better fitness than the parent local optimum. Otherwise, the reward equals 0. The learning rate parameters α and β are set equal to 0.05, the minimum probability of selecting an operator is $P_{min} = 0.1$.

Figure 1 and Table 2 show the experimental results for adaptive pursuit calling the local search operator 1000 times (AdaPILS). We also show the results of random selecting one of the 5 perturbation step sizes (ILSrand). The Wilcoxon rank sum test gave only in 3 cases a p-value different from 0: ILS02 vs. ILSrand (p-value = 0.44), ILS02 vs. AdaPILS (p-value = 0.03), and ILSrand vs. AdaPILS (p-value = 0.003). The adaptive pursuit ILS outperforms the ILS with $P_{mut} = 0.02, 003, 004$ and 0.05, while it is only a little worse than the best ILS with perturbation value $P_{mut} = 0.01$. The adaptive ILS however achieves these results without the need to experiment with different values of the perturbation step size, and is therefore computationally much more efficient. It is interesting to see how well a random selection of perturbation step sizes performs. ILSrand performs similar to ILS with perturbation step size $P_{mut} = 0.02$.

4   Conclusion

Iterated local search is a simple yet powerful metaheuristic, unfortunately it is very sensitive to the size of the perturbation step. Adaptive operator selection methods are on-line adaptive algorithms that adjust the probability of applying the search operators to the current solutions. We have demonstrated that the adaptive pursuit algorithm can be applied to automatically select the perturbation step size for ILS when optimizing a blind, single-constraint knapsack problem. The resulting adaptive ILS achieves almost the same performance as the ILS with the best perturbation step size but without the need to determine the optimal parameter setting, thus it is computationally more efficient.

References

1. Lourenço, H., Martin, O., Stützle, T.: A beginner's introduction to iterated local search. In: Proceedings of the 4th Metaheuristics International Conference (2001)
2. DaCosta, L., Fialho, A., Schoenauer, M., Sebag, M.: Adaptive operator selection with dynamic multi-armed bandit. In: Proceedings of the 10th Genetic and Evolutionary Computation Conference, pp. 913–920 (2008)
3. Thierens, D.: An adaptive pursuit strategy for allocating operator probabilities. In: Proceedings of the 7th Genetic and Evolutionary Computation Conference, pp. 1539–1546 (2005)

Improved Robustness through Population Variance in Ant Colony Optimization

David C. Matthews, Andrew M. Sutton,
Doug Hains, and L. Darrell Whitley

Colorado State University, Department of Computer Science,
Fort Collins, Colorado
{dvmtthws,sutton,dhains,whitley}@cs.colostate.edu

Abstract. Ant Colony Optimization algorithms are population-based Stochastic Local Search algorithms that mimic the behavior of ants, simulating pheromone trails to search for solutions to combinatorial optimization problems. This paper introduces Population Variance, a novel approach to ACO algorithms that allows parameters to vary across the population over time, leading to solution construction differences that are not strictly stochastic. The increased exploration appears to help the search escape from local optima, significantly improving the robustness of the algorithm with respect to suboptimal parameter settings.

1 Introduction

Stochastic Local Search (SLS) [1] algorithms are an effective means to solve combinatorial optimization problems [2]. The Traveling Salesman Problem (TSP) is a well known combinatorial optimization problem where the goal is to construct the shortest possible tour visiting each city only once. As the number of cities increases, the combinatorial size prevents a complete search of the entire solution space. SLS algorithms employ diversification methods to find promising areas in the solution space and intensification methods to focus the search in these promising areas.

Ant Colony Optimization (ACO) [3] algorithms are population-based SLS algorithms where a colony of ants communicates indirectly through pheromone trails over a series of iterations. Each ant in the colony randomly constructs a solution to the problem using the pheromone trails and problem heuristics as aids. After each iteration, pheromone trail updates based on the best solutions found help narrow the search.

The performance of SLS algorithms depends on proper parameter selection. While parameter recommendations exist for these algorithms, the optimal parameters are often problem specific. This paper focuses on a new method to improve ACO algorithm robustness, the ability to perform well for suboptimal parameter selections [1].

Existing ACO algorithms employ a homogeneous colony of ants. The ants in these colonies use identical parameters throughout a run. The Population

T. Stützle, M. Birattari, and H.H. Hoos (Eds.): SLS 2009, LNCS 5752, pp. 145–149, 2009.

Variance (PV) approach introduced in this paper employs a heterogeneous colony of ants where key solution construction parameters vary across the colony during the run. This approach improves exploration of the solution space by the ACO algorithm, resulting in more robust performance with respect to suboptimal parameter settings.

The remainder of this paper uses the Max-Min Ant System [4] and Traveling Salesman Problem [2] to perform an empirical study of the Population Variance approach. Section 2 introduces the Population Variance approach. Section 3 studies the robustness of algorithm parameters when using Population Variance. Section 4 summarizes our findings and suggests future work.

2   Population Variance

Population Variance introduces the functions $\alpha_k(t)$ and $\beta_k(t)$ to the computation of proportional probabilities (1) used in solution construction. These functions allow us to change the values of α and β by ant k or iteration t, varying the relative contribution of the pheromones τ and the heuristics η.

$$p_{ij}^k(t) = \frac{[\tau_{ij\alpha}(t)]^{\alpha_k(t)} \cdot [\eta_{ij}]^{\beta_k(t)}}{\sum_{l \in N_i^k} [\tau_{il\alpha}(t)]^{\alpha_k(t)} \cdot [\eta_{il}]^{\beta_k(t)}}. \tag{1}$$

In this paper, we incorporate Population Variance into the Max-Min Ant System (MMAS) [4]. We previously proposed an improved lower limit for pheromone trails (2) in MMAS that avoids stagnation when computing the proportional probabilities and significantly improved results when $\alpha \neq 1$ [5]. We used this improved lower limit with both the MMAS and Population Variance algorithms studied in this paper.

$$\tau_{min} = \tau_{max} \cdot \left[\frac{1 - \sqrt[n]{p_{best}}}{avg \cdot \sqrt[n]{p_{best}}} \right]^{\frac{1}{\alpha}}. \tag{2}$$

The improved lower limit for pheromone trails in (2) implies that pheromone tables are now α specific, hence the use of $\tau_{ij\alpha}$ in (1). Pheromone scaling defined in (3) allows us to maintain a single pheromone table for $\alpha = 1$ and scale the pheromones proportionally for other values of α. This increases the computation of each proportional probability a small amount.

$$\tau_{ij\alpha}(t) = \tau_{min,\alpha} + (\tau_{ij1}(t) - \tau_{min,1}) \cdot \left[\frac{\tau_{max} - \tau_{min,\alpha}}{\tau_{max} - \tau_{min,1}} \right]. \tag{3}$$

There are many possible methods to select $\alpha_k(t)$ and $\beta_k(t)$. In this paper we use a simple diversification method to increase exploration, varying these values independently by iteration with a uniform distribution of d discrete values over a defined range for each. All ants share the same values for a given iteration, allowing construction of a single proportional probability table $p_{ij}^k(t)$. The $\alpha_k(t)$

function in (4) selects d discrete values between α_{min} and α_{max}. The $\beta_k(t)$ function in (5) selects d discrete values between $\beta_{lim}(t)$ and β_{max}.

$$\alpha_k(t) = \alpha_{min} + \left\lfloor \frac{\alpha_{max} - \alpha_{min}}{d-1} \right\rfloor \cdot \lfloor random(0,1) \cdot d \rfloor. \tag{4}$$

$$\beta_k(t) = \beta_{max} - \left\lfloor \frac{\beta_{max} - \beta_{lim}(t)}{d-1} \right\rfloor \cdot \lfloor random(0,1) \cdot d \rfloor. \tag{5}$$

Early prototypes showed an inverse relationship between the value of β and the quality of the initial solution. To intensify the search, we use $\beta_{lim}(t)$ to restrict the initial range of β values to produce better starting tours so that early pheromone updates guide us to productive areas of the solution space. The lower limit $\beta_{lim}(t)$ in (6) uses an exponential moving average from with decay rate σ and $\beta_{lim}(0) = \beta_{max}$.

$$\beta_{lim}(t+1) = (1-\sigma)\beta_{min} + \sigma\beta_{lim}(t). \tag{6}$$

These simple mechanisms for diversification and intensification will demonstrate the robustness of the Population Variance method. We plan to study more sophisticated mechanisms in the future.

3   Robustness

We modified ACOTSP [6] to incorporate the Population Variance equations and accept α_{min}, β_{min}, α_{max}, β_{max}, d, and σ parameters. A series of tests using TSPLIB [7] problems compared the performance of MMAS and PV across a range of parameters intended to provide optimal and suboptimal paremters combinations.

For MMAS, tests were run for all combinations of $\alpha = 1, 2, 3, 4, 5, 6, 7$ and $\beta = 1, 2, 3, 4, 5, 6, 7$. For PV, tests were run for $\alpha_{min} = 1$, $\beta_{min} = 1$, $\alpha_{max} = 2, 3, 4, 5, 6, 7$, $\beta_{max} = 7$, $\sigma = 0.01$, and $d = 7$. For both algorithms, tests were run for all combinations of evaporation rates $\rho = 0.025, 0.05, 0.1, 0.3, 0.5$ and maximum pheromone selection probability $p_{best} = 0.00005, 0.0005, 0.005, 0.05, 0.5$ in addition to the α and β settings. All runs were limited to 10 tries of 2500 iterations. Local search was not employed so we could evaluate the effectiveness of the pheromone trail mechanism. All other parameters used their ACOTSP defaults.

PV exhibits more robust performance compared to MMAS across a range of parameter values for α_{max}, ρ, and p_{bests} as shown in Fig. 1 for problem $pcb442$ from TSPLIB. Similar results were obtained for other problems in TSPLIB. The MMAS tests for α_{max} include all tests with $\alpha \leq \alpha_{max}$ while the PV tests include a similar number of repeated tests for the given α_{max} value. The figure shows the same results for two ranges of percent deviation from optimal, $0 - 50$ and $0 - 10$. The range of PV results is much narrower and the PV medians are lower than the corresponding MMAS medians with a significance level less than 0.01 using the Mann-Whitney rank sum test. Tests varying other parameters

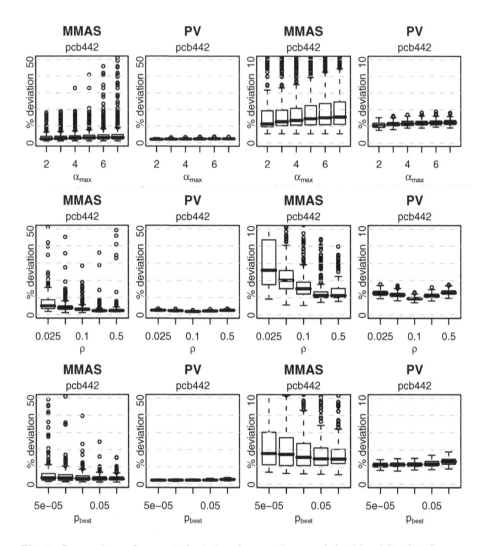

Fig. 1. Comparison of percent deviation from optimum of the Max-Min Ant System (MMAS) and Population Variance (PV) for ranges of α, ρ, and p_{best}

(pseudo random proportional selection, candidate list size, and number of ants) yielded similar improvements in robustness.

Some types of problems have no heuristics available to guide the search so we compared the performance of MMAS and PV using only pheromones in the random proportional selection, $\beta_{min} = \beta_{max} = 0$. The results in Fig. 2 shows four TSPLIB problems solved without the use of heuristics or local search, relying solely on the pheromone trails. These results suggest the PV methods for diversification and intensification are much more robust than MMAS.

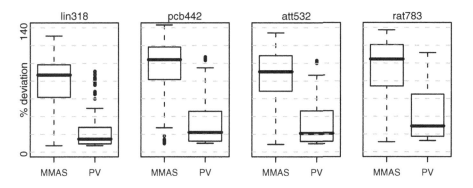

Fig. 2. Robustness for pheromone trails alone ($\beta = 0$)

4   Summary

This paper introduced a new method called Population Variance to increase robustness in ACO algorithms with respect to suboptimal parameter settings. This method varies the α and β parameters used during solution construction to improve exploration and escape local optima. The results of tests with problems from TSPLIB show significant improvements in robustness, particularly when heuristics are not available to aid the search.

Future work includes more sophisticated Population Variance functions $\alpha_k(t)$ and $\beta_k(t)$, interaction with local search, generalization to other ACO algorithms, and use with other types of combinatorial optimization problems.

References

1. Hoos, H.H., Stützle, T.: Stochastic Local Search: Foundations & Applications. Morgan Kaufmann, San Francisco (2005)
2. Garey, M.R., Johnson, D.S.: Computers and Intractability: A Guide to the Theory of *NP*-Completeness. W.H. Freeman, New York (1979)
3. Dorigo, M., Stützle, T.: Ant Colony Optimization. MIT Press, Cambridge (2004)
4. Stützle, T., Hoos, H.H.: MAX–MIN Ant System. Future Generation Computer Systems 16(8), 889–914 (2000)
5. Matthews, D.C.: Improved Lower Limits for Pheromone Trails in Ant Colony Optimization. In: Rudolph, G., Jansen, T., Lucas, S., Poloni, C., Beume, N. (eds.) PPSN 2008. LNCS, vol. 5199, pp. 508–517. Springer, Heidelberg (2008)
6. Stützle, T.: ACOTSP, http://www.aco-metaheuristic.org/aco-code
7. Reinelt, G.: TSPLIB,
   http://www.iwr.uni-heidelberg.de/groups/comopt/software/TSPLIB95/
   index.html

Mixed-Effects Modeling of Optimisation Algorithm Performance

Matteo Gagliolo[1,2], Catherine Legrand[3], and Mauro Birattari[1]

[1] IRIDIA, CoDE, Université Libre de Bruxelles, Brussels, Belgium
[2] Faculty of Informatics, University of Lugano, Lugano, Switzerland
[3] Institut de Statistique, Université Catholique de Louvain,
Louvain-la-Neuve, Belgium
{mgagliolo,mbiro}@iridia.ulb.ac.be, catherine.legrand@uclouvain.be

Abstract. The learning curves of optimisation algorithms, plotting the evolution of the objective vs. runtime spent. can be viewed as a sample of *longitudinal* data. In this paper we describe *mixed-effects* modeling, a standard technique in longitudinal data analysis, and give an example of its application to algorithm performance modeling.

1 Introduction

Models of algorithm performance can be useful for analysis purposes, but also for automating algorithm selection, or parameter tuning. The correct analysis technique depends on the kind of problem to be solved. For algorithms solving *optimisation* problems, in which each solution is characterized by a measure of its quality, the most general performance model is a bivariate distribution, relating runtime to solution quality. In order to gather performance data for a given algorithm, one can solve a benchmark of instances, storing a time, quality pair each time the best solution is improved. The resulting sample will be a set of observations of solution quality vs. time, grouped based on the individual runs of the algorithm. In statistical terminology, this is an example of *longitudinal data* [1], i.e. measurements of the same quantity repeated over time on each of a set of *subjects*. In the following, we describe parametric *mixed-effects* models, a standard technique in longitudinal data analysis (Sec. 2), and present preliminary experiments on performance data from a TSP solver (Sec. 3). Section 4 gives references for further reading, while Section 5 concludes the paper with a perspective on ongoing research.

2 Longitudinal Data Analysis

Consider a sample of measurements of a scalar y: for the i-th of a set of M *subjects*, or *individuals*, n_i values y_{ij} are collected at distinct times t_{ij}, with $j = 1, \ldots, n_i$. A pair (y, t) is termed an *observation*. The object of modeling is the distribution of y given t.

T. Stützle, M. Birattari, and H.H. Hoos (Eds.): SLS 2009, LNCS 5752, pp. 150–154, 2009.

In our case, y is the objective being optimized, and each y_{ij} records the value of the *best* solution found by a randomized algorithm within a time t_{ij}; the M subjects correspond to M distinct runs of the algorithm, which may be solving different problem instances, or differ only in the random seed used.

The main issue posed by longitudinal data is *within-subject* correlation: measurements taken on a same subject cannot be considered independent. To address this, in parametric *mixed-effects* models [1] the evolution of y for each subject is modeled by a separate curve, whose parameters are a random perturbation of those of a baseline curve, describing the overall behavior of the set of subjects. In a *nonlinear* mixed-effects model (NLME) [2],

$$y_{ij} = f(\boldsymbol{\alpha}_i, t_{ij}) + \epsilon_{ij}$$
$$\boldsymbol{\alpha}_i = \boldsymbol{\beta} + \mathbf{b}_i \tag{1}$$
$$\mathbf{b}_i \sim \mathcal{N}(\mathbf{0}, \boldsymbol{\Sigma}), \ \ \boldsymbol{\epsilon}_i \sim \mathcal{N}(\mathbf{0}, \sigma^2 \boldsymbol{\Lambda}_i),$$

the evolution of y is modeled by a parametric function $f(\boldsymbol{\alpha}, t)$, whose parameter vector $\boldsymbol{\alpha}$ is the sum of a subject-specific vector of *random effects* $\mathbf{b}_i$ and a common vector of *fixed effects* $\boldsymbol{\beta}$. The M vectors $\mathbf{b}_i$ are assumed to be generated independently, once for each subject i, from the same zero mean Gaussian distribution, whose covariance $\boldsymbol{\Sigma}$ is estimated along with the M $\mathbf{b}_i$ and $\boldsymbol{\beta}$. The arbitrary subject-specific covariance structure $\boldsymbol{\Lambda}_i$ can capture within-subject correlations that are not modeled by the random effects: in the simplest case, the ϵ_{ij} are homoscedastic, (i.e., their variance does not change with j), independent, and identically distributed, so $\boldsymbol{\Lambda}_i = \sigma^2 \mathbf{I}_{n_i}$ for all subjects i. Both stationary and time-varying covariates, as well as nested factors, can be easily included [3].

3   Experiments

One important issue in optimisation is that, while bounds may be easy to compute, the actual value of the global optimum is usually not available beforehand. Consider an algorithm solving a problem instance: in general, there is no way of telling whether the current best solution will be further improved, or the algorithm has already found the global optimum. Our interest in nonlinear models is motivated by the hope that they may allow to extrapolate the performance on a new instance, based on previous runs on similar instances. In order to test this idea, we collected performance data on a benchmark of small instances of the traveling salesman problem (TSP) [4], for which the global optima were available. The benchmark was composed of four groups of 100 symmetric Euclidean instances each, randomly generated, with 200, 300, 400, and 500 cities respectively. The solver used was ILS-FDD [5], an iterated version of the local search algorithm 3-opt, with fitness-distance diversification. Each instance was solved 25 times, with different random seeds. In the TSP, the objective is represented by the cost l of a path visiting all cities once, which has to be minimized. A lower bound l_b on l, and the global optimum l_o, were evaluated using Concorde. The value of the objective was collected, along with the runtime, each time an improvement was found, resulting in a sequence of (l, t) values for each instance and each random seed. In order to perform the modeling across different instances, the objective was scaled relative to the lower bound as $y = (l - l_b)/l_b$, and the corresponding sample of (y, t) values was used as longitudinal data. Modeling was performed using `nlme` [3], a software package for linear and nonlinear mixed effects, in its version for the R language [6]. As the data presented an exponential decay towards the optimum, which is typical of optimisation algorithms in general, we fit a model of the form $y = a + be^{-ct}$, implemented in `nlme` by the function `SSasymp`. A fundamental issue of the use of such model is that the NLME algorithm is based on a zero mean Gaussian noise model (1). In our case, this assumption is violated as the algorithm converges towards the optimum, as it cannot further decrease. As a solution, we used an heteroscedastic variance structure (`varPower`), expressing the variance as a function of time, $\text{Var}(\epsilon_{ij}) = \sigma^2 t_{ij}^{2\rho}$, with one parameter ρ being estimated, in order to be able to model a decreasing variance. For the correlation structure, we used the function `corCAR1` (continuous time $AR(1)$), $\text{Cor}(\epsilon_{ij}, \epsilon_{ik}) = \phi^{|t_{ij}-t_{ik}|}$, $0 < \phi < 1$, as we expected the correlation among y values to decrease with distance in time.

The aim of the following experiments was to find out if the estimated value of a could be used to approximate the global optimum l_o. Figure 1 reports results in terms of the relative deviation from the optimum, $d = (l_a - l_o)/l_o$, where $l_a = l_b(1 + a)$ is the asymptote of `SSasymp` scaled back. We first fit a separate model for each of the 400 instances, using data from all the 25 runs available. In this case the factor which identifies the subjects is the random seed. Random effects were negligible, and the model seemed to account for the variations among runs only with the variance-covariance structure. Here and in all other experiments, the value of ρ in `varPower` was estimated to be negative, giving a decreasing variance structure, and the correlation parameter ϕ was also significant. On some of the instances, `nlme` failed for numerical issues, namely the singularity of a matrix: this was observed mostly on the group of smaller instances, on which the algorithm was often too fast in converging, producing only a few (y, t) points for each run. The parameters estimated were found to be significant (p-value < 0.05), with the exception of c on some of the instances. Figure 1(a) plots statistics of the deviation from the optimum d, evaluated using the fixed effect of the asymptote a.

The next experiment was performed grouping the data based on the instance: 25 models were fit, one for each random seed, on the four separate groups of 100 instances each. This time the random effects were more remarkable, as each individual corresponded to a different instance, with a different optimum. In this case d was evaluated based on the mixed effect $(a + a_i)$, a_i being the random effect on the asymptote for instance i. Aggregated statistics of d are reported in Figure 1(b): the performance decreased visibly, but the estimates are still close to the real global optima.

The third experiment was a feasibility study for a model based stopping criterion, aimed at investigating the predictive power of our model. In a first phase, the model was trained based on data for a single random seed, grouped based

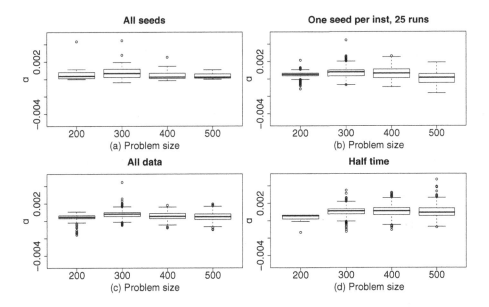

Fig. 1. All plots display statistics of $d = (l_a - l_o)/l_o$, the deviation of the estimate l_a from the actual optimum l_o. See text for details.

on the instance. In a second phase, a fresh model was trained on a subset of the same sample, obtained dropping the data from the second half of the time axis, for a half of the instances, randomly picked. The idea was to simulate a situation in which 50 "training" instances have been already solved to convergence, and the relative data recorded; while another 50 "test" instances are being solved, the algorithm is paused some time before convergence, and the model is used to predict the value of the optima, based on the previously solved instances, and on the learning curves observed so far. This scheme was repeated for each random seed, each time with a different random pick of the 50 test instances. Also in this case $(a + a_i)$ was used to evaluate l_a. Figures 1(c,d) report statistics of d for the two models, measured only on the test instances. The performance of the model from the first phase, which serves as an "oracle" for comparison, is clearly superior, but the one for the second phase is still reasonable.

4   Related Work

An up-to-date review of longitudinal data analysis, including nonparametric methods, can be found in [1]. We mainly followed [3] which is also rich in usage examples of nlme, from the same authors. The literature on algorithm performance modeling is mostly focused on decision problems, and the related concept of runtime distribution. Extreme value statistics was proposed in [7] to estimate the value of the global optimum for large problem instances, based on a sequence of suboptimal solutions; this method is integrated into local search in [8]. The learning curve of local search solvers is fit in [9] using a separate model for each run. Solution quality distributions are used in [10] to rank the performance of heuristic solvers. We refer the reader to [4] for further references.

5   Conclusions

We reviewed a class of models for longitudinal data, and showed how they can be used to model the performance of optimisation algorithms, investigating their predictive power with a preliminary experiment on data from a TSP solver. The results were quite promising, and we are currently analyzing other algorithm/problem combinations, as well as the impact of covariates. The models are quite general in this sense, as they allow time-varying covariates to be easily included: besides runtime, the distribution of solution quality could also be related to memory usage, bandwidth, or other resources, as well as dynamic variables of the algorithms. Adding algorithm parameters as stationary covariates could allow to tune them based on derivatives of the objective. Longitudinal data analysis could be useful to implement stopping criteria, or dynamic restart strategies, which take into account past experience in detecting the convergence of an algorithm; and to perform algorithm selection, or some more general form of resource allocation.

Acknowledgement. The first author was supported by the Swiss National Science Foundation with a grant for prospective researchers (n. PBTI2–118573).

References

1. Fitzmaurice, G., Davidian, M., Verbeke, G., Molenberghs, G.: Longitudinal Data Analysis. Chapman & Hall/CRC Press (2008)
2. Lindstrom, M.J., Bates, D.M.: Nonlinear mixed effects models for repeated measures data. Biometrics 46(3), 673–687 (1990)
3. Pinheiro, J.C., Bates, D.M.: Mixed Effects Models in S and S-Plus. Springer, Heidelberg (2002)
4. Hoos, H.H., Stützle, T.: Stochastic Local Search: Foundations & Applications. Morgan Kaufmann, San Francisco (2004)
5. Stützle, T., Hoos, H.H.: Analysing the run-time behaviour of iterated local search for the travelling salesman problem. In: Hansen, P., et al. (eds.) Essays and Surveys on Metaheuristics, pp. 589–611. Kluwer Academic Publishers, Dordrecht (2001)
6. R Development Core Team: R: A Language and Environment for Statistical Computing. R Foundation for Statistical Computing, Vienna, Austria (2009)
7. Dannenbring, D.G.: Procedures for estimating optimal solution values for large combinatorial problems. Management Science 23(12), 1273–1283 (1977)
8. Ovacik, I.M., Rajagopalan, S., Uzsoy, R.: Integrating interval estimates of global optima and local search methods for combinatorial optimization problems. Journal of Heuristics 6(4), 481–500 (2000)
9. Oppen, J., Woodruff, D.: Parametric models of local search progression. Technical Report 06-08, UC Davis Graduate School of Management Research (2008)
10. Schreiber, G.R., Martin, O.C.: Cut size statistics of graph bisection heuristics. SIAM J. on Optimization 10(1), 231–251 (1999)

Author Index

.